Counselling
Ethics
Casebook

Counselling Ethics Casebook

by *William E. Schulz, Ph.D.*

Partial funding for publication of the *Ethics Case Book* has been provided by a grant from the Canadian Guidance and Counselling Foundation.

Canadian Guidance and Counselling Association

Canadian Guidance and Counselling Association
600-220 Laurier Avenue
Ottawa, Canada K1P 5Z9

ISBN 0-9697966-0-9

To AERA presenters, Cambridge scholars
and people with high GRE scores.

CONTENTS

ACKNOWLEDGEMENTS

My sincere appreciation is extended to all those people who contributed to this casebook. First, and foremost, my thanks are extended to my many graduate students of 1992 who provided many cases. I am very grateful for their contributions.

My special thank you also to the many counsellor-educators who wrote essays for the five major sections of this casebook: Walt Pawlovich, Glen Sheppard, Bill Borgen, Norm Amundson, Marv Westwood, Bryan Hiebert, David Zinger, Paul Madak, Beth Haverkamp, John Gawthrop, and Max Uhlemann. They have raised a lot of issues related to professional practice in counselling, the counselling relationship, testing and research, consultation and private practice, and counsellor preparation standards.

Finally, my thanks go to Alice Turman, Gerald Beyak and Liz Bachmann who helped in the production of this casebook.

CHAPTER ONE

---- ❖ ----

Ethical
Decision-Making

---- ❖ ----

A real value in examining ethical dilemmas is
that, in the process of going through the steps
of ethical decision-making, counsellors can
promote their own professional growth.

INTRODUCTION

Objectives

In 1992, the Canadian Guidance and Counselling Association (CGCA) formed an Ethics Committee whose responsibility was to educate the CGCA membership regarding ethical guidelines, ethical issues and violations of counselling ethics. This casebook is one attempt to educate the membership, counsellor-educators and practitioners in the field.

Specifically, the objectives of this casebook are:

❖ To promote discussion of ethical issues in the professional practice of counselling, on the counselling relationship, on testing and research, on consultation and private practice, and on counsellor preparation standards;

❖ To provide specific case examples of both ethical and unethical behaviour in counselling;

❖ To provide material that will assist the Ethics Committee in dealing with complaints of ethical violations in a variety of situations;

❖ To be a guide to counsellors in their every day conduct and in the resolution of ethical dilemmas;

❖ To help define and facilitate counsellors' relationships with employers and supervisors; and

❖ To provide examples that will help clarify each of the 63 ethical guidelines in the Canadian Guidance and Counselling "Guidelines for Ethical Behaviour."

Organization of the Casebook

In the first chapter of this casebook the major focus is on examining a number of models for ethical decision-making. After detailing the decision-making models of Rest, the Canadian Psychological Association and Stadler, the author presents an integrated approach based on the previous three approaches.

Beginning with Chapter Two, specific cases are presented, designed to illustrate, clarify and analyze each of the 63 ethical guidelines in the

CGCA *Guidelines for Ethical Behaviour*. In Chapter Two, two ethical cases and two unethical cases are presented for each of the 11 guidelines of Section A. This section deals with the general issues of the professional behaviour of counsellors. Following these cases, a brief commentary is presented as well as a number of questions, designed to stimulate further discussion of the specific ethical guideline under review.

It should be noted at this time that the cases presented vary both in style and length, reflecting the fact that many people contributed cases for this casebook. Every attempt has been made to reflect a variety of work settings for counsellors. Some cases have been altered to reflect more accurately the guideline under discussion. All names used in the cases are fictitious. Also, cases have been labelled "+" and "-" to designate whether the case reflects positive behaviour or negative behaviour in accordance with the ethical guideline. No attempt has been made to specify the seriousness of any behaviour presented in the cases. As a result, some cases will exemplify very serious unethical behaviour while others will simply illustrate ignorance or questionable behaviour on the part of the counsellor. After the cases for Section A have been discussed, two essays dealing with Section A of the *Guidelines* are presented:

❖ Walt Pawlovich, "Establishing and Maintaining Competence: An Ethical Responsibility", and

❖ Glen Sheppard, "Counselling Ethics and Sexual Harassment."

Chapter Three of this casebook consists of cases related to Section B of the CGCA *Guidelines*; namely, "Individual and Group Counselling Relationships." The guidelines in this section deal with important issues related to confidentiality, record keeping, informed consent and many others. As was the case in the previous chapter, each of the 14 guidelines in this section are clarified by presenting two cases that reflect positive behaviour on the part of the counsellor, and two cases that demonstrate negative behaviour. Some commentary on the guideline and cases is presented. As well, four discussion questions are presented for each guideline, with the intention of furthering discussion of ethics and ethical guidelines. Two counsellor-educators have prepared essays for this section on individual and group counselling relationships:

❖ William Schulz, "Counselling Ethics and Confidentiality", and

❖ Marvin Westwood, Norm Amundson and Bill Borgen, "Group Counselling and Ethics."

The last three chapters are organized in the same way, with case presentation commentary, questions and essays. Chapter Four deals with Section C of the *Guidelines*, "Testing, Research and Publication." Again, two essays have been written for this section:

❖ Beth Haverkamp, "Psychological Testing: The Counsellor's Responsibility", and

❖ Paul Madak, "The Counsellor/Researcher and the Question of Ethics in Qualitative Research."

In Chapter Five, Section D of the *Guidelines* is presented; namely, guidelines exemplifying ethical behaviour in "Consulting and Private Practice." Essays for this section were written by:

❖ David Zinger, "Enhancing Ethical Awareness and Action With Comic Consciousness", and

❖ Bryan Hiebert, "Consulting and Ethics".

In the final chapter, cases are presented on "Counsellor Preparation Standards" (Section E of the *Guidelines*). Essays were prepared by:

❖ Max Uhlemann and John Gawthrop, "Ethics and Professional Education in Counselling Psychology," and

❖ Beth Haverkamp, "Teaching Ethics: Linking Abstract Principles to Actual Practice."

In the Appendices, the *Standards for the Clinical Practice of Mental Health Counseling* is presented in Appendix A and the *Guidelines for Ethical Behaviour* of the Manitoba School Counsellors' Association are presented in Appendix B. Appendix C contains the CGCA's "Procedures for Processing Complaints of Ethical Violations."

THE PROCESS OF ETHICAL DECISION-MAKING

In this section of the introductory chapter, the emphasis is on clarifying for counsellors some procedures for examining ethical decision-making. Counsellors will face moral, ethical and legal dilemmas in counselling. Some of the guidelines from the CGCA *Guidelines for Ethical Behaviour* are bound to come into conflict. Very frequently the ethical dilemmas will arise from cases where the guidelines on danger to clients and others, and the guidelines on confidentiality, are in conflict. How can counsellors resolve these ethical questions? A number of authors have produced models and procedures for examining ethical dilemmas. A number of these models will be discussed:

1. The Rest Model,
2. The Canadian Psychological Association Model,
3. The Stadler Model, and
4. An Integrative Approach.

1. The James Rest Model

James Rest (1979) has written about moral judgements and has examined many important issues, including ethical issues. He is concerned with the judgements people make regarding important but conflicting issues. He emphasizes the need to balance the interests of individuals involved in an ethical dilemma.

Rest (1984) developed a four-step model for ethical behaviour.

Step One

The counsellor recognizes that an ethical dilemma exists. Counsellors who are familiar with counselling codes of ethics, their responsibility to clients, and their need to be fair both to society and themselves, will recognize situations where confidentiality, danger to clients or others, client attraction and many other ethical problems come into conflict. In this step, then, the counsellor is aware of the ethical problem.

Step Two

This step involves the careful examination of the consequences of various courses of action.

These courses of action are based on some ordering or ranking of important principles that provide some guide to future action on the part of the counsellor.

Biggs and Blocher (1987) outline a number of these important, guiding principles:

1. Veracity – telling the truth,
2. Privacy – respecting other people and their property,
3. Autonomy – respecting people's rights to determine their fates,
4. Promise keeping – keeping promises,
5. Parentalism – safeguarding the rights of those who cannot do so themselves,
6. Self-improvement – improving ourselves,
7. Nonmaleficence – doing no wilful harm to others,
8. Equality – generally treating everyone equally, and
9. Sanctity of life – believing all living things are intrinsically valuable.

No attempt has been made to provide any ranking of these principles, and therefore counsellors need to examine carefully their values and the possible outcomes before weighing the principles to guide them in making an ethical decision.

Step Three

In the third step, counsellors' skills and attitudes become particularly important. During this step counsellors develop a plan of action whereby they attempt to resolve the ethical dilemma.

Step Four

The last step in the Rest process involves putting the plan of action into motion; that is, counsellors do what they have planned. Acting ethically may come at a price; a loss of a friendship, disappointment from clients or even the loss of a job. This final step, carrying out the ethical decision, is vital.

In using this four-step Rest Model, Biggs and Blocher (1987) have indicated that counsellors will need to ask themselves a series of questions as they work through the process:

1. How does the counsellor's behaviour effect others? To what extent?
2. Which of the nine principles apply in this ethical situation? Which are the most important principles?
3. What are the positive values that should be maximized? What negatives should be avoided?
4. What alternative courses of action are possible? What are the consequences of each action to the counsellor? To the client? To others?
5. How do these consequences compare in terms of the overriding principle in this situation?
6. What plan of action can be developed to implement the principles and values?
7. How can the counsellor act on these principles? What prices may the counsellor have to pay? How will the counsellor's actions reflect on the counselling profession and on the counsellor's future practice?

2. Canadian Psychological Association Model

In the *Canadian Code of Ethics for Psychologists* (1986) ethical principles and standards are articulated for psychologists. In spite of the fact that counsellors' role and functions are different than psychologists, these ethical principles and guidelines for decision-making are well worth considering.

Four ethical principles are presented and psychologists are implored to consider all principles in ethical decision-making. Unlike other ethical decision-making models, the four principles have been ranked according to the weight each principle should be given when the principles are in conflict. The rank order of principles is as follows:

PRINCIPLE I: *Respect for the Dignity of Persons*

This principle which includes factors such as respect for the client, non-discrimination, informed consent, consultation with others, confidentiality and responsibility, is given highest weight, except in instances when there is danger to known or unknown individuals.

PRINCIPLE II: *Responsible Caring*

Responsible caring receives second highest weighting and includes factors such as caring and promoting the welfare of client, professional knowledge and competence, and minimizing any possible harm. Responsible caring, in short, is carried out only in ways that "respect and promote the dignity of persons."

PRINCIPLE III: *Integrity in Relationships*

This next ordered principle includes factors such as the avoidance of fraud or misrepresentation, openness, freedom from bias, conflict of interest situations, and the withholding of information.

PRINCIPLE IV: *Responsibility to Society*

This principle is given lowest weighting when in conflict with the other three principles. Included in this principle are not only respect and responsibility to society, but, when appropriate and possible, enacting beneficial societal changes.

Not everyone, including psychologists, will agree with this ranking of principles. Pettifor (1991), in an article entitled "How well does the Canadian Code of Ethics Serve Community Psychologists?", questions the priority of placing Principle IV, "Responsibility to Society", fourth. As well, the 1987 *Ethical Guidelines for Feminist Therapists* have very proactive statements on the ethical duties of therapists and counsellors to advocate societal change.

In the *Canadian Code of Ethics for Psychologists* (1986), the following steps are suggested when ethical principles are in conflict and are not easily resolved:

Step One:
The ethically relevant issues and practices are clearly identified.

Step Two:
Alternative courses of action to resolve the conflict are developed.

Step Three:
Careful analysis of the likely short-term, ongoing and long-term risks and benefits of each course of action are examined. Effects of each

course of action are examined in terms of effects on the client, but also on any others such as the client's family, other employees, colleagues, society, the profession and the employing institution.

Step Four:
After conscientious application of the principles of respect for the dignity of persons, responsible caring, integrity in relationships and responsibility to society, application to counsellor, client and societal values, and application of ethical standards, a choice of a course of action is made.

Step Five:
Action is taken; and more, a commitment to assume responsibility for the consequences of the action is made by the psychologist.

Step Six:
The course of action is evaluated.

Step Seven:
Any negative consequences of the course of action are corrected. The member continues to assume responsibility for her or his actions. If the ethical issue is not resolved, the steps of this process are repeated.

Finally, psychologists are encouraged to consult with colleagues who can add objectivity and can help with this ethical decision-making process.

3. The Stadler Model

In 1985 the American Counselors Association (The American Association for Counseling and Development) provided funding for a series of video cassettes dealing with ethical issues. In the video *Confidentiality: The Professionals' Dilemma*, Holly Stadler provides the listener with her views on ethical behaviour and she outlines an ethical decision-making model. Her model consists of the following four steps:

1. Identify competing moral principles,
2. Implement moral reasoning strategy.
3. Prepare for action, and
4. Taking action.

Step One:
In the first step counsellors are asked to identify any competing moral principles. Four principles are described, and the rules of conduct that stem from each.

The principle of *nonmaleficence* brings forth the rule of "do not harm." This means that harm should not come to another person. Somewhat related to this first principle is the principle of *beneficence*. According to Stadler (1985), this principle guides counsellors to act in a proactive way in promoting good and preventing harm.

With the principle of *autonomy*, counsellors attempt to promote self-determination. Clients have the right to determine their own conduct and courses of action. The fourth principle, *justice*, is the rule to be fair.

A brief example can illustrate how these principles can give conflicting advice and give rise to ethical dilemmas. At the present time in Canada, some doctors, and many others, favour euthanasia (the act of putting to death painlessly a person suffering from an incurable disease). Is this a sufferer's *autonomous* right? Or, should helpers look at this situation from the perspective of the principles of *nonmaleficence* or *beneficence* and prevent "harm" (death) to the sufferer?

Step Two:
In the second step the counsellor implements a moral reasoning strategy. There are four sub-steps to this process. First, it is important that counsellors *secure additional information* concerning the ethical dilemma. This might include finding out more about the client, studying applicable ethical guidelines and examining relevant Canadian or provincial laws. The second sub-step includes the examination of *special circumstances* surrounding a particular case. The next sub-step in the process of implementing a moral reasoning strategy entails *ranking* the moral principles. Obviously, the way in which counsellors rank the principles will dictate subsequent actions. The fourth sub-step is to *consult with colleagues* for comments and additional ideas.

Step Three:
In the third step of ethical decision-making, counsellors prepare for action. To do this, a typical problem-solving approach is suggested:

   a) identification of hoped-for outcomes (e.g., protect the client or protect confidentiality),

b) listing of possible actions,

c) evaluation of the actions on the client, on related others and on society,

d) identification of any competing nonmoral values (e.g., financial or religious considerations)

e) choosing a specific course of action, and

f) testing that choice in terms of universality, publicity and justice.

Step Four:

In the final step, counsellors put into action their ethical decision. Stadler (1985) suggests that if the decision has been difficult, counsellors may need to engage in some ego-strengthening activities such as making a contract with a colleague to carry out the action, or to visualize the completed task with the results being favourable.

Next, concrete steps should be laid out on how to complete the task. Then the action is taken, and finally the action is evaluated.

4. An Integrative Approach

If an examination of models of ethical decision-making is to be truly useful, it is important that each counsellor examine various models of ethical decision-making, and then attempt to integrate the ideas into a model that makes sense to her or him. Following is my personal attempt to integrate the Rest, CPA and Stadler models so that I would be in a better position to understand and deal with ethical decisions. My first step in developing this integration was to highlight the major steps of the three approaches.

Three Model Overview

Rest	Can. Psych. Assoc.	Stadler
1. Recognition of the ethical dilemma.	1. Ethical issues are identified	1. Identifying competing moral principles: a) nonmaleficence, b) beneficence, c) autonomy, d) justice.
2. Courses of action based on principles: a) veracity, b) privacy, c) autonomy, d) promise keeping, e) parentalism, f) self-improvement, g) nonmaleficence, h) equality, and i) sanctity of life.	2. Alternatives are developed 3. Risks and benefits of each alternative are examined 4. Application of principles: a) respect for the dignity of persons, b) responsible caring, c) integrity in relationships, d) responsibility to society.	2. Implementing moral reasoning strategy: a) securing additional information b) examining special circumstances c) ranking d) consulting with colleagues
3. Develop a plan of action. 4. Doing it!	5. Action is taken 6. Action is evaluated 7. Negative consequences of the action are corrected	3. Preparing for action-problem-solving approach 4. Taking action: a) ego strengthening b) concrete steps c) act d) evaluate

Next, I examined more closely those steps and principles that I felt would be most useful for me. The first step of all three models is very much the same in that the ethical issues of a particular situation are identified. I believe an important second step consists of examining the moral and ethical principles that are important in the situation. The principles of the three models could be condensed to include an examination of the following six principles:

a) Sanctity of life,
b) Not wilfully harming others,
c) Keeping promises,
d) Responsible caring,
e) Responsibility to society, and
f) Respecting people's rights to determine their fates.

The third step consists of choosing the most important principles and beginning the action process by:

a) generating alternatives and examining the risks and benefits of each alternative,
b) securing additional information and/or consulting with colleagues, and
c) examining the probable outcomes of various courses of action.

Until this point, this decision-making process has concentrated on fairly cognitive, rational steps, so the fourth step should include involving feelings and emotions in the decision-making. Time permitting, counsellors should use emotional decision techniques such as the following:

a) Quest - a solitary walk in the woods or park where your emotions are allowed to interact with the ethical dilemma being faced;
b) Incubation - 'sleep on it'; or
c) Time projection - projecting the ethical situation into the future and thinking about the various fantasized scenarios.

The last, or fifth step, consists of taking some action. Counsellors should follow a concrete action plan, evaluate the plan, and be prepared to correct any negative consequences that might occur from the action taken.

A brief example will help to show how these five steps might work in actual practice. Questions are presented to help counsellors consider each of the steps in this five-step, integrated approach. A high school counsellor has seen a seventeen-year-old, grade eleven student, John, on numerous occasions. Initially, these counsellor visits came as a result of teacher referrals. Teachers found that John was a "nuisance in the classroom." Over the months, a good relationship developed between the counsellor and John, and frequently John just dropped in to chat. On one such occasion, John talked about his part-time job at a hardware store and how he made quite a bit of extra money "lifting" the occasional article from the store and selling it. When the counsellor got more of the details, he was convinced that considerable theft was involved. He didn't know what to do, since he had assured John on more than one occasion that "things said in my office will never leave this office."

What are the key ethical issues in this situation? The counsellor had promised confidentiality, yet the student's actions were illegal. In the long run, the thefts would probably be discovered and John would be in serious trouble. *What ethical principles are of major importance in this situation?*

Six principles were identified earlier, and the following principles are important in John's situation: keeping promises, responsible caring, not wilfully harming others, responsibility to society and respecting people's rights to determine their own fate.

What are the most important principles and *what are the risks and benefits if these principles are acted upon?* The counsellor examined each one of the principles and considered what would happen if he reported the theft, what would likely happen if he kept quiet and continued to work with John, and how could he best help John. Without identifying John, the counsellor discussed the situation with another counsellor, and was told that "to cover yourself you better tell the principal." The counsellor felt at this time that "responsible caring" and "responsibility to society" were of greatest importance. Before acting, the counsellor asked himself a fourth question: *Will I feel the same way about this situation if I wait a day or two before deciding?* The counsellor decided to "sleep on it" and the following day he took specific steps to deal with this ethical dilemma. *How can I best help John and at the same time stop any future theft?* The counsellor made an appointment with John and informed him that he would have to break confidentiality, since he felt that he just would not be acting responsibly if he allowed the stealing to continue. He tried to convince John that in the long run he might actually be helping him as well. John was given several options by the counsellor regarding the reporting of the theft: by himself, by the counsellor, or with the two of them seeing the appropriate authorities together.

References

Biggs, Donald, & Blocher, Donald. (1987). *Foundations of ethical counseling.* New York: Springer Publishing Company.

Canadian Psychological Association. (1986). *A Canadian code of ethics for psychologists.* Ottawa: Canadian Psychological Association.

Pettifor, Jean L. (1991). How well does the Canadian Code of Ethics serve community psychologists? *Psynopsis*, Winter, 11-12.

Rest, J. (1979). *Development in judging moral issues.* Minneapolis: University of Minnesota Press.

Rest, J. (1984). Research on moral development: Implications for training psychologists. *The Counseling Psychologist*, 12, 19-30.

Stadler, Holly A. (1985). *Confidentiality: The professionals' dilemma.* AACD Video Cassette Series. Alexandria, Virginia: American Association for Counseling and Development Foundation.

CHAPTER TWO

---------- ❖ ----------

Case Studies
In Professional
Behaviour

---------- ❖ ----------

Counselling is a professional occupation, and one of the unique roles of a profession is that members exercise independent judgment, make decisions and provide help.

❖ ❖ ❖ ❖ ❖ ❖ ❖ ❖ ❖ ❖ ❖ ❖ ❖ ❖

GUIDELINES

1 High standards of **professional competence** are expected by all members. Professional growth is exemplified by continuous effort to improve professional practices, teaching services and research. Members recognize the need for continuing education to ensure competent service.

❖

2 Members have a **responsibility** both to the individual who is served and to the institution within which the service is performed to maintain high standards of professional conduct.

❖

3 Ethical behaviour among **professional associates**, both members and non-members, must be expected at all times. Members are obligated, in situations where information is possessed raising serious doubts as to the ethical behaviour of other members, to take action that is conducive to rectifying these conditions.

❖

4 A member should not claim or imply **professional qualifications** exceeding those possessed and is responsible for correcting any misrepresentations of qualifications by others.

❖

5 In establishing **fees** for professional counselling services, members must consider the financial status of clients and locality. In the event that the established fee structure is inappropriate for a counsellee, assistance must be provided in finding comparable services of acceptable cost.

❖

6 Members, in **providing information** to the public or to subordinates, peers or superiors, have a clear responsibility to see that the information is accurate, unbiased and consists of factual, objective data. The manner of presentation should be conducted ethically and professionally as well.

❖

7 Members recognize their **boundaries of competence** and provide only those services and use only those techniques for which they are qualified by training or experience. Members should only accept those positions for which they are professionally qualified.

❖

8 In a counselling relationship, the counsellor is aware of the intimacy of the relationship and maintains respect for the counsellee and avoids engaging in activities that seek to meet the **counsellor's personal needs** at the expense of that counsellee.

❖

9 Members do not condone or engage in **sexual harassment** which is defined as deliberate or repeated comments, gestures, or physical contacts of a sexual nature.

❖

10 Through awareness of the negative impact of both racial and sexual **stereotyping and discrimination**, members guard the individual rights and personal dignity of the client in the counselling relationship.

❖

11 Products or services provided by the member by means of classroom instruction, public lectures, demonstrations, written articles, radio or television programs, or other types of **media** must meet the criteria cited in these standards.

❖

◆ ◆ ◆ ◆ ◆ ◆ ◆ ◆ ◆ ◆ ◆ ◆ ◆ ◆

CASE STUDIES

1 High standards of *professional competence* are expected by all members. Professional growth is exemplified by continuous effort to improve professional practices, teaching services and research. Members recognize the need for continuing education to ensure competent service.

Improving Professional Practices (+)

An experienced elementary counsellor, upon arriving in a new school in a different school division, realized that many of the children in her school had problems that were a result of poor parenting. Also, due to the high number of immigrant families in this counsellor's school, she attributed some of the children's problems to their families' unfamiliarity with Canadian customs.

The counsellor spent the remainder of the year with these children researching their needs, their parents' needs and the differences in these families' cultures in comparison to Canadian ways. She worked to improve her skills in cultural diversity in order that she could better serve her students.

After much research and consultation with other counsellors, she felt better qualified to facilitate evening parenting workshops for the community. Four such workshops were run throughout the school year dealing with topics such as discipline and family life education. All were highly regarded by parents, staff and administration.

Counsellor Networking (+)

A counsellor in a small rural school division organized counsellor peer group meetings so that she could meet with her colleagues on a regular basis. This group periodically joined forces with a group of counsellors from two neighbouring school divisions so that they could invite speakers from a major urban centre. The speakers kept them informed about urban counselling issues, new research and upcoming professional development opportunities. Other speakers and workshops helped them upgrade their skills. In their own divisional meetings they were able to consult with their colleagues about their clients while still maintaining confidentiality.

Insuring Children Receive Guidance From a Competent Counsellor (-)

An urban school division had more teachers returning from leaves than they had positions available for the 1992/93 school year. An extremely competent and highly regarded grade two teacher in the division returned from a two year leave of absence. She was given a few alternatives after she had notified the superintendent of her desire to return. Yet, being primary, the only position she felt remotely capable of accepting was a guidance position in a kindergarten through grade eight school. The school division did require that guidance counsellors be trained. The school with the opening was one of the toughest in the division. The previous counsellor had quit as a result of the stress he experienced from the job, and, internal advertising had resulted in no other interest from qualified staff. The superintendent awarded the primary teacher the position in spite of her having no training in counselling.

Professional Development Missing (-)

A school counsellor got his Master's degree in counselling in the 1970s. Over the next 20 years he took no additional course work in counselling, seldom went to counselling in-services and never attended a national counselling conference.

COMMENTS AND QUESTIONS

This first ethical guideline on the need for high standards of professional competence from counsellors raises a number of questions. Who determines a counsellor's competence? Should competence be determined by the counsellor or should it perhaps be other members? Should a client determine a counsellor's competence since it is the counsellee who can truly speak of the member's effectiveness?

Counsellors are professionals. Therefore, members and clients assume that counsellors are capable of determining their own competence. Professionals must be treated as professionals. They must be trusted to make sound judgments, to know their limitations and to know when consultation, re-training and/or additional education is necessary.

Still, counsellors are human and, humans are known to make mistakes and can be misunderstood. Thus, to protect counsellors and their clients the following two criteria are recommended before the public can enter into a counselling relationship:

a) **Professional Disclosure** – Prior to beginning a counselling situation, the client would be informed of the counsellor's qualifications, services offered, therapeutic process, nature of confidentiality, administrative procedures and finally, the client's own rights and responsibilities, and

b) **Written Contract** – After discussing the terms and coming to a mutual agreement of the upcoming counselling situation, the counsellor and the client should enter into a formal contract so that there will never be future questions of what was expected or promised by either partner in counselling.

1. How do counsellors recognize their own competence and how do they set limitations for themselves?

2. Degrees, licensing and/or certification do not insure competence of psychologists, social workers or counsellors, so what can clients do to insure they are receiving the best counselling available to them?

3. Is it ethically wrong to hire a teacher who is not certified as a trained counsellor for a school counselling position?

4. What are some things that counsellors could do to improve present professional practices?

2 Members have a *responsibility* both to the individual who is served and to the institution within which the service is performed to maintain high standards of professional conduct.

Suicide Threat (+)

Jane Sutherland has been engaged in counselling a client for two years as part of court-mandated treatment. Jane schedules a brief appointment at 4:00 P.M. and expects to be home with her family by 5:00. During this scheduled appointment, Jane is diverted by the comment "I don't know if I'll make it to September". Jane asks for clarification of the emotions behind the statement and determines that the client is depressed and has been contemplating suicide all week, having given hints to staff of a residential treatment centre where he has been staying for the last two months. The client has several plausible and available methods to meet his intentions. No intensive or extensive intervention has been done to that point by the facility staff. Jane Sutherland continues with a suicide check and is unable to move the client toward committing to living another day. She tells the client that she has no choice but to escort him to the hospital for follow-up. Jane notifies agency staff of the predicament and transports him to the hospital where a series of interviews occur and suicidal ideation diminishes. Jane remains as a support for the client during the hospital intake/treatment period.

Theft Disclosure (+)

A client discloses to his counsellor that he has stolen something from his employer. This disclosure occurs well after qualitative gains have been made in counselling. The counsellor is torn by his commitment to the client and confidentiality and the legalities of knowing about an illicit activity. The counsellor works for an agency funded by the Justice Department. The agency guidelines to counsellors indicate that all known or potential criminal activity is to be reported. The counsellor encourages the client to turn himself over to authorities and indicates that he will accompany him to the police, acting as a support.

Gathering Court Data (-)

A counsellor is instructed to compile a report for the court regarding a subject charged and having plead guilty to sexually assaulting an 11 year old girl. As part of the report, a victim impact statement is to be included in the report. The counsellor will be required to obtain information regarding the psychological and physical damage to the victim. This agency has guidelines regarding the interviewing of any victim who may be further traumatized by having to reiterate already available information. The counsellor contacts the victim directly to arrange an interview. The interview takes place at the counsellor's office, where a series of questions is asked. Examples of these questions include: "What emotional impact has this assault had on you?", "What physical impact has this assault had on you?", "Why did you allow the assault to occur?", "What attempts did you make to stop the assault?", "Why did you wait so long to report the assault?", "Are you sure about the assault occurring?". During the course of the interview the victim becomes overwhelmed by the focus of the questions, but, the counsellor continues with the battery of questions slated for the agenda.

Inadequate Information (-)

A counsellor is employed at an agency which provides pregnancy information services to adolescents. The agency is of the opinion that clients have the right to be advised of all available resources in the community and be referred to these if they so choose. A female adolescent comes to the counsellor and requests information on different options regarding her pregnancy. The counsellor who is pro-life fails to provide the client with information on abortion, but provides information related to adoption and keeping her expected baby.

COMMENTS AND QUESTIONS

This ethical guideline provides a clear understanding that the professional member must demonstrate "responsible" behaviour to the counsellee as well as to the institution within which the counsellor is working. Despite this crucial and well-meaning mandate, it would be rare to find a counsellor who has not been challenged at some level where he or she would be required to reflect on this ethical guideline and seek a creative response to remain ethical.

Counsellors will invariably find conflict in responsibility to clients or the institution they serve. This may arise when an employer or institution requests a specific level of service for its clients that is not commensurate with professional standards and therefore represents a breach of responsibility. The question remains as to who is ultimately responsible: the employer who is underfunded to provide the actual number of staff or services to meet the needs of the client population? or, is it the counsellor who gives in to the supervisor's advice to provide limited service to the majority of clients. It is likely that in many cases the supervisor and counsellor follow the same code of ethics; or at least, a similar series of ethical instructions. It would be easy to say that the supervisor should cut down the number of cases the agency is willing to handle. This may be appropriate for private agencies, however, government agencies may not have this option. They are expected to provide the service despite the lack of staff or resources.

1. In the third case, what should the counsellor have done as a responsible measure in his treatment of the victim?

2. Is it realistic, with large client caseloads, to expect the counsellor to provide full services to all clients? What would you do if you were a counsellor in an agency that received too many clients?

3. What type of orientation should counsellors receive in regards to the ethic of 'responsibility to client and institution'?

4. Based on the examples cited, how important do you feel it is to maintain the ethic of 'professional conduct and high institutional standards'? Why? If you were a staff trainer, how would you demonstrate the proper implementation of ethical conduct?

3 Ethical behaviour among *professional associates*, both members and non-members, must be expected at all times. Members are obligated, in situations where information is possessed raising serious doubts as to the ethical behaviour of other members, to take action that is conducive to rectifying these conditions.

Reporting of Abuse (+)

After an appointment with a school counsellor, a fifteen year-old male student sought an interview with another counsellor who discovered during the conversation, through student disclosure and physical evidence, that the student had been physically abused by his guardian the previous evening. The student volunteered further information that indicated that he was no longer permitted to enter his home and that no action had been taken by the school counsellor to secure his safety and well-being. Following guidelines for legal responsibilities and school division protocol, the teacher contacted Child and Family Services to report suspected abuse, informed the principal of this action, then sought out the school counsellor to advise him of the actions that had been taken. Once approached on the issue of abuse, the counsellor and teacher discussed the school policy regarding ethical responsibilities and the importance of reporting information to proper authorities.

Mentorship Program (+)

A high school principal acknowledged that some of the new counsellors he had recently hired were having difficulty integrating the ethical guidelines set forth by the CGCA, the school's policies and procedures, and the provincial laws. In order to address this issue, he implemented a mentorship program whereby experienced counsellors were paired with novice counsellors. The ultimate goal of the program was to promote and encourage ethical behaviour within the classroom and within the school. Through modeling, supervision, and consultation, the experienced and exemplary counsellors guided the novice counsellors to resolve ethical dilemmas as they occurred naturally.

Conduct of an Associate (-)

During a routine counselling session prior to graduation, a distraught grade twelve student confided to her counsellor that one of her teachers had abruptly ended an intimate relationship with her. She indicated that her life was "falling apart" and she didn't know what she was going to do after graduation. The student requested that no action be taken since she would be graduating in two weeks and she did not want to harm anyone's reputation. The counsellor consoled the student and the request by the student for no further action was granted.

Dating a Student (-)

A teacher is secretly dating one of his grade twelve students. The school counsellor, who happens to be one of the teacher's good friends, sees them out together once and dismisses it. As the school year continues, the counsellor sees them together on numerous other occasions. The counsellor realizes the teacher-student relationship of dating is inappropriate. However, he chooses to remain silent and ignore the matter, for fear of jeopardizing the teacher's job and losing a good friend.

COMMENTS AND QUESTIONS

This ethical guideline is a mandate to guide counsellors in their everyday conduct and in the resolution of ethical dilemmas. It assists in the evaluation of questionable behaviour by colleagues. The basic principles underlying this guideline are the respect for the dignity and integrity of persons, responsible caring in counselling relationships and responsibility to society.

Doubts should be raised as to the ethical or non-ethical behaviour of professional associates, both members and non-members, in the following situations:

a) where the welfare of a student is at risk,

b) where the reputation of a school could be compromised, and

c) where confidence in the counselling profession could be diminished.

Questions to consider, in reference to this ethical guideline and the cases presented, include:

1. What are some common feelings and/or thoughts experienced when a counsellor has serious doubts about the ethical behaviour of a colleague?
2. Has the CGCA set up guidelines to follow when unethical behaviour is suspected? If so, what *are* the guidelines?
3. What is the protocol for reporting known unethical behaviour of a colleague?
4. What are the likely short-term, on-going, and long-term risks and benefits (i.e. consequences) of each course of action (e.g. reporting, not reporting) on the individual(s)/ group(s) involved or likely to be affected (e.g. student, school, colleague, profession, society, self)?

4 **A member should not claim or imply** *professional qualifications* **exceeding those possessed and is responsible for correcting any misrepresentations of qualifications by others.**

No Master's Degree (+)

A private counselling agency hired a person with a Master's degree in Social Work. He claimed to have attended a particular university in England. During the time he was employed in the agency he became the assistant to the director and was expected to become director. In anticipation of his taking this position, his credentials were checked. For some reason this had not been done when he was first hired. He had never attended the university and did not have a degree at all. He was fired from his position and a procedure was instituted so that all prospective employees had their credentials confirmed before they were offered a position.

Needed Referral (+)

Gail Bruce had counselled her client for twelve sessions with limited progress. During this time she was able to build a good rapport with her client and she felt this rapport was the strongest part of the counselling. Gail Bruce believed that the client needed treatment that was beyond the scope of her training. Although the client was given an information and consent form before counselling began, Ms. Bruce did not believe the client fully understood her qualifications. She felt she had two choices: to continue to treat her client to the limits stated on her consent form, or to refer the client to another counsellor who was known to be successful in using the treatment procedures needed by the client. Gail Bruce felt she was ethically bound to do what was best for her client and referred the client to her associate.

Cultural differences (-)

A Native child was referred to Bob Smith for consultation. Though he had never worked with Natives before, Bob was confident in his ability to help Nancy work through her problems. He learned that Nancy had lived with her family on a reserve her entire life and had recently moved to the city to live with her grandmother. He also learned of the importance of culture in Nancy's life. After fifteen sessions, Bob Smith was at a loss as to what to do. He was not making any progress with Nancy using techniques he had been successful with in the past. His success in the past had been with white, middle-class clients. He found it difficult to establish a relationship with Nancy due to his limited knowledge of her culture. He consulted with his associates, but they did not feel confident to counsel Nancy. They encouraged him to remain in the relationship as he had a good success rate with his therapeutic process in the past. Pushing his doubts aside, Bob did as the associates suggested. He continued to be unsuccessful with Nancy and was later informed she was returning to her home reserve. Bob Smith was relieved to discover he would not be counselling Nancy again; but at the same time he felt he should have sought help in working with Nancy or referred her to someone with experience in working with clients other than 'white, middle-class'.

Continuing Education (-)

Fred Campbell was licensed in 1955 during a time when there were many advancements being made in counselling. He often attended workshops and lectures to keep up-to-date on any developments in his field. During his career, Dr. Campbell was often asked to present at various workshops due to the success of his work and research. When he was approached to join a private practice in 1980, he did so due to his failing health. Over the years Fred Campbell continued with his private practice, but he failed to keep abreast of any new developments in counselling. He felt he had devoted enough of his life to theories and wanted to end his career applying those theories to clients. While discussing a recent development presented at a workshop, Fred's associates were surprised to discover he knew nothing about this information. The associates encouraged him to update his knowledge and skills, but he declined. Fred insisted he had sufficient counselling knowledge to treat his clients. The associates did not force the issue and Fred Campbell continued to remain on the counselling insti-

tute's information form; a form that informed clients that all counsellors were continuing their education in counselling.

COMMENTS AND QUESTIONS

As professional counsellors become more popular and powerful in people's lives there is a greater need for guidelines to protect both counsellor and client. Upon meeting a new client, counsellors should be responsible for providing an information form that is mutually beneficial. The consent forms would contain all pertinent information about counsellors and their practice. It would be the counsellor's responsibility to clearly define and explain all information on the document to client satisfaction. Ideally, a professional counselling association would certify all counsellors and verify the information on the consent form to protect both the client and counsellor.

Some questions that could be considered when examining the ethics involved in professional qualifications are:

1. Should it be necessary to continue training after certification to maintain qualifications?
2. Is it realistic to list specific requirements that need to be met every two to five years in order to continue practising?
3. What rights, beyond terminating counselling, does a client have if he or she discovers that the counsellor's stated or implied qualifications are inaccurate?
4. What questions should a client ask upon entering a counselling relationship?

5 In establishing *fees* for professional counselling services, members must consider the financial status of clients and locality. In the event that the established fee structure is inappropriate for a counsellee, assistance must be provided in finding comparable services of acceptable cost.

Establishing Fees (+)

An economically disadvantaged client who is also deaf had sought out counselling on his own because he was experiencing problems with anxiety attacks, insomnia, and anger, and he had become fearful of the consequences of these episodes. He was assessed at the lowest rate on the counsellor's fee schedule. In order to communicate with the counsellor, he required the services of a deaf interpreter at the rate of $50 per hour. The funding arrangement of the interpreter was external to this agency and could therefore not be adjusted to meet the client's economic needs. Despite the additional cost, the client signed all necessary 'commit-ment-to-pay' forms and began attending counselling sessions, paying for all the counselling services on a regular basis.

Referral (+)

An upper middle class couple was seeking help with parenting and marital issues. This couple had recently filed for bankruptcy and, as well, were having difficulties dealing with their adult children who were non-working and refusing to leave the relative comforts of home. Parenting issues on how best to deal with these children and the marital discord stemming from the couple's conflict over these matters were the motivating factors for this couple seeking counselling. The fee had been adjusted to a modest level to accommodate their current economic circumstances. The couple insisted that they could not afford any fee as a result of their bankruptcy. The counsellor suggested that the couple receive counselling at one of the public counselling clinics or at a family services agency.

Fee Collection (-)

A young woman has sought help from a counsellor in private practice for problems with self-image and self-confidence. The fee schedule was discussed, and even though the client disclosed that she was in a particularly stressed position financially, the therapist's regular fees were agreed upon. Sessions commenced and the client realized an improvement. However, the counsellor allowed the client to become four sessions behind in payments. When the debt was discussed, the counsellor aggressively insisted that since she (the counsellor) was working only part-time due to the recent delivery of her first child, she needed the full fee immediately.

No Credit (-)

John and Ellen, a couple who have been married for 15 years, are receiving marriage counselling. Ellen's father, who lives in another city, is very ill and John and Ellen take time off from work to visit him. When they return, they plan to resume counselling, but being quite short of money, they ask the counsellor if they can pay him at the end of the month, some three weeks away. The counsellor tells them he does not counsel any clients who can't afford his fees and tells them to go elsewhere.

COMMENTS AND QUESTIONS

This guideline clearly states that counsellors should consider the ability of the client to pay fees when charging for professional services. Furthermore, should a client not be able to pay, it is the responsibility of the counsellor to help the client find some other services.

Successful counsellors in private practice, who have more demand for their services than they can realistically handle, can easily decide to see only those clients who can pay the highest fees. Is there a danger of the poor eventually receiving counselling from the less successful (possibly less qualified) counsellors who charge lower rates?

1. Should provinces introduce fee regulations for counsellors? Would service decline as a result?
2. What does the private counsellor do when someone is not in a position to pay fees, yet there is no "comparable service" available?

3. Should counselling services be part of our medical services available to all Canadians?

4. What range of fees should counsellors with a Master's degree or a Ph.D. be allowed to charge?

6 Members, in *providing information* to the public or to subordinates, peers or superiors, have a clear responsibility to see that the information is accurate, unbiased and consists of factual, objective data. The manner of presentation should be conducted ethically and professionally as well.

Reporting a Counselling Failure (+)

In a rural high school, the senior counsellor was told by a grade nine counsellee, whom he had been seeing for two-and-one-half years, that she had been, for a year, the victim of sexual abuse by her uncle. Reviewing her records in preparation for deposition to the child welfare authorities, the counsellor realized that about a year ago the girl had demonstrated significant behaviour, language, and attitudinal changes which the counsellor had not pursued; changes which could clearly have signalled abuse. In the deposition, the counsellor made a full report on all these details, aware of the importance they might have in a potential criminal action.

Reporting Objective Data (+)

A composite high school in the city core of a large metropolitan area found that it had been experiencing increasing demands from government agencies for reports on specific cases. While some of these demands were internal, most came from outside the school system, as changing social conditions involved students in custody cases and with juvenile courts and child welfare agencies. The counselling department head recognized this growing trend early in its development and engaged the counsellors in establishing protocols to ensure that reports would consist only of factual, objective data. Advice from the Canadian Guidance and Counselling Association was sought, counsellors were in-serviced in observational skills, and a record-keeping system was devised which would aid counsellors in discerning between the various degrees of objectivity, from scientific data to impressionistic comments. A protocol was established, ensuring that the more impressionistic observations were excluded from reports.

Unethical Presentation (-)

A large urban school division, experiencing its third year of zero growth in provincial grants, was undertaking an intensive programme evaluation in order to prioritize elements of its operations. The superintendent required that the counselling section of educational support services provide data concerning the classes of cases and the counsellor time spent on the cases. In full knowledge that in 1988 both the severity of cases and their number was atypically low, the director of counselling chose that year as her baseline year, giving the impression of significant growth in demand for services in the recent three years.

A Biased Programme (-)

During the late 1980s public awareness of the threat of AIDS had grown significantly in a large rural town. The single high school in the town found itself under pressure from the school board, dominated by clerics of the evangelical religions most common in the area, to create a student AIDS awareness programme which did not deal with the known primary sexual risks and did not mention the non-abstinence means of reducing risk. The counselling department was aware that part of the board's agenda was generally to reduce student sexual activity. The counselling department prepared and promoted the programme as the school board had required.

COMMENTS AND QUESTIONS

Like all professions, counselling has two primary interests: that of the well-being of the client and that of its own improvement and perfection as a human art. This CGCA ethical guideline is directed towards ensuring that counselling will be improved by being founded upon truth. Threats to truth in reporting come from three areas: carelessness and sloppiness in observation and in reporting; the exertion upon the counsellor of external political pressure which places the counsellor in a "conflict of values" situation; and the seeking of political or other advantage by the counsellor. The last case is a purely ethical case involving the coun-sellor's personal moral stature and involves other CGCA guidelines. The other cases require counsellors to be sensitive to their environment and personal competence, to be able to make careful and truthful judgments and to strive for accuracy and honesty.

1. What distinctions might be helpful to the counsellor in separating out the degrees of difference between fact and opinion?
2. What political considerations might occur which would pressure the counsellor to tell less than "the truth, the whole truth, and nothing but the truth" in reporting?
3. What biases, institutional and personal, might come into play to limit the counsellor's ability to be truthful in reporting?
4. What special obligations do counsellors have when reporting to the public; that is, to people without specific background in the issues and methods of social sciences?

7 Members recognize their *boundaries of competence* and provide only those services and use only those techniques for which they are qualified by training or experience. Members should only accept those positions for which they are professionally qualified.

Referral (+)

A beginning counsellor is speaking with a student about the student's recently declining grades. In the course of the discussion, they get into reasons why the student's school work is down and in a moment of disclosure the student admits to abuse in the home. The counsellor immediately recognizes that this is beyond the scope of his abilities and he notifies the proper authorities and refers the student to qualified counselling facilities specifically geared for dealing with abuse cases such as this.

Career Counsellor (+)

A graduate student, from a Department of Educational Psychology in a Canadian university, decides to begin her own private counselling service. In spite of the fact that many clients ask to see her for marriage counselling, she refuses all these clients, pointing out that her own training and practicum experiences were mainly in employment and career counselling.

Avoiding Teacher Lay-Offs (-)

A school division has had a declining student population for the past three years. The school superintendent makes the decision that 15 teachers will have "to be terminated". At the same time, this division makes the decision to have a school counsellor in each of their 18 elementary schools. Teachers with counsellor training or without training apply for the counselling positions. The counselling jobs are offered to several trained counsellors, but 12 of the new elementary school counselling positions are offered to teachers in the division with no counsellor training. All 12 teachers accept the counselling positions for which they have no training.

No Training in Marriage Counselling (-)

An employment counsellor with eight years experience decides to begin private counselling on a part-time basis. Her first clients are a couple who wish to receive marriage counselling. The counsellor happily accepts these clients for counselling even though she has had no training in marriage counselling.

COMMENTS AND QUESTIONS

This ethical guideline clearly dictates that counsellors need to evaluate their abilities and level of experience. When situations arise which are beyond the training or experience of a counsellor, it is unethical to proceed blindly into counselling. As Section B, Guideline 6 indicates, consultation with other professionals about such situations is both ethical and recommended. Furthermore, counsellors should consider even casual discussions with colleagues an important means to determine others' experience and expertise and then should not hesitate to tap into these resources whenever the need arises. This guideline suggests that counsellors provide only those services for which they are qualified. A natural extension of this guideline is that counsellors maintain active enrolment in professional groups, (determine areas of expertise among colleagues, and services available) and participate regularly in professional development activities.

Lastly, the guideline clearly states that counsellors accept only those positions for which they are professionally qualified. This means that teachers should not become school counsellors if they have not received counsellor training.

1. Is it better to provide some counselling if no other services are available?
2. How do counsellors determine their "boundaries of competence"?
3. What should be the training of a "professionally qualified" counsellor?
4. How can counselling organizations stop the practice of school divisions giving teachers (with no counsellor training) positions in counselling?

8 In a counselling relationship, the counsellor is aware of the intimacy of the relationship and maintains respect for the counsellee and avoids engaging in activities that seek to meet the *counsellor's personal needs* at the expense of that counsellee.

Being Objective (+)

A youth counsellor working in a church setting frequently counsels young people regarding their concerns or problems. Joyce, a 19 year old university student, reveals to the counsellor that she is pregnant and that she wants information on the effects of adoption and abortion on women. Although the counsellor personally is opposed to abortion in most situations, she objectively attempts to present the issues and effects on women of both abortion and adoption.

Client Dependence (+)

A counsellor has been seeing a client for some time. They have a good relationship and the client has expressed her admiration for the counsellor and gratitude for the help being given. The counsellor begins to feel that the client is not making any progress on the issue of making her own decisions and acting on them. The client seems overly dependent on the approval of the counsellor when making decisions and does not take action on these decisions unless urged to do so by the counsellor. The counsellor explains his concern over the lack of progress in this area and the issue of dependency and suggests various options available to the client.

Beyond Counselling (-)

A counsellor in private practice is asked by parents of a twelve year old boy to counsel him relating to severe behaviour problems that are causing him trouble both at school and in the community. The counsellor develops a liking for the boy and begins to see him outside of the counselling sessions, taking him to movies, etc. This practice continues as the counsellor finds that he enjoys spending time with the boy and the child seems to be responding well

to the attention. The parents are also pleased with the arrangement as it provides some respite from the tensions in their home. The relationship continues to grow until the boy is spending weekends at the home of the counsellor, a single man.

Counsellor's Needs (-)

A husband and wife have been seeing a marriage counsellor for about three years. The sessions began where the counsellor was seeing each spouse separately, then they came to the sessions together for a short while. On a rare occasion, in the last year and a half, the couple sees the counsellor together. The wife continues seeing the counsellor once a week. The counsellor, even though he realizes that the wife is becoming emotionally dependent on him, makes no mention of this issue and continues the sessions.

COMMENTS AND QUESTIONS

Counsellors are professionals who are ethically obliged to act in the best interests of the client. Because of the nature of the counselling relationship counsellors are in a position of power, while the clients are in a very vulnerable position. If counselling is to be an effective activity the public must be able to trust that a counsellor will avoid situations where there is a conflict between the best interests of the client and those of the counsellor. The individual counsellor must consider how his or her actions reflect upon the profession as a whole. The trust of the public can be lost over the unethical, unprofessional or irresponsible behaviour of one member of the profession.

The counsellor should endeavour to become aware of his or her own needs and how these could interfere with the counselling relationship. This does not imply that the counsellor must be without personal problems or areas that he or she needs to deal with, but that the counsellor should be aware of these issues and not bring them into the counselling relationship. Counsellors have responsibilities to themselves and their clients to seek help in dealing with problems that could interfere with their functioning within a counselling relationship, and to consult with colleagues or supervisors in cases where they are unsure about the extent to which their own needs are interfering with their ability to be effective in the counselling relationship. If counsellors become aware that they are using the counselling relationship to meet their own needs rather than the needs of the client, counsellors have a responsibility to refer clients to another counsellor and to terminate the relationship.

1. How can counsellors distinguish between trust and warmth in a counselling relationship and counsellors' needs for closeness in interpersonal relationships?
2. Should counsellors (see the third case) spend time with clients "outside the office"?
3. Are there some personal needs that you have that would interfere with your being an effective counsellor?
4. Should counsellors deliberately keep somewhat distant from clients to avoid any possibility of too much intimacy in the counselling relationship?

9 Members do not condone or engage in *sexual harassment* which is defined as deliberate or repeated comments, gestures, or physical contacts of a sexual nature.

Not Condoning (+)

At a junior high school, the guidance counsellor has had a number of female students coming to see him regarding a certain science teacher on staff. This staff member has always taken a great interest in promoting science interest among girls and encouraging the girls to become actively involved in their own science education. To this end, he has set up a special science club for the girls in his classes, and has made participating in the club a requirement for extra marks. He has club meetings after school and has each of the girls in the club working on a project, for marks. Recently, he has suggested that some of the girls see him on an individual basis for extra help with their projects. He has given the girls various reasons; for example, one girl was told she had exceptional abilities and he wanted to help her develop these talents. Another was told she was not going to pass science unless she came for extra help. All of the girls report that in these individual meetings, Mr. X becomes overly friendly, sitting very close to the students, sometimes touching their arms or putting an arm around their shoulders. The girls are feeling very uncomfortable about this, but nothing overtly improper in nature has occurred. The guidance counsellor decides to have a talk with Mr. X to inform him of the concerns of the female students, and to let him know that his behaviour could be construed as sexual harassment. The counsellor suggests to Mr. X that he should probably cease insisting on having private meeting with female students after school hours, and if a student requires help, he should have the meeting in a more public forum, such as the office or library, rather than in his classroom. The counsellor also informs Mr. X that she will continue to check in with the students in question, to ensure they are feeling more comfortable in Mr. X's science classes. Privately, she makes a notation of the date and nature of the conversation, as well as plans to check with the students periodically to ensure that there are no further incidents. She decides that should she have any more complaints, she will make a report to her department head and the administration.

Education (+)

The guidance counsellor at a certain high school has become increasingly concerned about the issue of sexual harassment, and knows that while many staff members are aware of the issue, most are not knowledgeable about the type of behaviours which could be construed as sexual harassment. He decides to approach the administration of the school about holding a workshop at the upcoming school inservice. He plans to invite speakers to explain to staff members what types of actions or comments constitute sexual harassment, how to respond to student concerns regarding the behaviour of fellow students or teachers, and how to handle situations in which they (teachers) feel they are the victims of harassment, by both students or other people with whom they may come in contact. His rationale for suggesting the inservice presentation is that once teachers have clear guidelines for proper behaviour, they will be less likely to find themselves in a compromising position, and hopefully, they will pass their new knowledge on to their students, who in turn, will become more aware of behaviours which may make others uncomfortable.

Condoning (-)

In a junior high school, the physical education teacher, who also happens to be the guidance counsellor, notices a problem developing in one of the co-educational gym classes. One of the students, a boy named Justin, has been harassing some of the more physically mature girls during the ten-minute run at the start of every class. He began by staring overtly at their chests as they ran by him, and has now progressed to making suggestive comments. The girls are clearly uncomfortable with the attention, and have become increasingly resistant to doing the run. The gym teacher feels that Justin is just being a typical adolescent boy, preoccupied with his sexuality, and this will pass in time. On the other hand, he feels the girls are over-reacting to a situation that they will have to get used to anyway, since boys will be boys, and he lets the girls know that he will impose penalties if they refuse to participate in the ten-minute run at the beginning of the class.

Student Discomfort (-)

The guidance counsellor in a high school has been asked to teach the new "Life Skills" course to all grade 10 students. The course includes a unit on human sexuality, and is designed to be taught in co-educational classes. The counsellor believes students get the most out of classes if they are made to feel as though they are active participants, and follows this philosophy in teaching the human sexuality component of the course. He begins the unit by having each student fill out an explicit questionnaire on his/her sexual maturation, asking such questions as when the girls first started menstruation, and when the boys first noticed they were maturing sexually. He then uses the results to compare students to one another in a discussion of how maturation occurs at different times for different members of the class. Even when he notices some of the students becoming embarrassed at having such personal details revealed to the class, he persists in making reference to the questionnaire results at various times during the ensuing weeks. He continues to make sexual comments about specific students in spite of the fact that students are openly uncomfortable with his sexual descriptions.

COMMENTS AND QUESTIONS

Harassment has been defined as disturbing or troubling another person by persistent, repeated attacks. This guideline is clear, members do not condone or engage in sexual harassment. Members of a professional counselling association are expected to do something about colleagues involved in sexual harassment. This action may consist of confronting a colleague on her or his sexual harassment, and it may mean reporting continued harassment to appropriate authorities.

1. What is your definition of sexual harassment? Give some specific examples.

2. What resources or assistance is available for members who must deal with sexual harassment?

3. What are some of the risks involved in reporting a case of sexual harassment? What are the benefits?

4. If a colleague appears to be sexually harassing another person, would you confront the individual or would you report the individual? Comment.

10 Through awareness of the negative impact of both racial and sexual *stereotyping and discrimination*, members guard the individual rights and personal dignity of the client in the counselling relationship.

Counselling Services (+)

At a division meeting of administrators and school counsellors, the counsellors submitted to the administration that their schools must make every attempt to provide students with as many options as possible. The submission included recommendations regarding the equitable hiring of qualified male and female counsellors, providing each student the opportunity to seek counsel from someone they felt comfortable approaching, regardless of their gender. It was also suggested that the division expand the current facilities to allow for the increase in personnel and the appropriate confidential space required by each counsellor.

Sexual Stereotyping (+)

During a grade eight team meeting, teachers, administrators and counsellors examined the results of the eighth grade on the Canadian Tests of Basic Skills. Comments were made about the low scores in mathematics by many of the females. One male teacher said these results were not unexpected and that "girls never do as well as boys in mathematics" since they don't understand mathematics. Several teachers agreed. The counsellor felt this was unfair to the girls and talked to the group about their attitudes towards females and mathematics.

Stereotypical Jobs (-)

When considering post-secondary education, a graduating female student made an appointment with the guidance office to discuss the options available to her. She was referred to the female counsellor. While waiting in her office, she noted that most of the literature that the counsellor had displayed was in the areas of education, nursing, and secretarial studies, all of which could be labelled as traditional female employment. When she posed the question about alternative career choices in other fields, the counsellor responded with skepticism about non-traditional jobs for females and stated that she was not familiar with the requirements for fields such as engineering or medicine nor would she advocate the pursuit in such a career for any young woman.

Discriminatory Counselling (-)

During a rash of break and entry crimes in a small town, local authorities suggested that the high school provide guidance and counselling for the student body to discuss the problem as well as outline the possible outcomes of such behaviours. The school agreed and the counsellor proceeded to organize group counselling sessions for the aboriginal students within the student population. The session was announced over the school's public address system as being mandatory for all aboriginal students, but no provisions were made for counselling other students because it was assumed that they would probably not be involved in the break and entry crimes.

COMMENTS AND QUESTIONS

With the global community gradually becoming a reality, the importance of multiculturalism in counselling is increasingly important. The Canadian Charter of Rights and Freedom does not allow for discrimination and guards the rights of all Canadians. Racial and sexual stereotypes and discrimination must not be allowed. Counsellors can not be "culturally encapsulated" and rely on stereotypes when working with culturally diverse clients.

1. What efforts are being made in your counselling centre to promote non-traditional work for women and men?

2. Is it the responsibility of counsellors to educate others regarding sexual and racial stereotyping?

3. What are the more subtle forms of racial and sexual stereotyping that counsellors must guard against?

4. Should re-education or education of counsellors on multicultural issues be mandatory?

11 Products or services provided by the member by means of classroom instruction, public lectures, demonstrations, written articles, radio or television programs, or other types of *media* must meet the criteria cited in these standards.

Boundaries of Competence (+)

A school counsellor is a guest on a radio program and receives a call from a listener asking advice about her troubled marriage. The counsellor has very little experience in marriage counselling and explains that he is not qualified to comment, but refers the caller to an appropriate agency for information and help.

Professional Qualifications (+)

A family counsellor was prepared to speak at a public lecture. The counsellor was introduced by the lecture coordinator who gave a short personal history of the counsellor and listed the counsellor's qualifications and experience. The counsellor realized that her educational qualifications had been incorrectly stated and corrected the error for the audience before starting her lecture.

Post-Secondary Career and Educational Information (-)

The post-secondary career and educational information in one high school was provided by the counselling department. This information was placed on display and was available for viewing by the entire student body. Unfortunately, the information available only applied to a small percentage of students, those wishing to attend university. The information did not apply to vocational training or job training for those students not aspiring to university. Also, the counselling offered about this information was only available to those meeting requirements for university.

Psychodrama (-)

A counsellor-educator has been invited to demonstrate several new psychodrama techniques in front of a large audience. She asks for volunteers on whom to demonstrate the techniques.

The demonstration begins without any arrangements having been made regarding confidentiality, audience involvement or follow-up.

COMMENTS AND QUESTIONS

Counsellors must make every attempt to insure that media materials:

a) are appropriate for the reading level and maturity of the audience,

b) are accurate, unbiased and gender and culture fair,

c) are distributed with appropriate explanations, and

d) are giving a fair representation of all sides of an issue.

1. What range of materials should be available in a high school, junior high school, and elementary school counselling office regarding sensitive life issues, future education options, and future job opportunities?

2. How can educators and counsellors increase the availability of media materials that are more culturally aware?

3. What factors would you need to consider when using media materials to discuss a cultural issue?

4. What precautions should be taken to make sure that all media meet ethical standards?

❖ ❖ ❖ ❖ ❖ ❖ ❖ ❖ ❖ ❖ ❖ ❖ ❖ ❖

ESSAYS

Establishing And Maintaining Competence: An Ethical Responsibility

Walt Pawlovich
University of Saskatchewan

Competence and the Rights of the Client

Professional competence has been defined as the provision of quality services through the application of professional knowledge, skills and abilities (Overholser & Fine, 1990). Incompetence occurs when professionals continue to provide services that they are not fully capable of performing (Keith-Spiegel & Koocher, 1985). Failure to recognize one's fallibilities and limitations as a professional and as a person are also elements of incompetence (Van Hoose & Kottler, 1977). Therefore, as a basic ethical principle, competence involves the expectation for therapists to recognize their own personal and professional limitations. Ethical counsellors should not employ diagnostic or treatment procedures that are beyond the scope of their training, nor should they accept clients whose personal functioning is seriously impaired, unless they are qualified to work with those clients.

The duty to be competent and maintain competence is absolute because clients have a right to receive services of consistently high quality and to have that service provided by an individual who is competent (Rosenbaum, 1982). Incompetent counsellors have actually harmed their individual or group clients, largely because of the trust given to them as "experts" (Thompson, 1990). The duty to be competent entails the duty to respect the rights of individual clients and in part to understand what constitutes morally legitimate decisions (Carroll, Schneider and Wesley, 1985).

Elements of Competence

In order to establish competence, it is first necessary to recognize and understand what is required in all areas of counselling in order to ensure professional competence to the fullest extent. Competence should be established not only in the domains of skill and knowledge acquisition, but in areas involving professional and personal judgment. Norman (1985) proposed a categorization scheme describing five domains of professional activities deemed essential to competent performance: knowledge and understanding, clinical skills, technical skills, problem solving and clinical judgment, and personal attributes.

Counsellors are expected to attain and maintain adequate levels of knowledge regarding the scientific basis of the services they provide (Overholser & Fine, 1990). It is essential not only to attain adequate knowledge, but to maintain it over time. Therefore, it is important that counsellors know, understand, and use the published literature that pertains to a particular diagnosis and its treatment (Sheldon-Wildgen, 1982). Professional knowledge also includes the ability to recognize the limitations of one's knowledge and expertise. Thus, it is vital for counsellors to recognize and limit their practice to areas for which they have sufficient expertise to perform in a competent manner. It is also the responsibility of the therapist, in collaboration with the client, to evaluate the progress that has been made, and if deemed inadequate, to change modalities or terminate therapy and refer the client elsewhere (Keith-Spiegel & Koocher, 1985).

Counsellors and therapists also need to have general clinical skills and the basic interviewing skills necessary to assess and treat clients. In psychotherapy and counselling, adequate levels of empathy, warmth, and genuineness are often considered important for positive therapeutic outcomes regardless of theoretical orientation. Other relevant skills include composure and sensitivity, the ability to communicate with a variety of clients, and the ability to maintain an appropriate professional relationship with clients (Overholser & Fine, 1990).

The technical skills necessary for competence include the ability to use special procedures or techniques in the clinical setting. This may involve special assessment procedures or treatment techniques specific to a particular treatment orientation. Specialized techniques require specialized training in the theory and application of such interventions. Competent counsellors have the ability to determine what techniques are most appropriate for the client's particular problem (Carroll et al., 1985). This involves being able to understand what counts as improvement and to change behaviour in light of this understanding.

Competence also pertains to problem solving and clinical judgment, which refer both to the ability to apply knowledge and clinical skills to assess or treat a particular client and the ability to make reasonable judgments in resolving the dilemmas which arise in therapy (Carroll et al., 1985). Responding well to different situations requires knowledge of relevant legal and ethical guidelines, training in how to manage them, and judgment regarding effective ways to respond.

The interpersonal attributes of the professional are essential to his or her competence. Professional demeanour, including one's appearance and attire as well as a calm and confident manner, plays an important role in therapy. As well, personality characteristics, social skills, and emotional problems may affect the ability to function in a professional capacity. The manner in which individuals take care of themselves and the lifestyles they maintain directly influence not only their personal happiness but their productivity as well (Thoreson, Miller & Krauskopf, 1989). Recent concern over the incidence of impaired practitioners has suggested that personal and emotional problems may interfere with effective professional functioning. Although it is not a sign of incompetence for professionals to suffer emotional problems, it is considered incompetence if they continue to provide services when unable to function adequately (Overholser & Fine, 1990).

Does Licensing Ensure Competence?

A commonly accepted requirement of competence emphasizes the training of counsellors or therapists. However, it must first be specified what counts as relevant training. Although typically assumed otherwise, academic degrees, credentials, and courses or workshops completed are not necessarily good indicators of competence (Bervan & Scofield, 1987). Professionals who point to degrees and certificates as "proof" of their competence may only be deluding themselves. Licence and certification are not necessarily useful as criteria of compe-

tence. Licences mainly assure the public that the licencees have completed minimum educational programs, have had a certain number of hours of supervised training, and have gone through some type of evaluation and screening (Corey, 1991). Licences imply that their holders have had a certain level of professional training, but they do not assure the public that practitioners can effectively and competently do what their licences permit them to do (Corey, Corey, and Callanan, 1979). Most licences are generic in nature; they usually do not specify the types of clients or problems the licencee is competent to work with, nor do they specify the techniques that a practitioner is competent to use. A licence permits the professional to provide a wide range of services, yet it is the professional's responsibility to determine which services he or she is actually competent to provide.

Alternative Methods to Establish and Maintain Competence

Counsellor competence could and should be maintained through both an external and internal frame of reference. Licensing is an external frame of reference necessary to ensure that the professional has met the required minimum standards of the profession. From an external perspective, it is important for counsellors to realize that processes such as reviewing, evaluating, examining, and screening will continue to be handled by external forces such as licensing boards and professional groups (Gross & Robinson, 1987).

Counselling education programs are also needed as an external verification of competence. In order to provide adequate training and supervision to establish competence, counselling programs need to incorporate both academic and experiential phases, and provide appropriate supervision for the sake of both the client's welfare and the intern's professional growth. The problem of incompetence can be reduced if graduate training programs promote an interest in learning and an emphasis on professional development as a lifelong process (Corey, 1991).

From an internal perspective, it is the counsellor's responsibility as a professional to gain the skills and knowledge basic to the profession as well as maintain the personal and professional ethics necessary to work within the boundaries of his or her competence. This can be done through continuing education, professional disclosure and consultation and referrals.

It is important for the professional to realize that pre-doctoral training is not sufficient to guarantee a high level of competence in professional areas of functioning (Corey, Corey & Callanan, 1979). Even the best present education and training will become obsolete within a relatively short period of time unless counsellors make a very determined effort to expand their professional base of knowledge and techniques. Therefore, continuing education is needed to prevent the obsolescence of a professional's knowledge (Jensen, 1979). It is essential for keeping up-to-date with new knowledge in professional specialties. Counsellors have an ethical responsibility to engage in continuing education in order to maintain high levels of competence, and consequently, counsellors who fail to keep informed about new developments in both theory and research can be vulnerable on both ethical and legal grounds.

Another internal frame of reference for competence works as an alternative to the present licensing practices. This involves requiring practitioners to fully disclose information about themselves and their practice. Professional disclosure should ideally contain the following: informing prospective clients about one's qualifications, describing the counselling services offered with an explanation of the therapeutic process, describing the rights and responsibilities of clients, clarifying the nature of confidentiality and the release of information, and outlining the administrative procedures relating to time and money (Lovett & Lovett, 1988). The rationale is that clients must have this information to make intelligent decisions about the use of practitioners' services. It is the responsibility of the therapist to provide clients at the outset of treatment with specific information regarding training, status and competency.

Professional disclosure has benefits for both clients and practitioners. It provides a basic assessment of how well services are being provided, as well as setting up a structure by which consumers can protect themselves, implying an informed or informable public. Self-report on the part of professionals reflects honesty and may be the only criterion available from the consumer's or client's point of view (Gross, 1977).

Counsellors not only have the responsibility to accurately express their qualifications and competencies, but to be aware of and make clients aware of, their professional limitations. It is not an infrequent situation for therapists to find themselves operating out of their area of expertise. Counsellors who become aware of their lack of competence in a particular case have the responsibility to seek consultation with colleagues or a supervisor (Corey, 1991). Competent counsellors are also aware of the available resources and are prepared to make referrals when they do not feel competent or prepared to help (Van Hoose & Kottler, 1977). Counsellors should continually assess competence through conferring with colleagues to share perceptions of what is occurring with their clients, themselves, and between them and their clients (Corey, 1991). At times it can be appropriate to work as a "team", and seek out a group of colleagues whose judgment is trusted and regularly present difficult cases to this "team".

Competence as an Ethical Responsibility

Counsellors must become aware of the boundaries of competence and seek qualified supervision or refer clients when they recognize that they have reached their limit. They must also become familiar with community resources so they can make appropriate referrals (Corey, 1991). This ethical ideal of competence reflects the expectation that professionals in the counselling field must possess an ability to evaluate honestly and objectively their own skills and make reasonable, responsible decisions of both a professional and moral nature. As counsellors, it is important to be able to recognize and accept the position they are in regarding the well-being of those whom their actions may affect (Carroll et al., 1985).

Competence ultimately involves a willingness to continually question whether counsellors are doing their work as well as they might and search for ways of becoming more effective as therapists (Corey, Corey and Callanan, 1979). In order to do this, it is essential to have an understanding of the importance of the elements of competence in all areas of counselling including skills, knowledge, judgment abilities and interpersonal attributes. The continual maintenance of competence will consist of external references, such as training and licensing, but more importantly, will require the counsellor to participate in continuing education, professional disclosure and seek consultation and make referrals when necessary.

The ultimate duty of the counsellor is to protect and benefit clients. The establishment of all elements of competence and the maintenance of competence through both external and internal sources will ensure that this duty is fulfilled for the client in the counselling experience.

References

Bervan, N. & Scofield, M. (1987). Ethical responsibility in establishing and maintaining professional competence. *Journal of Applied Rehabilitation Counseling, 18*, 41-44.

Carroll, M., Schneider, H., and Wesley, G. (1985). *Ethics in the practice of psychology.* New Jersey: Prentice-Hall.

Corey, G. (1991). *Theory and practice of counseling and psychotherapy.* Pacific Grove: Brooks/Cole Publishing Company.

Corey, G., Corey, M., & Callanan, P. (1979). *Professional and ethical issues in counseling and psychotherapy.* Monteray: Brooks/Cole Publishing Company.

Gross, S. (1977). Professional disclosure: An alternative to licensing. *Personnel and Guidance Journal, 55*, 586-588.

Gross, D., & Robinson, S. (1987). Ethics in Counseling: A Multiple Role Perspective. *TACD Journal, 15*, 5-15.

Jensen, R. (1979). Competent professional service in psychology: The real issue behind continuing education. *Professional Psychology, 10*, 381-389.

Keith-Spiegel, P., & Koocher, G. (1985). *Ethics in psychology: Professional standards and cases.* New York: Random House.

Lovett, T., & Lovett, C. (1988). Suggestions for continuing legal education units in counselor training. Paper presented at annual meeting of American Association of Counseling and Development, Chicago; cited in Corey, G., (1991), *Theory and practice of counseling and psychotherapy.* Pacific Grove: Brooks/Cole Publishing Company.

Neufeld, V., & Norman, G. (Eds.) (1985). *Assessing clinical competence.* New York: Springer.

Norman, G. (1985). Defining competence: A methodological review. In V. Neufeld and G. Norman (Eds.), *Assessing clinical competence.* New York: Springer.

Overholser, J., & Fine, M. (1990). Defining the boundaries of professional competence: Managing subtle cases of clinical incompetence. *Professional psychology: research and practice, 21*, 462-469.

Rosenbaum, M. (1982). *Ethics and values in psychotherapy.* New York: The Free Press.

Sheldon-Wildgen, J. (1982). Avoiding legal liability: The rights and responsibilities of therapists. *The Behaviour Therapist, 5*, 165-169; cited in Overholser, J., & Fine, M. (1990), Defining the boundaries of professional competence: Managing subtle cases of clinical incompetence. *Professional Psychology: Research and Practice, 21*, 462-469.

Thompson, A. (1990). *Guide to ethical practice in psychotherapy.* New York: John Wiley and Sons.

Thoreson, R., Miller, M., & Krauskopf, C. (1989). The distressed psychologist: Prevalence and treatment considerations. *Professional Psychology: Research and Practice, 20*, 153-158.

Van Hoose, W., & Kottler, J. (1977). *Ethical and legal issues in counseling and psychotherapy.* San Francisco: Jossey-Bass.

Boundary Violations In Counsellor-Client Relationships

Glenn W. Sheppard
Memorial University

> Boundary violations are acts that breach the core intent of the professional-client association. They happen when professionals exploit the relationship to meet personal needs rather than client needs. Changing that fundamental principle undoes the covenant, altering the ethos of care that obliges professionals to place clients' concerns first. In fact, all of the boundaries in a professional-client relationship exist in order to protect this core understanding (Peterson, 1992, p. 75).

Peterson uses the term 'boundary violations' to refer to a wide range of behaviours all of which constitute a violation of the ethical codes of conduct which are intended to set boundaries for relationships between human service professionals and their clients. In her book, *At Personal Risk: Boundary Violations in Professional-Client Relationships*, Peterson (1992) elaborates on four broad categories of relationship violations. They are:

- **A reversal of roles.** This refers to situations in which the professional helper, in order to satisfy his or her personal needs, switches places with the client so that the client becomes, to a significant degree, the caregiver. Such role reversals violate the primary ethic of care in which the client's needs must remain paramount. They also blur the relationship boundaries between the client and helper and leave the client vulnerable to abuse;

- **The secret.** Here, Peterson is referring to the professional's withholding of information which is vital to the client and the concealment of which may be damaging to the client's well being in the relationship. The lack of disclosure may also compromise the client's ability to exercise informed consent. Typically, in such circumstances, the helper has dual agendas which contribute to maintaining the secret;

- **The double bind.** This type of boundary violation occurs whenever the client is placed in a 'no-win' situation because of some request or demand by the professional helper. These are situations which present a conflict of interest for the client who feels trapped as a consequence of such a request because there is uncertainty as to implications for the therapeutic relationship of refusing or acceding to it; and

- **The indulgence of personal privilege.** Violation of this nature occurs whenever the professional decides to use his authority or position in the relationship to fulfil a personal agenda. This could range all the way from using information gained from the client to pursue some personal benefit outside the relationship to establishing a sexual relationship with a client.

Whether or not one accepts precisely Peterson's conceptualization of ethical boundaries and their violations within professional relationships, it is clear that it is grounded on the fundamental principles on which a professional code of ethical conduct is based. These ethical principles, according to Kitchener (1984, 1985) who has analyzed many human service ethical codes, are: do no harm; benefit others; respect autonomy; be fair; and be faithful.

Most human service professional associations give supremacy to the ethical concept of *nonmalefience* which has its origins in the history of medical ethics (Childress, 1981; Beauchamp & Childress, 1979). This principle is more commonly stated as "above all do no harm." It obligates professional helpers not only to avoid inflicting harm intentionally but to refrain from engaging in any activities in which there is a high risk of harm to their clients without any offsetting benefits. Clearly, when professional relationship boundaries are violated, clients are vulnerable to abuse, and helpers may fail to keep their ethical obligation to 'do no harm.'

These ethical principles and concepts are now receiving increased attention within the counselling profession and are reflected in the various ethical codes or standards of practice of national counselling associations (BAC, 1990; CGCA, 1989; AACD, 1988). Also, many scholars are making a significant contribution to advancing our understanding of this critical dimension of professional life (Corey, Corey & Callahan, 1993; Pope and Vasquey, 1991; Eberlein, 1988; Kitchener, 1988; Tymchuk, 1986). This may be an indication of the growing maturity of the profession as well as a response to the public demand for accountability in the provision of quality mental health services. Whatever its origin, it is consistent with the Gibson and Mitchell (1990) observation that, "A profession's commitment to appropriate ethical and legal standards is critical to the profession's earning, maintaining, and deserving the public's trust" (p. 45).

Historically, the counselling profession was quick to publicly express an understanding of its legal and ethical obligations. The American Personnel and Guidance Association produced the first code of ethics for counsellors in 1961, just ten years after its founding. In fact, it established an ethics committee just one year following its formation as a professional association (Gibson & Pope, 1993). This first code has been published in three revised editions since 1961 (AACD, 1988). The much younger Canadian Guidance and Counselling Association adopted its first code of ethics in 1981 and approved a revised code in 1989 (CGCA, 1981, 1989). This latest edition acknowledges that the determination of appropriate ethical behaviour must frequently be made when the issues are complex and in circumstances in which conflict between several competing ethical principles must be resolved. For this reason, it outlines several ethical decision-making models for the consideration of counsellors.

The new *CGCA Guidelines for Ethical Behaviour* specifically addresses many of the boundary violation issues raised by Peterson. For example, in *Section A, Number 8*, it states:

> In the counselling relationship, the counsellor is aware of the intimacy of the relationship and maintains respect for the counsellee and avoids engaging in activities that seek to meet the COUNSELLOR'S PERSONAL NEEDS at the expense of that counsellee.

This clause reminds counsellors of the intimate and private nature of counselling and the need, therefore, to be aware of and sensitive to the complex ethical issues and risks relating to closeness, intimacy and distance in counselling (Wilmer, 1991). Clients are often at their most vulnerable state when they seek out counselling. As they share the most private details of their lives, counsellors listen empathically to their clients' pain, confusion, anxieties, and failures as well as to their hopes and dreams. Such sharing can result in feelings of intimacy and closeness.

The individual attention and understanding of a counsellor may be unique in the life of a client. It is not surprising then that this may engender strong feelings which may distort the client's view of the counsellor. In fact, some theoretical constructions of counselling acknowledge such distortions as expected and normal *transference* phenomenon (Pope, and Vasquey, 1991; Corey and Corey, 1989).

Transference usually means the transfer by the client to the counsellor and to the counselling relationship of emotions, needs, and conflicts experienced with significant others in their lives. These theorists believe that counsellors must learn to recognize the many manifestations of transference and manage this phenomenon for the benefit of client insight and growth. Transference, it is assumed, can be evident in a wide range of strong client feelings towards the counsellor, such as love, anger, and ambivalence. Clients, for example, may develop an excessive need to please their counsellors in order to feel liked or valued by them.

From this theoretical perspective, there is also the complementary counsellor process of *countertransference*. This refers to the counsellor transferring to the client feelings, thoughts, and behaviours which stem from the counsellor's life experiences. Such transfer might result from unresolved personal issues or from unmet needs in the counsellors' life. Gerald Corey (1986) talks about the potential in counselling for countertransference to occur:

> I found that when I began counselling others, old wounds opened and feelings that I had not explored in depth came to the surface. Being a therapist forces us to confront our unexplored blanks related to loneliness, power, death, sexuality, our parents and so on (p. 362).

Counsellors who work with children and adolescents may face unique challenges to the ethical obligation expressed in Section A, to be aware of the "intimacy of the relationship" and "to avoid activities which seek to meet the counsellors' personal needs at the expense of the counsellee." Children and young adolescents share concerns with adult counsellors which often center around interpersonal conflicts and hurtful experiences with parents, teachers and other adults. Counsellors may violate relationship boundaries by an excessive need to be overprotective of their young clients. Children may also distort the counselling relationship out of their need to receive from the counsellor nurturance and caring lacking from other adult caregivers in their lives. Clearly, it is the responsibility of counsellors to protect children from abusive experiences. However, this responsibility can be extended beyond acceptable relational boundaries if counsellors, out of their unmet needs, unwittingly develop unhealthy dependency within their clients and when the dynamics of their counselling are transformed into those of a needy, overprotective parent.

Eliana Gil (1991) cautions about the strong risks of countertransference when counsellors work with abused children:

I have alluded to countertransference issues throughout the book but deal with them at length here to emphasize the relevance of countertransference to work with abused children. These children are extremely vulnerable, with tumultuous histories of abuse, neglect, and deprivation. Consequently, they elicit a multitude of responses from the therapist, including intense hostility, sadness, protective impulses, and/or feelings of helplessness.

Occasionally, a child's plight demands special attention, and highly qualified professionals may find themselves behaving in unexpected ways. For example, one clinician treating an abused child got herself licensed as a foster parent and entered into a dual role with the child. Another clinician, whose rescuing instinct was strongly evoked, adopted a child. While these may be extremes, the clinician must carefully assess any personal conduct that threatens to develop outside the boundaries of a strict therapeutic relationship (p. 192).

Of course, working with adult clients who have been sexually abused as children may be just as challenging. Briere (1992), author of a number of publications dealing with therapy for sexually abused adults, is cognizant of the risks of boundary violations. It is his view that:

Perhaps the most dangerous form of abuse-related countertransference is that of boundary violation. Examples of therapist boundary confusion include any type of sexual behaviour with clients, obviously inappropriate personal disclosures during therapy, excessively intrusive questions or statements, and most generally, the therapist's use of the client to gratify the therapist's own needs (p. 160).

Whether or not one accepts the theoretical construct of transference, most counselling practitioners and theorists would agree that the counsellor's unmet needs can sometimes be so enmeshed in the counselling relationship as to obstruct his or her objectivity. Most individuals who enter the counselling profession have a strong motivation to help others and they receive satisfaction from being instrumental in helping others to make positive personal change. These are acceptable and even desirable motivations, but it requires that counsellors be "...aware of their own needs, areas of unfinished business, potential personal conflicts, defenses and vulnerability" (Corey, 1986, p. 369). By continuing to develop their self-understanding, counsellors minimize the risks of relationship violations and avoid abuse of their power within counselling.

One of the most serious boundary violations which continues to be of grave concern to counsellors, clients and the general public is sexual contact between helpers and their clients. Such unethical and illegal behaviour continues to occur despite the fact that ethical codes of conduct for all the helping professions explicitly prohibit it (Vasquey and Kitchener, 1988). Very early in the history of the helping professions, sexual contact between helpers and their clients was considered to be unacceptable. If fact, the medical profession has had this prohibition since it was included in the

Hippocratic Oath over two thousand years ago (Edelstein, 1943). Despite this longstanding taboo, sexual exploitation continues to occur within all helping professions (Gabbard, 1989; Pope, 1990; Screenivasan, 1989; Wilson, 1993).

The *CGCA Guidelines for Ethical Behaviour* states the prohibition against sexual contact between counsellors and clients in *Section B, Statement 9*, "Members will avoid any type of sexual intimacies with counsellors. *SEXUAL RELATIONSHIPS* with counsellors are unethical." This ethical clause is similar to those found in the ethical codes of other professions. For example, in its position paper (Screenivasan, 1989), the Canadian Psychiatric Association states, "Erotizing the physician/patient relationship is unacceptable under any circumstances and cannot be rationalized as therapy" (p. 234). The Code of Ethics (1981) of the National Association of Social Workers stipulates, "The social worker should under no circumstances engage in sexual activities with clients." In several additions to the principles of medical ethics adapted by the American Psychiatric Association (APA, 1985), practitioners are alerted to the potential for sexual misconduct, "...the necessary intensity of the therapeutic relationship may tend to activate sexual and other needs and fantasies on the part of both patient and therapist, while weakening the objectivity necessary for control" (p. 4). Also, like most codes, it states that, regardless of the behaviour of the client, it is the clear and unequivocal responsibility of the professional under all circumstances to maintain this fundamental relationship boundary.

According to a study by Gibson and Pope (1993), counsellors continue to support this basic ethical standard and disapprove of a wide range of behaviours which they consider to be a violation of this relationship boundary. These researchers report that one-fourth of the 21 behaviours judged to be unethical by the 579 certified counsellors in their study were of a sexual nature. There is a growing public and professional awareness of the disturbing extent of sexual abuse within society in general including abuse within professional-client relationships.

The prevalency rates for this most serious boundary violation are difficult to establish. However, a number of national surveys based on self-reports conducted in the U.S. have been summarized by Pope and Bouhoutsos (1986). They conclude that sexual intimacies between clients and male therapists happen at a rate of from 9 to 12 percent and from 2 to 3 percent between female therapists and their clients. Another U.S. study conducted by Bajt and Pope (1989) reports that an alarming proportion of sexual contact between therapists and clients include children and adolescents. They report that 56 percent of the victims in this study were young clients including girls between the ages of 3 and 17 years with a mean age of 13 years and boys ranging from 7 to 16 years with an average age of 12 years.

Some commentators, particularly feminist therapists, have expressed the view that sexual contact within counselling, the victims of which are largely female clients, can only be properly understood within the context of larger societal problems which result in the abuse of women (Gartell, Herman, Olarte, Feldstein, Localio, 1986). Others believe that counsellors and counsellor-educators should be particularly well qualified and committed to the advancement of our recognition, understanding, and change of the societal structures and processes which lead to the victimization of women (Frazier and Cohen, 1992).

Regardless of the reasons advanced or debated to explain the sexual misconduct by professional helpers, clearly this critical problem requires urgent attention. In the counselling profession, as in other human service groups, it demands increased recognition as an issue of immediate concern and requires the attention of individual practitioners, counsellor-educators and professional organizations.

One strategic element in an overall initiative to address the risks of sexually-based boundary violations has been proposed by Corey (1991). He argues that counsellor education programs do not adequately prepare counsellors to deal appropriately with sexual feelings which they may experience towards their clients. Corey proposes that, "Educational programs must provide a safe environment in which trainees can acknowledge and discuss feelings of sexual attraction. If counsellors do not learn how to deal with these feelings, they are more likely to become involved in seductive exchanges. Ideally, practitioners will be able to accept their sexual feelings and desires toward certain clients and at the same time see the distinction between having these feelings and *acting* on them" (p. 68).

Counsellors may experience feelings of sexual or romantic attraction towards clients more frequently than has been previously acknowledged (Gottlieb, Sell, Schoenfeld, 1988). In a U.S. survey, 87% (95% of men, 75% of women) of the 575 psychotherapists responding to a questionnaire reported that they had been sexually attracted to their clients on at least one occasion (Pope, Keith-Spiegel, Tabachnick, 1986). Pope and his associates (Pope, Sonne, Holyroyd, 1993) have recently published a book entitled *Sexual Feelings in Psychotherapy: Explorations for Therapists and Therapists-in-Training.* This publication is based on the author's research on sexual attraction in therapeutic relationships. It should serve as a useful resource in responding to Corey's call to deal with this important dimension of counselling in graduate training and in continuing professional development programs.

The CGCA ethical guidelines obligate members, "in situations where information is possessed, raising serious doubts as to the ethical behaviour of other members, to take action that is conducive to rectifying these conditions" (Section A, Number 3). This obligation would certainly include having a knowledge that a member had violated the ethical boundary which prohibits sexual contact between counsellor and client as well as awareness of any other violations of the ethical standards. The guidelines do not elaborate on what specific action a member is obligated to take in any such circumstances. However, it must be sufficient to 'rectify' the situation.

Some professionals, (Gartell, Herman, Feldstein, Localio, 1987) advocate that professional human service associations should adopt a policy of mandatory reporting to ethics committees or licensing boards of all complaints heard from clients of being sexually abused by their counsellors. In fact, a number of U.S. states have legislated such mandatory reporting (Appelbaum, 1990). In Canada, two recent provincial commissions examining sexual mis-

conduct in the medical profession have each recommended mandatory reporting by medical practitioners whenever a patient alleges that they were sexually abused by a member of that profession (Hardy, 1993; Wilson, 1993).

The potential risks and benefits of mandatory reporting will continue to be debated. However, in future revisions of the CGCA *Guidelines*, there is likely to be more elaborated and specific detail regarding the obligation to act on knowledge of a member's unethical conduct.

In addition to the increased attention to sexual dual relationships between counsellor and client, in the past decade, there has been a dramatic increase in the professional concern over non-sexual dual relationships in counselling. According to St. Germaine (1993), counsellors are in a dual relationship with clients whenever they have a "...relationship that involves a connection beyond that associated with the therapeutic setting" (p. 3).

The *CGCA Guidelines for Ethical Behaviour* (1989), following the lead of the AACD Code of Ethics (1986), addresses the duality of relationships as follows:

> When members have other relationships, particularly of an administrative, supervisory, and/or evaluative nature with an individual seeking counselling services, members must not serve as counsellor but should refer the individual to another professional. Only in instances where such an alternative is unavailable and where the individual's situation warrants counselling intervention should the member enter into and/or maintain a counselling relationship. DUAL RELATIONSHIPS with clients that might impair members' objectivity and professional judgment (e.g., as with close friends or relatives) must be avoided and/or the counselling relationship terminated through referral to another competent professional. (Section 3, Number 8)

This new ethical standard reflects a growing awareness that dual relationships increase the potential for boundary violations and may compromise the counsellor's ability to place the welfare of the client first. According to a report by the American Psychological Association (April, 1988), ethical complaints reflect an increase in the number of allegations of misconduct arising from dual relationships.

This code also implicitly recognizes that there is not mutuality within counselling relationships, but that they are characterized by a significant power differential. Clients are typically at their most vulnerable state when seeking help. They are expected to be open and self-focused in the counselling encounter. This is not the emotional status or behaviour expected of the counsellor. Indeed, such openness and self-preoccupation could very well constitute ethical misconduct. It is this inherent power imbalance which can make dual relationships so challenging to the maintenance of appropriate relational boundaries.

With our heightened awareness of this new area of concern, it is surprising just how many relationships might now be seen as resulting in problematic duality. St. Germaine (1993) has generated the following long list of counsellor behaviours, all of which, in her view, constitute a dual relationship with clients:

- buying a product or service from a client.
- selling a product to a client.
- entering into a business or financial arrangement with a client.
- attending social events of a client or inviting a client to social events.
- developing a friendship or social relationship with a client or former client.
- accepting gifts from a client.
- counselling clients close friend, family member, or lover.
- counselling a close friend or family member or the lover of a friend or family member.
- counselling an employee or student, or a close friend or family member of an employee or student (p. 29).

Counsellor-educators may be particularly at risk of unwittingly entering into dual relationships since they often fill many roles, including supervisor, administrator, teacher and counsellor. As others have pointed out (Corey, Corey & Callahan, 1987; Stadler, 1986), counsellor-educators and supervisors need to be alert to the potential ethical pitfalls of dual relationships if they engage in counselling their students or supervisees. The risks of blending

these roles, according to Kitchener (1988), are, "...confidentiality may be compromised, student autonomy sacrificed, the therapy process impaired, and objectivity damaged..." p. 217.

The British Association of Counselling in its various codes of ethics addresses the ethical concern over dual relationships (B.A.C. 1986, 1990). For example, in the *Code of Ethics and Practice for the Supervision of Counsellors* (1986) it states:

> Supervisors and counsellors are both responsible for setting and maintaining clear boundaries between working relationships and friendships or other relationships, and making explicit, the boundaries between supervision, consultancy, therapy and training (2.3, p. 175).

The British codes recognize the potential for a conflict of interest when those with managerial responsibility for counsellors also serve as supervisors. It sets out the following ethical guideline to avoid the potential risks in such duality of roles:

> The counselling supervisor role should be independent of the line manager role. However, where the counselling supervisor is also the line manager, the counsellor should also have access to independent consultation support (B.3.3, BAC, 1990).

There is also a growing recognition of the potential for boundary violations associated with the experiential components of programs to prepare group counsellors as well as with the personal growth experiences required in some counsellor education programs (Forester-Miller, Duncan, 1990). The American Counselling and Development Association in its Ethical Standards (AACD, 1988) recognized the need to establish an ethical guideline for the delivery and management of any such experiential learning requirements. The guidelines are expressed as follows:

> Members must assure that forms of learning, focusing on self-understanding or growth are voluntary, or if required as part of the education program, are made known to prospective students prior to entering the program. When the educational program offers a growth experience with an emphasis on self-disclosure or other relatively intimate or personal in-

volvement, the member must have no administrative, supervisory, or evaluating authority regarding the participant. (Sec. H.12)

The Association for Specialists in Group Work also address the dual relationship issues in its *Ethical Guidelines for Group Counsellors* (ASGW, 1989). To minimize the risks to students, it set the following standard of conduct for counsellor-educators:

Students who participate in a group as a partial course requirement for a group course are not evaluated for an academic grade based upon their degree of participation as a member in a group. Instructors of group counselling courses take steps to minimize the possible negative impact on students when they participate in a group course by separating course grades from participation in the group and by allowing students to decide what issues to explore and when to stop. (#9 [g])

School counsellors need to be particularly cognizant of the ethical challenges associated with the duality of roles, since they frequently have to balance their responsibilities to students, parents, colleagues and the community (Hardy, 1986). Ethical dilemmas can emerge when the expectations of these groups are in conflict. For example, if school counsellors are expected to accept school disciplinary functions, it may compromise their obligations to place the welfare of clients first, since it is difficult to reconcile the dual roles of disciplinarian or informant and counsellor. In a position statement on the potential for role duality inherent in the position of school counsellor, Michael Dougherty takes a firm position:

I believe that school counsellors should avoid roles such as disciplinarian, substitute teacher, and lunchroom/bathroom/bus monitor that conflict with their primary role as counsellors to students. The unique role of the counsellor in the school makes the taking on of such roles highly questionable as they are likely to violate some of the basic tenets of the counselling relationship (e.g., confidentiality). As a consequence, new counselling relationships with students may be inhibited and existing ones may be compromised (p. 175).

School counsellors can avoid some of those ethical dilemmas by being sensitive to and

anticipating the potential complications arising from attempting to fulfil multiple roles. They can, in collaboration with their professional colleagues, reach a shared view of their role and responsibilities and ensure that it is clearly communicated to students, teachers, administrators, and parents.

Of course, as Keith-Spiegel and Koocher (1985) acknowledge, helping professionals who work in small communities and in institutions such as schools and hospitals cannot always avoid multiple relationships with clients. Kitchener (1988) has proposed a number of guidelines which might help counsellors and other helpers, working in such environments, to recognize those dual relationships which have a high probability of leading to ethical difficulties. She suggests the use of these three guidelines:

First, as the incompatibility of expectations increases between roles, so will the potential for misunderstanding and harm; for example, the incompatibility of the expectation of a therapist and a supervisor.

Second, as the obligations of different roles diverge, the potential for divided loyalties and loss of objectivity increases.

Last, as the power and prestige between the professional's and consumer's roles increases, so does the potential for exploitation and an inability on the part of the consumers to remain objective about their own best interests.

These three taken together suggest that the relationship has a high potential for misunderstanding, confusion and damage (p. 219).

Herlihy and Corey (1992) conclude their comprehensive treatment of dual relationships in counselling with the following succinct, thematic summary of the state of our current understanding of this complex area of ethical concern:

• dual relationship issues effect virtually all counsellors and human development specialists, regardless of their work setting or clientele. No helping professional remains untouched by potential dual role conflicts and dilemmas.

- nearly all codes of ethics caution against dual relationships.
- not all dual relationships can be avoided, nor are they necessarily always harmful.
- with the exception of clear agreement that sexual dual relationships with current clients are unethical, there is little consensus about most dual relationship issues.
- dual role relationships challenge us to monitor ourselves and to examine our motivations for our practices.
- when we are considering becoming involved in a dual relationship, it would be wise to seek consultation from trusted colleagues or a supervisor.
- there are few absolute answers that can neatly resolve dual relationships dilemma.
- the cautions for entering into dual relationships should be for the benefit of our clients, rather than to protect ourselves from censure.
- in determining whether to proceed with a dual relationship, consider whether the potential benefit of the relationship outweighs the potential for harm.
- whenever we are operating in more than one role and when there is potential for negative consequences, it is our responsibility to develop safeguards and measures to reduce the potential for harm.
- it is the responsibility of counsellor preparation programs to introduce issues pertaining to dual relationships and to teach students ways of thinking about alternative courses of action.
- counsellor education programs have a responsibility to develop their own guidelines, policies, and procedures for dealing with dual relationships within the program. (pp. 223-228)

This inventory of key beliefs about the nature of role duality in counselling is a cogent reminder of the dynamic and emerging nature of our ethical strivings within the counselling profession. It also underscores the necessity for counsellors to exercise a high level of ethical reasoning in fulfilling their obligation to maintain appropriate relational boundaries with clients. In fact, most instructional models advocated for the teaching of professional ethics emphasize the need to teach the process of ethical reasoning and decision-making (Gawthrop & Uhlemann, 1992; Elliot, 1991; Kitchener, 1984).

The *CGCA Guidelines of Ethical Behaviour* now declare that members, counsellor-educators, as well as others, have a responsibility to induct students into the ethical standards of the profession. It states:

> Members must make students aware of the ethical responsibilities and standards of the profession.

This ethical requirement is intended to ensure that the counselling profession meets a fundamental condition of professionalism; having a membership with a thorough understanding of and adherence to a shared code of ethical conduct. Although such codes are essential to the maintainence of the integrity and accountability of the profession, boundary violations as well as other ethical misconduct, can only be prevented when counsellors have the ability and courage to exercise a high level of ethical judgement. As Pope and Vasquey (1991) express it:

> Such codes...cannot do our thinking, feeling and responding for us. (They) can never be a substitute for the active process by which the individual therapist or counsellor struggles with the sometimes bewildering, always unique constellation of responsibilities, contexts, and competing demands of helping others (p. xi).

References

Adler, J., and Rosenberg, D. (1992). Psychotherapy. *Newsweek*, April 13, 53-58.

American Association for Counseling and Development. (1988). *Ethical standards.* Alexandria: CA: Author.

American Psychiatric Association. (1985). *Principles of medical ethics with annotations especially applicable to psychiatry.* Washington, D.C.: Author.

American Psychological Association, Ethics Committee. (1988). Trends in ethics uses, common pitfalls, and published resources. *American Psychologist,* 43(7), 564-572.

Appelbaum, P.S. (1990). Statutes regulating patient-therapist sex. *Hospital and Community Psychiatry*, 41, 15-16.

Association for Specialists in Group Work. (1989). *Ethical Guidelines for Group Counselors*. Alexandria, VA: Author.

Bajt, T.R. and Pope, K.S. (1989). Therapist-patient sexual intimacy involving children and adolescents. *American Psychologist*.

Beauchamp, T.L. & Childress, L.F. (1979). *Principles of biomedical ethics*. Oxford: Oxford University Press.

Beck, M., Springen, K., Foote, D. (1992). *Newsweek*, April 13, 53-58.

Briere, J.N. (1992). *Child abuse trauma: theory and treatment of the lasting effects*. Newbury Park, CA: Sage Publications.

British Association for Counselling (1990). *Code of ethics and practice for counsellors*. Rugby: England. Author.

British Association for Counselling (1986). *Code of ethics and practice for the supervision of counsellors*. Rugby: England. Author.

Canadian Guidance and Counselling Association (1989). *Guidelines for ethical behavior*. Ottawa: Author.

Canadian Guidance and Counselling Association (1981). *Guidelines for ethical behavior*. Ottawa, Author.

Canadian Psychological Association (1986). *A Canadian code of ethics for psychologists*. Old Cheben, Quebec: Author.

Childress, L.F. (1981). *Priorities in biomedical ethics*. Philadelphia: Westminister Press.

Corey, G. (1991). *Theory and practice of counseling and psychology*. Belair, CA. Brooks/Cole Publishing Company.

Corey, G. (1986). *Theory and practice of counseling and psychotherapy*. Monterey, CA: Brooks/Cole.

Corey, M. & Carey, G. (1989). *Becoming a helper*. Pacific Grove, CA: Brooks/Cole.

Corey, G., Corey, M.S. & Callahan, P. (1993). *Issues and ethics in the helping professions (2nd ed.)*. Pacific Grove, CA: Brooks/Cole.

Corey, G., Corey, M.S. & Callahan, P. (1987). *Issues and ethics in the helping professions*. Pacific Grove, CA: Brooks/Cole.

Eberlein, L. (1988). The new CPA code of ethics for Canadian psychologists: An education and training perspective. *Canadian Psychology*, 29(2), 206-212.

Edelstein, L. (1943). The Hippocratic Oath: Text, translation and interpretation. *Bulletin of the History of Medicine, Supplement 1*. Baltimore: Johns Hopkins Press.

Elliot, M.M. (1991). *Ethical decision-making and judgements of psychologists: An exploratory study*. Unpublished doctoral dissertation, University of Alberta, Edmonton.

Forester-Miller, H., and Duncan, J.A. (1990). *The Ethics of Dual Relationships in the Training of Group Counselors: The Journal for Specialists in Group Work*, 15(2), 88-93.

Frazier, P.A., Cohen, B.B. (1992). Research on the sexual victimization of women: Implications for counselor training. *The Counselling Psychologist*, 20, 141-158.

Gabbard, G.O. (1989). *Sexual exploitation in professional relationships*. Washington, D.C.: American Psychiatric Press, Inc.

Gartell, N., Herman, J., Olarte, S., Feldstein, M. & Localio, R. (1986). Psychiatrist-patient Sexual Contact: Results of a National Survey. I: Prevalence. *American Journal of Psychiatry*, 143, 1126-1131.

Gartell, N., Herman, J., Olarte, S., Feldstein, M., & Localio, R. (1986). Reporting Practices of Psychiatrists Who Knew of Sexual Misconduct by Colleagues. *American Journal of Orthopsychiatry*, 57, 287-295.

Gawthrop, J., & Wilemann, M. (1992). Effects of the problem-solving approach in ethics training. *Professional Psychology: Research and Practice*, 23, 1, 38-42.

Gibson, W.T., & Pope, K.S. (1993). The Ethics of Counseling: A National Survey of Certified Counselors. *Journal of Counseling and Development*, 71, 330-336.

Gibson, W.T. and Pope, S.K. (1993). The Ethics of Counseling: A National Survey of Certified Counselors. *Journal of Counseling and Development*, 71, 330-336.

Gibson, R.L., & Mitchell, M.H. (1990). *Introduction to counseling and guidance* (3rd. ed.). New York: Macmillan.

Gil, E. (1991). *The healing power of play: Working with abused children*. New York, NY: Guildford Press.

Gottlieb, M.C., Sell, J.M. & Schoenfeld, L.S. (1988). Social/romantic relationships with present and former clients: State licensing board actions. *Professional Psychology: Research and Practice*, 19, 459-462.

Green-Vasan, U. (1989). Sexual Exploitation of Patients: The Position Paper of the Canadian Psychiatric Association. *Canadian Journal of Psychiatry*, 34, 234-235.

Hardy, G. (1993). Mandatory reporting of sexual abuse: Physicians say regulations go too far. *Evening Telegram*, January 7, p. 12.

Herlihy, B., & Corey, G. (1992). Dual relationships in counseling. Alexandria: VA. *American Association for Counseling and Development.*

Huey, W.C. (1986). Ethical Concerns in School Counselling. *Journal of Counseling and Development*, 64, 321-322.

Hyattsville, M.D. *American Psychological Association.*

Keith-Spiegel, P., & Koocher, G.P. (1985). *Ethics in Psychology*. Hillsdale, N.J.: Lawrence Eribaum.

Kitchener, K.S. (1988). Dual Relationships: What Makes Them So Problematic? *Journal of Counseling and Development*, 67, 217-221.

Kitchener, K.S. (1985). Ethical principles and ethical decisions in student affairs. In H.J. Canon & R.D. Brown (eds.), *Applied Ethics in Student Services*. San Francisco: Jossey-Bass.

Kitchener, K.S. (1984). Intuition, initial evaluation and ethical principles: Foundation for ethical decisions in counseling psychology. *The Counseling Psychologist*, 12, 43-55.

National Association of Social Workers. (1981). *Code of ethics*. Washington, DC: Author.

National Association of Social Workers (1979). *Code of ethics*. Washington, DC: Author.

Pettifor, J., & Pitcher, S. (1982). Ethics training in Canadian graduate schools. *Canadian Psychology*, 23(4), 235-242.

Peterson, M.R. (1992). *At personal risk: Boundary violations in professional-client relationships*. New York, NY: W.W. Norton & Co., Inc.

Pope, K.S. (1985). How Clients are Harmed by Sexual Contact with Mental Health Professionals: The syndrome and its prevalence. *Journal of Counseling and Development*, 67, 222-226.

Pope, K.S. (1990). Therapist-patient sexual involvement: A review of the research. *Clinical Psychology Review*, 10, 477-490.

Pope, K.S., & Bouhoutsos, J.C. (1986). *Sexual intimacy between therapists and patients*. New York: Praeger Press.

Pope, K.S., & Vasquey, M.J.T. (1991). *Ethics in psychotherapy and counseling*. San Francisco: Jossey-Bass.

Pope, K.S., Sonne, J.L. & Holyroyd, J. (1993). *Sexual feelings in psychotherapy: Explanations for therapists and therapists-in-training.*

Pope, K.S., Keith-Spiegel, P., Tabachnick, B.G. (1986). Sexual attraction to clients: The human therapist and the (sometimes) inhuman training system. *American Psychologist*, 41, 147-158.

Sell, J.M., Gottlieb, M.C., Schoenfeld, L. (1986). Ethical considerations of social/ romantic relationships with present and former clients. *Professional Psychology: Research and Practice*, 17(6), 504-508.

Screenivasan, U. (1989). Sexual Exploitation of Patients: The Position of the Canadian Psychiatric Association. *Canadian Journal of Psychiatry*, 34, 234-235.

St. Germaine, J. (1993). Dual relationships: What's wrong with them? *American Counselor*, 2, 25-30.

Stadler, H.A. (1986). To Counsel or not to Counsel: The Ethical Dilemma of Dual Relationships. *Journal of Counseling and Human Service Professions*, 1(1), 134-140.

Tymchuk, A. (1986). Guidelines for ethical decision making. *Canadian Psychology*, 27(1), 36-43.

Vasquey, M.J.T. and Kitchener, K.S. (1988). Introduction to Special Issue. *Journal of Counseling and Development*, 67, 214-216.

Wilmer, H.A. (1991). *Closeness in personal and professional relationships*. Boston, Mass: Shambhala Publications, Inc.

Wilson, D. (1993). B.C. doctors to adopt sex-abuse proposal. *The Globe and Mail*, July 9, p. 10.

Chapter Three

---- ❖ ----

Case Studies In Counselling Relationships

---- ❖ ----

Counsellors must be aware that at all times their primary obligation is to help their clients. Counsellors must recognize that they have limited confidentiality and must always inform clients of counselling conditions.

GUIDELINES

1 Members' **primary obligation** is to respect the integrity and promote the welfare of counsellees, whether counsellees are assisted individually or in groups. In a group setting, the member-leader is also responsible for protecting the individuals from physical and/or psychological trauma resulting from interaction within the group.

❖

2 The counselling relationship and information resulting therefrom must be kept **confidential** in a manner consistent with the obligations of the member as a professional person. In a group setting the member is expected to set a norm of confidentiality regarding all group participants' disclosures.

❖

3 When the counsellee's condition indicates that there is clear and imminent **danger** to the counsellee or others, the member must take reasonable personal action or inform responsible authorities. The member should consult with other professionals and should only assume responsibility for the counsellee's action after careful deliberation.

❖

4 **Records** of the counselling relationship including interview notes, test data, correspondence, tape recordings, and other documents, are to be considered professional information for use in counselling and they are not part of the official records of the institution or agency in which the counsellor is employed. Revelation to others of counselling material should only occur upon the express consent of the counsellee.

❖

5 The counsellee should be **informed of counselling conditions** at or before the time the counsellee enters such a relationship. Particular care should be taken in the event that conditions exist about which the counsellee would not likely be aware. In individual or group situations the member-leader is obligated to make clear the purposes, goals, techniques, rules of procedure, and any limitations that may affect the continuance of the relationship.

❖

6 The member reserves the right to **consult** with any other professionally competent person about the counsellee. In choosing professional consultants the worker must avoid placing the consultant in a conflict of interest situation. If the identity of the counsellee is to be revealed, it should be done with the express consent of the counsellee.

❖

7 If members determine an inability to be of professional assistance to counsellees, members must either avoid initiating the counselling relationship or immediately terminate that relationship. In either event, members must **suggest appropriate alternatives.** Members must be knowledgeable about referral resources so that a satisfactory referral can be initiated. In the event the counsellees decline the suggested referral, members are not obligated to continue the relationship.

❖

8 When members have other relationships, particularly of an administrative, supervisory, and/or evaluative nature with an individual seeking counselling services, members must not serve as counsellor but should refer the individual to another professional. Only in instances where such an alternative is unavailable and where the individual's situation warrants counselling intervention should the member enter into and/or maintain a counselling relationship. **Dual relationships** with clients that might impair members' objectivity and professional judgment (e.g.., As with close friends or relatives) must be avoided and/or the counselling relationship terminated through referral to another competent professional.

❖

9 Members will avoid any type of sexual intimacies with counsellees. **Sexual relationships** with counsellees are unethical.

❖

10 Members have the responsibility to screen prospective **group members**, especially when group goals focus on self-understanding and growth through self-disclosure. Members ensure that there is professional assistance available during and following the group experience.

❖

11 When **computer applications** are used as a component of counselling services, members must ensure that: (a) the counsellee is intellectually, emotionally and physically capable of using the computer applications; (b) the computer application is appropriate to the needs of the counsellee; (c) the counsellee understands the purpose and operation of counsellor-assisted and/or self-help computer applications; (d) a follow-up of client use of a computer application is provided to assess subsequent needs; (e) computer-stored data is limited and appropriate, is destroyed after ceasing to have value in providing services, and is restricted to appropriate staff members.

❖

12 Members shall decline to initiate or shall terminate a counselling relationship when the member cannot be of professional assistance to the counsellee either because of lack of competence or **personal limitation.** In such instances, the counsellee shall be referred to an appropriate (professional) specialist. If the counsellee declines the suggested referral, members are not obligated to continue the relationship.

❖

13 If after entering a counselling relationship the member discovers the counsellee is already in a **counselling relationship with another counsellor,** the member is responsible for discussing the issues related to continuing or terminating counselling with either one or both counsellors.

❖

14 Should members be engaged in work settings which call for any variation from the above principles, members are obligated to ensure that such **variations** are justifiable under the conditions and that they are clearly specified and made known to all concerned with such counselling services. ❖

◆ ◆ ◆ ◆ ◆ ◆ ◆ ◆ ◆ ◆ ◆ ◆ ◆

CASE STUDIES

1 Members' *primary obligation* is to respect the integrity and promote the welfare of counsellees, whether counsellees are assisted individually or in groups. In a group setting, the member-leader is also responsible for protecting the individuals from physical and/or psychological trauma resulting from interaction within the group.

Respect of counsellee (+)

The counsellor came highly recommended to a woman whose marriage was in trouble due to many factors, but most significantly, due to emotional and verbal abuse from her husband. The abuse had gone on for several years without the wife being able to persuade the husband to seek any kind of help. The counsellor recognized the hurt the woman was feeling and that she had a plan which she seemed to have difficulty carrying out. The counsellor did not tell her what to do or question whether what she revealed to him were her true inner feelings. He seemed to accept what she was saying and to recognize that the feelings that she was displaying were real to her. This counsellor made the woman feel comfortable; the rapport between the two that was established during their first session was so positive that it left the door wide open for more revelations. The counsellor's genuineness was picked up by the woman early on in the first session. He showed understanding of the inner conflicts the woman had regarding whether or not she and her children should remain in the abusive situation. The counsellor was able to explain the cycle of abuse and the consequences of remaining in the situation, and to restate the alternatives the woman had decided were open to her. Most importantly the counsellor helped her see that the time had come for her to make a decision.

Disclosure in a Group (+)

In a group session involving six students, all of whom come from non-abusive alcoholic homes, one of the students confides that he "can not take any more". He is 16 years old and is intending to take his father's car and run away to the nearest big city. He has no money, no skills, and no friends or relatives with whom to stay. It is his intention to live on the street. He is aware that many his age do and he feels it is better than the life he is living. Despite all arguments against this course of action from the other members of the group and the counsellor, the boy staunchly adheres to his position. Knowledge of the family situation leads the counsellor to believe that apart from the concern for the stolen car, little will be done for the student if parents were notified. The counsellor calls Child and Family Services and requests their help in working with the student and his family.

Alone (-)

A male teacher, Frank, who is in his early forties, came home one day and learned that his wife had taken their two children and left him. In the subsequent divorce case, his wife was given custody of the children. Frank has been seeing a counsellor for weekly sessions for several months. He continues to express much anger, pain and loneliness during his hourly sessions. During the last session, the counsellor stopped the session after ten minutes and told Frank that he was "behind schedule" even though Frank had made his usual hourly appointment.

Doubting Counsellor (-)

In a small, remote community, a 14 year old grade nine student, Mary, told her female school counsellor that she desperately needed to talk to her in confidence as soon as possible. The counsellor felt the student was probably overreacting about something and did not meet with her immediately. A week later the student once again approached her counsellor and explained that she had been sexually abused by her stepfather. The counsellor was not convinced that the student was speaking the truth, and felt the student was out to attack her stepfather with these allegations. The counsellor told the student that she would look into the matter, but never reported it to the proper authorities for further investigation.

COMMENTS AND QUESTIONS

Counselling is a personal matter that involves personal relationships. Honesty, sincerity, acceptance, understanding, and spontaneity are basic ingredients for a successful relationship between the counsellor and counsellee. The degree of caring, counsellor interest and ability in helping the counsellee, and counsellor genuineness are all factors that influence this relationship and enhance the positive aspects of this ethical guideline. These characteristics were definitely lacking in the two negative cases.

Group counselling gives clients a place to express conflicting feelings, explore self doubts and come to the realization that they may share these concerns with their peers. A group may allow counsellees to openly question their values and to modify those that may need to be changed.

In a group setting, if members are to drop their defenses and reveal their "selves", they need assurances that the group is a safe place in which to do this.

It is the responsibility of counsellors to make sure that they "promote the welfare of counsellees", whether this is in individual or group counselling. This guideline has been placed first in this counselling relationship section; first, because counsellors must never forget that their primary obligation is to help their clients. It is necessary that counsellors act in ways that will further the best interests of clients. Counsellors must a) be willing to consult with colleagues, b) keep themselves informed about laws affecting counselling practice, c) keep current, d) reflect on the impact their values have on counselling, and e) be willing to engage in honest self-evaluation.

1. What do you do when the school or agency that you work for has policies that do not appear to be helpful for your client?
2. What are some ways in which counsellors can enhance the welfare of clients?
3. Can you 'promote the welfare' of a client by breaking confidentiality? Explain.
4. How can group leaders protect group members from "physical and psychological" harm?

2 The counselling relationship and information resulting therefrom must be kept *confidential* in a manner consistent with the obligations of the member as a professional person. In a group setting the member is expected to set a norm of confidentiality regarding all group participants' disclosures.

"What's Happening?" (+)
Fred Davis is a counsellor in a family counselling agency. One day he receives a phone call from the wife of one of the clients he is counselling. The wife indicates that she has seen some changes in her husband and asks the counsellor for information as to what her husband is saying during counselling. The counsellor, in a kind but firm manner, explains to the woman that the matters discussed during counselling are confidential.

Limited Confidentiality (+)
Fifteen year old Sally has been referred to the high school counsellor, Ms. Smith, by her English teacher because her grades are falling and she is very inattentive in class. She will end up failing the course if she doesn't do something to pull up her grades. During the course of the conversation between Sally and Ms. Smith, it becomes evident that Sally's performance in her other classes is similar to her performance in her English class and that she will more than likely fail the year if she isn't able to improve her grades. Sally discloses that she has been feeling depressed lately and cannot seem to concentrate on her school work. After further probing, it becomes evident to Ms. Smith that Sally is being sexually abused by her father. Sally admits to the abuse but says she is afraid of what might happen to her if her father finds out she has disclosed this information to anyone. Ms. Smith tells Sally that she is required to report the matter to Child and Family Services and assures her that it is in Sally's best interest that she do so. Ms. Smith then calls Child and Family Services and waits with Sally for the social worker to arrive.

Inappropriate Chatter (-)

An anger management group at a local high school was co-lead by two counsellors. At a social gathering one evening, the one counsellor was the focus of attention as he shared antics and incidents that had occurred during the group sessions.

Breaking Confidentiality (-)

Sixteen year old Mary Lou made an appointment with Ms. Jones, the high school counsellor, to discuss what courses she should take in Grade XII in order to prepare her for entering university the following year. During the course of their conversation, Mary Lou disclosed to Ms. Jones that she was having problems with her mother because her mother was always trying to control her life. Because she was of the belief that whatever she told Ms. Jones would be held in strictest confidence, she further disclosed that she has been lying to her mother, telling her that she was studying at the library evenings when in fact she was spending time with a young man whom, she felt, her mother would disapprove of. Shortly after the session was over, Ms. Jones made a call to Mary Lou's mother and informed her of Mary Lou's involvement with the young man and how she has been lying to her. Ms. Jones hoped she would be helping Mary Lou by informing her parents.

COMMENTS AND QUESTIONS

Confidentiality protects clients from unauthorized disclosures without informed consent. Confidentiality is crucial to establishing and maintaining a strong counsellor/client relationship. With confidentiality counsellors are not only respecting clients' ability to control their own lives, but also respecting all human relationships.

Counsellors will agree that the material of the counselling session belongs to the client. Confidentiality is, nevertheless, not absolute. There are times when confidentiality must be broken, and there are other times when breaking confidentiality remains unclear. Some of the exceptions to confidentiality include:

a) The client is a danger to self or others,

b) The courts order release of counselling information,

c) Support staff who process information and papers,

d) Legal and clinical consultation, and

e) During clinical supervision of counsellors.

1. What are additional exceptions to confidentiality?

2. How can we increase the chances of confidentiality in a group?

3. What is your responsibility as a counsellor when you hear other staff members discussing clients over coffee?

4. How should counsellors explain to clients that there are limits to their confidentiality?

3 When the counsellee's condition indicates that there is clear and imminent *danger* to the counsellee or others, the member must take reasonable personal action or inform responsible authorities. The member should consult with other professionals and should only assume responsibility for the counsellee's action after careful deliberation.

The Counsellee is Protected (+)

A fourteen year old grade nine student has been seeing her school counsellor for the past several months. She has not shared much information about her home life, but complains often about depression and a feeling of detachment from her peers. The counsellor has developed a good rapport with the young student who has expressed that she feels much more comfortable lately in their counselling sessions. The young girl has recently revealed that she does not feel loved and does not have a good relationship with her parents. During one of the counselling sessions, she became tearful and expressed to the counsellor that she did not feel safe at home because she had been sexually abused by her father. The counsellor explained to her that his first priority was her safety and that he had an obligation to protect her. This obligation would mean that he would have to contact an agency that works to protect children from abuse (Child and Family Services). He assured her that she would now be safe and protected from any further harm and that her father would now get help with his problem.

Potential Suicide (+)

A suicide note was left by a grade seven student indicating her intention of suicide. The note was brought to the attention of the guidance department head since the girl's counsellor was out of the building at the time. Later, the counsellor spoke to the girl. The counsellor contacted her parents regarding the note, but they did not seem too concerned but agreed to phone the counsellor or school principal if help was needed. Next, the counsellor met with the student and talked to her about her note and

her suicide intention. It seemed that she had considered suicide, but had not thought of how to carry out the plan. She did have a very close friend, someone that she trusted and felt that she could talk to at all times. The counsellor gave the grade seven student the phone number of a suicide prevention centre, as well as her own home number to call.

Informing Others (-)

A fifteen year old student in a large high school had begun to see his school counsellor because of problems he was having with his girlfriend. The counsellor enjoyed the relationship he had with the students in the school and felt that he had gained their trust and respect. During one of their sessions, the boy expressed to the counsellor that many of the students trusted him and felt that he was really on their side. He also told the counsellor that he and his girlfriend had tried "crack" on several occasions. She had first been hesitant to try the drug but after some pressure she gave in and in fact enjoyed it. The counsellor discussed the dangers of the drug as well as the strain the boy was putting on his girlfriend and their relationship.

The counsellor debated whether he should inform the girl's parents or the principal but felt that the trust he had gained among the students was very important. He decided to continue his sessions with the boy and did not inform the responsible authorities. He was informed several days later that the girl had nearly died of an overdose of drugs at a party on the weekend. The counsellor was given a short term suspension from his position at the school for not following the school's policy on reporting drug use.

Selling Drugs (-)

Alan tells his counsellor that his friend Joe told him about a big drug deal that is going to go down that evening at the arcade. He mentions Darryl, a good looking, well dressed, senior student who is always surrounded by a group of friends, as being the person who will purchase a large amount of "crack". Alan says Darryl plans to sell the drugs to the other students at school. The counsellor knows Darryl's parents, his father is a teacher, and feels that this could not be true. Alan, however, insists that he knows all of the details of the transaction from Joe, and he wants the counsellor to do something. The counsellor continues to listen to Alan and reflects his concerns about the situation, but he tells Alan that he can not get involved in something that is only hearsay evidence.

COMMENTS AND QUESTIONS

It is important for counsellors to inform clients, at the beginning of their sessions, of their obligation and responsibility to break confidentiality when counsellors feel that their clients or others are in potential danger. By informing clients of their limited confidentiality, counsellors can alleviate the sense of betrayal that clients may feel if they were under the impression that anything said to the counsellor would be kept confidential. Warning of danger must be presented in such a way that it is seen as a caring act on the part of the counsellor.

Counsellors should be aware that there may be certain repercussions that result from informing responsible authorities. There is the danger that other clients may feel that the counsellor can not be trusted, or the client may even feel a sense of anger or betrayal toward the counsellor.

Counsellors must be aware of institutional policies and the responsible parties to whom they have an obligation to contact when they feel the client or others are in danger. Parents have a right to be informed if their child may be harmed, and parents should be informed of additional resources within the community, or professional organizations, that can help with a potentially dangerous situation.

1. What can be done to alleviate a possible sense of betrayal that the students may feel if they become aware of the member breaking the confidentiality between the member and the counsellee?

2. Under what circumstances and in what situations should the counsellor assume responsibility for the counsellee's actions?

3. If there is a case in which the counsellor has been made aware of a possible danger to the client or others, but does not feel that the danger is probable, do they still have an obligation to inform responsible authorities?

4. Are counsellors legally obliged to inform responsible authorities of the clients' involvement in illegal activities if counsellors feel that it would be detrimental to the clients? Counsellors may feel they have a better chance of helping clients by encouraging them to stop their involvement in illegal activities within the framework of their counselling relationship.

4 *Records* **of the counselling relationship including interview notes, test data, correspondence, tape recordings, and other documents, are to be considered professional information for use in counselling and they are not part of the official records of the institution or agency in which the counsellor is employed. Revelation to others of counselling material should only occur upon the express consent of the counsellee.**

Counsellor Files (+)
In a family counselling agency records are kept of all the clients coming to the agency for counselling. These individual files contain only basic biographical information. Each counsellor at the agency keeps her or his own files on all clients that she or he is counselling. These personal counsellor files contain interview notes and are intended only for the use of the counsellor who is counselling a particular client.

Tape Recordings in a Practicum (+)
In a counselling practicum, students are required to submit audio and video tapes of counselling sessions with clients. The practicum instructor has developed appropriate forms that explain the purposes of the audio and video recordings. All clients and student counsellors sign the forms giving permission for the practicum instructor and counselling student to view the tapes for learning purposes. After the viewing, the tapes are erased.

The Police Are Calling (-)
A marriage counsellor is contacted by the police regarding one of her clients. The police ask for any information the counsellor can give them from the interviews with this particular client. The counsellor, realizing the police are asking, goes to her files and tells the inquiring policeman the essence of the interviews.

The Principal's Policy (-)
The policy of one school principal is to have one set of files in his school. He insists that all counsellors write interview notes for each client that they see, and that these notes be placed in the school files. As a result of the protests from counsellors, the principal has "compromised" by telling counsellors that their interview notes "may be brief," but that they must submit a report on each student interviewed. In spite of the fact that the files are accessible to all the teachers, secretaries and clerks in the school, the counsellors continue to file their interview notes in the school files.

COMMENTS AND QUESTIONS
Client records belong to the client. These records include test data, letters of correspondence, any video or audio recordings and the counsellor's interview notes. These materials belong to the client and are for the use of the client and counsellor. These personal records "are not part of the official records of the institution or agency in which the counsellor is employed." Permission from the client is necessary before these "client records" are shared with others.

1. What type of record keeping policy is in place at your counselling centre?
2. Do some schools have records policies similar to those of the principal depicted in the last case?
3. Should counsellors-in-training be allowed to keep their audio or video recordings of clients?
4. Should counsellors give police or lawyers records of their interviews?

5 The counsellee should be *informed of counselling conditions* at or before the time the counsellee enters such a relationship. Particular care should be taken in the event that conditions exist about which the counsellee would not likely be aware. In individual or group situations the member-leader is obligated to make clear the purposes, goals, techniques, rules of procedure, and any limitations that may affect the continuance of the relationship.

A Plan of Action (+)

Jane is a 14 year old grade eight student who comes to the school counsellor in a panic, thinking she is pregnant. The counsellor is a long-time staff member and well-liked by the student. Given the rapport between the two, it is not too long before the student is calm and rational enough to listen to the counsellor. The counsellor indicates there are ways in which a pregnancy can be confirmed and the plan of action would depend on the results. If negative, Jane would educate herself with regard to avoiding future unwanted pregnancies. If positive, Jane would have one of three choices: keep the baby, give the baby up, or abort, and the consequences of each choice would be discussed. Furthermore, Jane's parents would have to be informed. Should this moment arrive, the counsellor offered to either tell her parents himself or to be with her when she told them. Jane decided to work through her problem with the guidance of her counsellor.

Informed On Confidentiality (+)

Joyce meets with her school counsellor and tells the counsellor that she has a very serious concern, but before she will tell the counsellor, Joyce insists that the counsellor keep everything she says in strictest confidence. The counsellor carefully explains that she will keep matters confidential, but that there are limits to her confidentiality. The counsellor explains what these limits are. The counsellor then encourages Joyce to talk more about her demand for absolute confidentiality, and to then make a decision whether she wishes to tell the counsellor in spite of the limits that the counsellor has placed on confidentiality.

Secret Phone Call (-)

During the course of the counselling sessions the counsellor discovers that part of the reason for the boy's aggression in class toward his teacher and peers is the fact that he has been physically abused by his father. The counsellor contacts a Child Guidance Clinic to give them this information. But because he is afraid the child and the child's mother will want to stop the counselling to protect the father, the counsellor does not indicate to either the boy or his mother that he has contacted the Child Guidance Clinic.

Principal's Orders (-)

Jocelyn, a grade eleven student, was referred to the counsellor by a teacher who was having difficulty "controlling Jocelyn and her disruptive behavior in the classroom." Jocelyn and the counsellor established a good relationship, but the disruptive behavior continued and the principal was called in to take more severe action. The principal told the counsellor that he would be taking action in this situation and he asked the counsellor to turn any records of her meetings with Jocelyn over to him, so that he could get a better understanding of the situation. In spite of the fact that the counsellor had shown Jocelyn a counselling consent form that promised confidentiality (except when there was danger to the client and others), the counsellor gave the principal all her private documentation of her meetings with Jocelyn.

COMMENTS AND QUESTIONS

It is important that counsellors inform clients at or before counselling as to what they typically do in a counselling session. Counsellors should prepare a personal statement (informed consent) on their counselling. Such an informed consent form would contain a short statement about the counselling sessions, the nature of the counselling, the length and the type of follow-up used. This informed consent form would also contain information on the counsellor's qualifications. There would also be a statement regarding confidentiality and the client's rights.

1. If it is true that the majority of school counsellors and employment counsellors do not have informed consent forms, what do you think are the reasons for this?
2. Besides the areas mentioned in the preceding comment, what other items should be part of a counsellor's personal statement?
3. Should group facilitators have different consent forms than individual counsellors?
4. What are some limitations that may result in the discontinuance of counselling? Should this information be part of the consent form?

6 **The member reserves the right to *consult* with any other professionally competent person about the counsellee. In choosing professional consultants the worker must avoid placing the consultant in a conflict of interest situation. If the identity of the counsellee is to be revealed, it should be done with the express consent of the counsellee.**

Consultation With Consent (+)

David had been counselling Marty for several weeks without making much progress. He felt that Marty's home situation had much to do with Marty's problems in school. David felt it would be of benefit to him and to Marty if he consulted with another professional about Marty. David concluded that the social worker in the community would be a professionally competent person with whom to consult. David approached Marty with his intentions of consulting with the social worker. Marty gave his consent to this, and David then consulted with the social worker concerning Marty.

Consultation With Another Counsellor (+)

Janice has been counselling Miguel, a grade 6 student, for several sessions. Miguel and his mother had recently moved to Canada to live with his aunt and uncle. Miguel liked his new home but he really missed his home and his family. School was very different for Miguel, and he was having some difficulty adjusting to this new environment. He had made no close contacts or friendships with other students. He maintained the distance between himself and others.

Janice was concerned about Miguel's situation. She had counselled counsellees similar to Miguel before, but Miguel had made little progress and she felt she needed advice from someone more experienced in this field. Janice felt that it would be of benefit to her professionally, and of benefit to Miguel, if she consulted with another professional who had more experience with immigrant children.

Murray was a very experienced counsellor and had done much counselling of this type himself. Janice felt that he would be able to give some evaluation and advice on Miguel's situation and her counselling action.

Janice approached Murray and asked him if he would be willing to consult with her on one of her cases. Murray was willing to help. Janice explained Miguel's situation and her concerns to Murray. He gave Janice his opinions and ideas, and they discussed the situation. Miguel's identity was not revealed in this consultation.

Client Uninformed (-)

Through counselling sessions with Janice Wells, a junior high student, Tanya, had shown some improvements in her attitudes toward school. As counselling continued, Tanya began to disclose more, and she made reference to her involvement in "hanging out" with high school age students and drinking and doing drugs. The counsellor felt that she should consult with Tanya's teacher concerning Tanya's situation. She felt that by consulting and collaborating with the teacher, she could get further insight into the counsellee's situation and devise a plan of action for herself that would best help Tanya.

Once Janice Wells decided that this consultation should be the next step, she went immediately to the teacher to discuss Tanya's situation. Tanya was not made aware of this consultation, and did not consent to such action.

Uninvolved "Client" (-)

An English teacher in an urban high school contacts one of the school counsellors about the strange behavior of one of her students. She also tells the counsellor that in a recent autobiographical paper that the student submitted, the student had written that it "would be wonderful not to be in this world anymore." Without stopping to talk to the student, the counsellor immediately informed his department head, the school principal and the parents of the student.

COMMENTS AND QUESTIONS

Consultation needs to be an integral part of counselling. Counsellors must realize their own attitudes and limitations in working with clients. Consulting with a professionally competent person can present new ideas and attitudes, and offer new ways of thinking to the counsellor. Often when working with a problem in a certain manner, counsellors may not easily recognize another effective approach. Consultation can provide a varied array of approaches and ideas. Counsellors may also receive needed reinforcement, support or evaluation of their ideas and practices through consultation.

Counsellors must remember that their primary obligation is to the client and any additional help from another professional may help the client.

It is crucial that when consulting another person, the counsellor maintain the highest ethical standards. In terms of ethical guidelines regarding consultation, the counsellor must not reveal the identity of the client unless the client is aware of the consultation.

1. What does a counsellor do if the client refuses consent for consultation?

2. Do you agree that with most consultation it is not necessary to reveal the name of the client?

3. How best can a counsellor avoid a conflict of interest situation when consulting with teachers?

4. What are some situations where a consultant can be put into a conflict of interest situation?

7 If members determine an inability to be of professional assistance to counsellees, members must either avoid initiating the counselling relationship or immediately terminate that relationship. In either event, members must *suggest appropriate alternatives*. Members must be knowledgeable about referral resources so that a satisfactory referral can be initiated. In the event the counsellees decline the suggested referral, members are not obligated to continue the relationship.

Awareness of Skills (+)

A client that a counsellor has been counselling regarding a family matter (death of a parent) discloses that he is drinking heavily and realizes that it is a problem that is getting worse. Upon discussion with the client, the counsellor and client agree that referral to Alcoholics Anonymous would be advisable in order to monitor his progress in this area, and to set up a support group.

Strong Personal Bias (+)

A teenager comes for counselling and discloses that she is pregnant and wants an abortion. After discussion with the client, the counsellor refers the girl to a pregnancy and abortion clinic due to strong pro-choice feelings on the part of the counsellor and the inability to be objective in her professional assistance.

Referral Required (-)

A family counsellor had just moved to a new city and had joined a family counselling centre. He had worked with a client for several sessions when he learned of the client's problems of dealing with alcohol abuse in her family. The family counsellor, unaware of an excellent alcohol counselling program in the city, continued the counselling, in spite of his total inexperience with 'alcohol counselling'.

Suicidal Tendencies (-)

Kayla Thompson had just graduated with a Master's degree in counselling psychology. Her total counselling experience consisted of an eight-month field experience in an elementary school, working with an elementary school counsellor. Kayla joined a three-person counselling service and began her private practice.

One of her first clients was a young man who told of his "useless life", his feelings of "hopelessness", and his envying his cousin who had recently committed suicide. Kayla, in her zeal to begin counselling, never questioned her own ability to help her client, in spite of her total lack of training in helping suicidal clients. She continued her once-a-week, Rogerian-like sessions, and after the third session she learned that her client had had an unsuccessful suicide attempt.

COMMENTS AND QUESTIONS

It is not enough for counsellors to "just counsel"; they need to be knowledgeable in the areas in which they counsel. This guideline is very specific on this matter; namely, that if counsellors can not be of professional help they should not initiate counselling, but should refer the client to someone else with expertise in the problem area. It is very important that counsellors are knowledgeable about referral resources.

1. How can counsellors know whether they can be of "professional assistance" at the beginning of counselling?

2. Is "relationship counselling" sufficient in most cases?

3. What resources are available for counsellors to help them be more informed about referral resources?

4. How have you learned about referral resources?

8 When members have other relationships, particularly of an administrative, supervisory, and/or evaluative nature with an individual seeking counselling services, members must not serve as counsellor but should refer the individual to another professional. Only in instances where such an alternative is unavailable and where the individual's situation warrants counselling intervention should the member enter into and/or maintain a counselling relationship. *Dual relationships* with clients that might impair members' objectivity and professional judgment (e.g.., As with close friends or relatives) must be avoided and/or the counselling relationship terminated through referral to another competent professional.

Referrals (+)

When two close friends of a marriage counsellor decide to divorce, they both seek their counsellor friend for counselling. The counsellor, knowing the ethical boundaries of dual relationships, decides it's best not to mix her personal relationship with a professional relationship. The member explains her dilemma to the couple and makes appropriate referrals to other marriage counsellors that she knows.

Counselling Students? (+)

A counsellor-educator is asked by one of her graduate students to help her with her severe depression. The counsellor-educator explains to the student that she is her teacher and evaluator of her work and that it would be inadvisable for them to have a counselling relationship as well. The counsellor-educator recommends several counsellors who she feels could help the graduate student.

Counselling A Relative (-)

A counsellor is approached by his niece regarding her personal problem. She is under all kinds of pressure from her family to leave the man she is dating, and who wishes to marry her. The man she is dating is of a different race, and her family strongly disapproves. The counsellor agrees to counsel his niece, since she has come to him with her concerns. Though he attempts to help his niece with her dilemma, his professional judgement becomes influenced. He tells his niece that she should leave her boyfriend and find a man from within her own race.

Counselling Co-Workers (-)

The director of a ten-counsellor counselling centre is approached by one of the counsellors at her centre regarding her own marital problems. The two counsellors are good friends, even though the director of the centre is required to send annual reviews of each counsellor to a board of directors. In spite of the different roles that the director has, she agrees to counsel her friend and co-worker.

COMMENTS AND QUESTIONS

Counsellors should be aware of the problems that can arise when dual relationships come into play. Frequently, dual relationships can impair counsellors' professional judgement and objectivity. School administrators who may have to discipline students are in a dual relationship if they also take on counselling responsibilities with the students. Marriage counsellors who work with couples who are their friends may encounter ethical dilemmas in their dual relationship. It is very difficult to balance a professional relationship during counselling with a personal relationship outside of counselling. For this reason, this ethical guideline clearly states that 'dual relationships must be avoided.'

1. Whose needs are being met when a counsellor counsels a close friend or relative?

2. What is the best way to avoid getting into a counselling relationship with friends?

3. When it is difficult or impossible to refer a potential client (with whom you have a supervisory or administrative relationship) to another counsellor, what are some precautions you should take in this counselling relationship?

4. Is it not possible that counselling a friend will enhance the friendship?

9 **Members will avoid any type of sexual intimacies with counsellees.** *Sexual relationships* **with counsellees are unethical.**

Counselling Relationship Explained (+)

Bryan Adamar is an employment counsellor in a large employment counselling centre. A woman, seeking to re-enter the workforce after having stayed home to raise three children, greatly appreciates the time and effort Bryan takes on her behalf. He spends many sessions with her, helping her to gain confidence in her ability to take on a job. Since the woman has recently left her husband, she feels she needs much emotional support. Thinking that Bryan Adamar is also attracted to her, she suggests they meet for dinner. Bryan, in a kind but firm way, explains that their meeting socially would interfere with their counselling relationship and that intimate behavior with clients was unethical.

"Just Say No" (+)

A female counsellor in a high school setting works regularly with a 17-year-old male student. During one session, the student places his hand on the counsellor's leg and leaves it there. The counsellor removes the student's hand, informs him that his action is inappropriate, and advises him that if it happens again she will have to terminate their relationship and refer him to another counsellor in the school.

Boundaries I (-)

A male elementary school counsellor frequently gives his students pats on the back or hugs, recognizing how deprived of affection many of them are. One of his clients is an attractive, 13-year-old grade six girl whose father has recently deserted the family. During one session, the girl breaks down and begins to cry. The counsellor attempts to comfort her and she ends up sitting on his lap as he strokes her back. Although the counsellor recognizes that he is being sexually stimulated by this contact, he does nothing to end it, and in fact encourages her to come back any time she needs a shoulder to cry on.

Boundaries II (-)

A male counsellor in private practice has a female client whose marriage has recently ended. He is seen to be a caring, compassionate counsellor who regularly holds clients' hands or gives hugs when he feels it is helpful. On one occasion with this client, the hug becomes more than simply an affectionate gesture. At present, although they have not engaged in actual intercourse, a certain amount of sexual activity is now a regular part of each counselling session. The therapist justifies his actions by claiming that the client is a consenting adult and that his attention to her physical needs is part of the healing process for her.

COMMENTS AND QUESTIONS

This ethical guideline is an absolute mandate for counsellors to avoid any type of sexual intimacy or sexual relationship with clients. It is important that counsellors recognize and accept that sexual attractions are human responses, but it is just as important that counsellors are aware of other options such as the following:

a) modelling sensitive but non-exploitive behavior,

b) willingness to consult with colleagues,

c) recognizing and dealing with their own issues of sexuality, and

d) recognizing the distinction between having sexual feelings and acting on them.

1. What feelings or thoughts would be experienced if you were sexually attracted to a client?

2. What feelings or thoughts would you experience if a client were sexually attracted to you?

3. What approach would you take in either case?

4. What training would be helpful for you as a counsellor to assist you in this situation?

10 Members have the responsibility to screen prospective *group members*, especially when group goals focus on self-understanding and growth through self-disclosure. Members ensure that there is professional assistance available during and following the group experience.

Screening Prospective Group Members (+)

A counsellor about to start a social skills group in her school meets with the students individually to talk with them about the goals and expectations of the group. During the screening interviews, the counsellor and one of the students, Elaine, discuss areas Elaine wishes to focus on. It becomes evident that Elaine is having a major problem with another child also referred to the group. Elaine is reluctant to participate in the same group since she feels the conflict cannot be resolved at this time. Since several of these social skills groups are being facilitated by the counsellor, it is possible to separate these two students yet allow them both to experience group counselling.

Prior Screening (+)

Several weeks before the group begins to meet, the counsellor interviews each member individually. He ascertains why the prospective members want to be a part of the group, if they have ever been involved with a group before and how they think this group will benefit them. On one occasion, the counsellor was challenged by a potential group member as to the need for a screening. The counsellor decided not to include this person in a group whose goals were self-understanding through self-disclosure.

Insufficient Screening (-)

A teacher referred a student, Susan, to a counselling group which was focusing on building empathy and anger control. Susan is an extremely angry acting out student who has not learned to accept responsibility for her actions. Whenever she is in trouble, she diverts the blame elsewhere. Susan does not admit she has difficulty dealing with anger. Although a limited screening interview took place prior to placement of the child in group, no discussion regarding goals of the group took place. Susan was unaware that she was expected to talk about her anger in this group setting. When she was confronted with her anger during one session, the results were traumatic for her and the other members of the group.

Group Follow-Up Counselling Needed (-)

A young boy in an elementary school refused to attend a counselling group after having a conflict with another member. The conflict arose as the boy was extremely angry due to rejection of his parents. He took it out on another group member who appeared to come from a stable, caring environment. The group leader felt rejected by this youngster's refusal to come to group. As a result he ignored the child and did not arrange for counselling to assist the child in dealing with the rejection he was experiencing.

COMMENTS AND QUESTIONS

This ethical guideline denotes a responsibility for the counsellor to screen prospective group members, particularly when the group goals focus on self-understanding through self-disclosure, and for the counsellor to ensure that there is professional assistance available to any one who needs assistance both during and following the group session.

Group members should be informed of their responsibility when entering the group. These responsibilities might include taking risks, self-disclosure, giving and receiving feedback, and keeping confidentiality. Group members should be made aware of the possible advantages and disadvantages of participating in a group. They need to know the possible psychological risks and how the group might disrupt their lives. They need to be informed that often friends and families may not support the changes they make.

It is also extremely important to ensure there is professional assistance available during and following the group experience. Individual group members may need assistance coming to terms with painful issues resulting from the group process or other events in their lives.

Sometimes these issues are of a highly complex and personal nature and it is not appropriate to deal with them in a group setting. Furthermore, upon conclusion of the group, referrals should be made when and if group members have issues they wish to discuss further.

1. What types of questions should be asked during a group screening interview?
2. What behaviors or comments in a screening interview would keep you from including a person in your group?
3. What type of professional assistance would you arrange if you were planning to lead a personal growth group?
4. What types of follow-up activities are needed for group members?

11 When *computer applications* are used as a component of counselling services, members must ensure that: (a) the counsellee is intellectually, emotionally and physically capable of using the computer applications; (b) the computer application is appropriate to the needs of the counsellee; (c) the counsellee understands the purpose and operation of counsellor-assisted and/or self-help computer applications; (d) a follow-up of client use of a computer application is provided to assess subsequent needs; (e) computer-stored data is limited and appropriate, is destroyed after ceasing to have value in providing services, and is restricted to appropriate staff members.

Computerized Career Information (+)

At one employment counselling centre, a computerized career information system is used to help clients make career decisions. The director of this centre insists that all counsellors are thoroughly familiar with the computer system, and that all clients receive at least an initial and follow-up session so that counsellors can both explain the computer counselling tool and can discuss the results with the clients afterwards.

High School Career Information (+)

At a large high school in a large city in Eastern Canada, all the students in their final year of high school are given the opportunity of spending an hour or more on the computer terminal and work with an interactive career information program designed to help them explore future career directions. The high school has a full-time guidance technician who assists the students with the computerized program. Following this session with the computer, all the students are scheduled for an appointment with one of the counsellors of their choice to make any additional plans regarding their possible career directions.

Open Computer Access (-)

In a small remote Northern town, the area employment office is equipped with the latest in computer equipment. The manager makes sure that all the information on each client — biographical, work history, and counselling interview information — is stored in the computer. All this data in the computer, including the counselling interview material, is accessible to all the staff members including secretarial staff and clerks.

Emotional and Career Needs (-)

In a career counselling program designed to help 35-45 year old women (with limited education and formal work experience) enter or re-enter the world of work, one counselling outreach program had designed a program that consisted mainly of computer interactions. Although some of the women were interested in "what the computer said", many others had other counselling needs that required attention prior to sitting in front of a computer terminal and examining career information.

COMMENTS AND QUESTIONS

As computer applications become more sophisticated there is the danger that the "computer becomes the counselling", rather than a tool, to help the counsellor help clients. Computerized career guidance programs must be restricted to those clients that can truly benefit from such programs. Besides making sure that clients fully understand computer applications, counsellors must guarantee that follow-up counselling is provided after clients use the computerized career guidance programs.

1. In a school or employment counselling centre, should counsellors store interview data in the computer?

2. What data is appropriate to store in a counselling computer system?

3. What use should be made of guidance technicians when it comes to using computerized counselling systems?

4. How long should client information be stored in the computer?

12 Members shall decline to initiate or shall terminate a counselling relationship when the member cannot be of professional assistance to the counsellee either because of lack of competence or *personal limitation*. In such instances, the counsellee shall be referred to an appropriate (professional) specialist. If the counsellee declines the suggested referral, members are not obligated to continue the relationship.

Aggressive Client (+)

A counsellor has had four sessions with a client. With each succeeding session the client becomes more aggressive, hostile and verbally abusive towards the counsellor. The counsellor decides to terminate the counselling relationship after the client refuses to cease the verbal abuse directed toward the counsellor. The counsellor suggests further expertise is required and offers to make a referral. The client agrees and the case is appropriately referred.

Intoxicated Client (+)

A counsellor is working with a client concerning alcohol dependency. It becomes apparent after three sessions the client attends counselling sessions intoxicated. The counsellor informs the client he cannot work with his client under these conditions, but suggests he will refer his client to an agency skilled in the area of alcohol abuse. The client refuses to accept the referral. The counsellor then explains he must terminate the relationship and follows through with this.

Referral Refused (-)

After counselling a client for several months concerning issues of intense grief, loss, and abandonment, the counsellor decides that she can be of little further help and recommends that she receive intense grief therapy with a specialist in this area. After discussing this decision with her client, the client refuses the suggestion and states she views this as further rejection and abandonment. She reproaches the counsellor for even suggesting a referral. The counsellor, not wishing to upset her client any further, forgets the referral and continues working with her client.

Unresolved Counsellor Issues (-)

A counsellor who is recently separated carries unresolved marital issues and over-identifies with a recently separated client. The counsellor is unable to be objective and is not performing her role competently. There is no clear differentiation of boundaries between client and counsellor. The counsellor continues the therapeutic relationship despite the circumstances.

COMMENTS AND QUESTIONS

This ethical guideline provides a clear mandate for counsellors to recognize their own boundaries of professional competence and personal limitations. It is necessary for counsellors to keep in mind that their primary obligation is to the client. Counsellors must maintain a relationship with the client only if it is beneficial to the client. Being always accountable to the client, counsellors must at all times evaluate their own abilities as counsellors. When and if counsellors are in situations where they lack competence, they must recognize this and refer the client to a specialist or terminate the therapy. Counsellors should be aware of the services and resources in their community in order to refer clients when necessary. Counsellors should also be aware of their own abilities and limitations and share their struggles with their supervisors and colleagues. Most importantly, they should realize that referring clients or terminating therapy when necessary is sound judgment. Ethically, members must admit to themselves and to their clients when they are not competent to continue the therapy. When the client refuses the referral or termination, the counsellor is still obligated to terminate the relationship. This guideline makes counsellors accountable to clients and to themselves. Continual self-awareness is the key to effective counselling.

1. How can a counsellor know when to terminate counselling?

2. Would you continue counselling a client if he or she refused your referral?

3. Is counselling that does not seem to be accomplishing anything better than no counselling at all?

4. How can counsellors determine if they are being of "professional assistance"?

13 If after entering a counselling relationship the member discovers the counsellee is already in a *counselling relationship with another counsellor*, the member is responsible for discussing the issues related to continuing or terminating counselling with either one or both counsellors.

Permission to Counsel (+)

Frank Owens has been seeing a counsellor in private practice for several months. Frank decides to go back to university to finish the last year of his degree, a degree program that he had interrupted for eight years. He learns of the counselling service at the university and sees a counsellor about some educational/career matters. When the university counsellor learns of Frank receiving counselling elsewhere, she says that she needs permission from the counsellor in private practice before she can continue counselling Frank. Frank agrees to this request and upon receiving permission the university counsellor and Frank continue their counselling relationship.

Group and Individual Counselling (+)

Freyda Elliott asks a group leader about joining her "confidence building" group. In the ensuing screening interview the group leader learns that Freyda is currently under the care of a local psychiatrist. With Freyda's permission, the group leader contacts the psychiatrist regarding Freyda's joining her group. The psychiatrist feels that the group experience may be very helpful to Freyda and encourages her entering the confidence building group.

Counselling Plus (-)

Joan and Bob have been seeing a marriage counsellor for over six months. One day Joan learns from her good friend about a counsellor who is very good. Besides seeing the marriage counsellor with her husband Bob, Joan also begins seeing the counsellor, Joyce Reynolds, that her friend recommended. When Joyce Reynolds learns that Joan is also seeing a marriage counsellor, she asks Joan for permission to discuss this dual counselling with the marriage counsellor. Joan tells Joyce that she does not want the other counsellor to know. She also tells Joyce how much she is gaining from their individual counselling sessions. Joyce decides to continue their counselling.

Two Counsellors For Bobby (-)

Bobby has been in trouble with the law regarding drug use, and his parents have arranged for him to see a counsellor with knowledge in working with adolescents using and abusing drugs. Since Bobby is on the volleyball team, he establishes a close relationship with the coach who is also the school counsellor. Bobby begins seeing the school counsellor. Even though both counsellors are aware that they are both counselling Bobby, neither counsellor makes any attempt to discuss the issue of "two counsellors for Bobby".

COMMENTS AND QUESTIONS

It is important that counsellors do not work at cross purposes with a client. To help avoid any problems that might arise if two or more counsellors are working with the same client, it is vital that counsellors discuss issues related to dual counselling. The client must give permission for counsellors to contact each other, and if this permission is not granted, counselling by at least one of the counsellors should be terminated.

1. What are some of the problems that can arise if a client is seeing two counsellors at the same time?
2. If both counsellors agree, should a client see two counsellors?
3. Is it the counsellor's responsibility to ensure that her or his client is not receiving other counselling?
4. What would you do as a counsellor if you were convinced that you were helping a client; the client said that you were being helpful; the client did not want to stop seeing another helpful counsellor; you discussed the issues with the other "first" counsellor, and he insisted that you stop seeing his client?

14 Should members be engaged in work settings which call for any variation from the above principles, members are obligated to ensure that such *variations* are justifiable under the conditions and that they are clearly specified and made known to all concerned with such counselling services.

Anti-Abortion (+)

A pregnancy information centre is funded in part by several church groups. Members of these church groups constitute the majority of the board of directors for this centre. Their policy regarding pregnancies is to have counsellors advise all clients against abortion. The director of counselling insists that all the counsellors have informed consent forms that clearly state the abortion philosophy of the centre.

Open Records? (+)

In a large family counselling centre, the director has established a policy whereby all counselling records are open to all the workers in the centre. One counsellor, in particular, feels strongly that there is a real danger of breaking confidentiality unnecessarily. She voices her concerns at a regular counsellors' meeting and asks the director and others to reconsider their policy. In the meantime she informs all of her clients of the method of record keeping at the centre.

Principal's Wishes (-)

In spite of a general policy of confidentiality in a school counselling department, few efforts are made to assure what is said in counselling sessions is kept confidential. The school principal insists that all records, including counsellors' interview records, be kept in a central file open to all teachers. Although the counsellors do not like the policy, they go along with the principal's wishes.

Acquiescence (-)

In one junior high school, counsellors are required to do a number of administrative duties. As well, if teachers have students who have discipline problems, the "first step of defense", says the principal, is to have the counsellors deal with these discipline problems. The counsellors see these disciplinary relationships as having the potential to interfere with counselling relationships. The counsellors grumble and complain a great deal among themselves, but they do not talk to the principal about their concerns.

COMMENTS AND QUESTIONS

This guideline states that counsellors should adhere to the ethical guidelines related to confidentiality, records, danger to clients and others, consultation, sexual and dual relationships, and many others. If the counsellor is in a work situation where any of the guidelines must be compromised in some way, the counsellor is obligated to examine carefully whether any variation to the ethical guideline is justifiable. Should these variations to the ethical guidelines be justifiable, counsellors must inform not only their clients, but also inform administrators, support staff, other counsellors and board of directors.

1. How will counsellors know which ethical "variations" are justifiable?

2. What part does an informed consent form play in this ethical guideline?

3. Is a flagrant ethical violation justifiable if keeping your job depends on it?

4. Of what help are the guidelines for reporting ethical violations to the counsellor when ethical guidelines are compromised?

❖ ❖ ❖ ❖ ❖ ❖ ❖ ❖ ❖ ❖ ❖ ❖ ❖ ❖

ESSAYS

Counselling Ethics and Confidentiality

William E. Schulz
University of Manitoba

The Importance of Confidentiality

Some time ago I was asked what I would do if I were the high school counsellor in the following situation. A high school student, Frank, gradually developed a good relationship with his counsellor and having been told that their conversations were confidential, Frank told his counsellor that he had made a good deal of money selling drugs both in his and other schools. Frank said he had made a lot of friends through his drug sales and he now had money to buy many things he wanted. Upon hearing Frank make this disclosure, the counsellor showed a great deal of surprise and disappointment, and Frank quickly reminded his counsellor that "you promised to keep everything confidential."

One suspects that this counsellor was very lax in his "informed consent" to students and probably did not inform Frank of the limits of confidentiality. Putting this aside, this case does raise a number of additional issues related to confidentiality. First of all, counsellors' "primary obligation is to respect the integrity and promote the welfare of counsellees" (CGCA *Guidelines for Ethical Behaviour*, Section B-1). Should Frank's counsellor continue the developing counselling relationship and hope that Frank will alter his behaviour as he begins to understand more fully his illegal, destructive actions? Would this best "promote the welfare" of Frank? The CGCA *Guidelines for Ethical Behaviour* (Section B-3) also state that when "there is clear and imminent danger to the counsellee and others", the counsellor needs to inform responsible authorities. Does the protection of students who are buying drugs from Frank take precedence over a promise to keep all interviews confidential? Possibly, there is even a middle approach between continuing to counsel Frank and reporting Frank's drug selling activities. Maybe Frank can be convinced by the counsellor to stop selling drugs, knowing that if he does not, the counsellor will inform both the school principal and Frank's parents.

These questions and issues, and many others, arise when confidentiality in counselling is considered. Confidentiality is crucial in establishing and maintaining a strong counsellor/client relationship. Bok (1983) has clarified the real importance of confidentiality by pointing out that through confidentiality counsellors are respecting clients' ability to control their own lives and have autonomy. With confidentiality, counsellors show respect for all human relationships and the information shared during a counselling interview. A further premise underlying confidentiality is its utility. That is, clients who need help are much more likely to seek help if they know that what they say will be kept confidential. Would Frank have sought out his counsellor and talked about his activities so freely had he known that the interview would not be confidential?

Confidentiality and Privileged Communication

Confidentiality relates to matters of professional ethics. Confidentiality protects clients from unauthorized disclosures of any kind on the part of the counsellor without first obtaining the permission of the client. Privileged communication is a legal right which protects clients from having any confidences revealed during legal proceedings. The only privilege granted in Canadian law is that which exists between a lawyer and client (Whitley, 1992). When legal issues come into conflict with ethical issues, the law prevails.

Several Canadian court cases in the last decade clearly point out the differences between privileged communication and confidentiality. In the MacDonald vs. MacDonald case (January 14, 1987 in British Columbia) an application was made where a wife and husband, experiencing marital difficulties, would attend counselling and that all discussions with the counsellor be privileged for purposes of possible future litigation. The husband agreed to attendance for counselling but refused to agree that all discussions should be privileged. The Court did not grant privilege saying that even if there was a greater prospect of successful counselling with privilege, this possible greater success was not sufficient reason to grant a new kind of privilege for the future.

In another case (R. vs. Fehr, December 8, 1983), an accused, charged with doing an indecent act, talked to a counsellor. This conversation was ruled not privileged as it did not fall within the ambit of solicitor-client privilege. The counsellor was not a barrister or solicitor, nor did he purport to act for a lawyer. Wigmore's four conditions necessary to be met for establishing privilege had not been satisfied in this case. These four fundamental conditions are:

i) The communications must originate in a *confidence* that they will not be disclosed.

ii) This element of *confidentiality must be essential* to the full and satisfactory maintenance of the relation.

iii) The relation must be one which in the opinion of the community ought to be sedulously *fostered*.

iv) The *injury* that would inure to the relation by the disclosure of the communication must be *greater than the benefit* thereby gained for the correct disposal of litigation.

Counsellors do not have privileged communication and confidentiality is not absolute. At best the CGCA *Guidelines for Ethical Behaviour* serve as "guidelines" in numerous areas and offer some protection to counsellors. These ethical guidelines serve as a basis of comparison in that counsellors are expected to adhere to the same behavioral standards as other counsellors with similar duties and training.

Limited Confidentiality

As indicated earlier, in order for counselling to be most effective, clients must feel that what they reveal to the counsellor will be kept confidential. In actual practice, the counsellor will soon realize that there are real limits to confidentiality. There are times when complete confidentiality is undesirable or even unethical. These exceptions to confidentiality include the following (Remley, 1990):

1. A client is a danger to self or others.

2. A client requests release of information.

3. A court orders release of information.

4. Clients raise the issue of their mental health in a law suit.

5. During the systematic clinical supervision of a counsellor.

6. A third party is present in the room.

7. Clerical assistants who process information and papers.

8. During legal or clinical consultation.

Many examples exist to exemplify each of these exceptions to confidentiality. The confidentiality exception of danger to others, is raised in the well-known Tarasoff case, in which Prosenjit Poddar informed his counsellor that he was planning to kill his girlfriend, Tatiana Tarasoff. Poddar killed Tarasoff, and her parents filed suit against the university for failing to notify their daughter of the danger. The court confirmed the guiding principle that confidentiality must yield to the extent to which disclosure is essential to protect others. Counsellors have an ethical responsibility to take some direct action when they feel a client is likely to cause harm to self or others.

Several of the exceptions to confidentiality refer to court orders and law suits. Counsellors do not have legal privileged information and must yield to court requests for interview information. Counsellors should, however, explain to the court their reasons for their reluctance to break confidentiality. The premise for the counselling relationship is confidentiality and the counsellor's role is to provide a safe, confidential setting to explore feelings, examine information and consider options (Whitley, 1992).

Other exceptions to confidentiality relate to the clinical supervision of a counsellor and/or when a "third party is present in the room". Confidentiality belongs to the client, and in these cases it is important that the client gives permission for being part of the supervision process of another counsellor, or for being observed by a third person.

High levels of confidentiality are expected from secretaries and clerical assistants who have access to confidential interview material. It is the responsibility of counsellors to educate support staff on the importance of maintaining *confidentiality*.

When counsellors are involved in legal or clinical consultation, it usually is not necessary to reveal the identity of the client. If it becomes necessary to reveal the identity of the client, counsellors should again keep in mind that confidentiality belongs to the client, and counsellors should inform clients of their intention of consulting with others.

Avoiding Ethical Violations

To avoid ethical violations, particularly as they relate to confidentiality, counsellors should know the "Three R's" of counselling; namely, rapport with clients, reasonable behaviour, and the rights and duties of informed consent. Counselling is more effective if there is rapport or a good working relationship between the counsellor and client. Clients who feel positive toward their counsellors are not likely to give their counsellors problems related to confidentiality.

What is reasonable behaviour on the part of the counsellor? One over-simplistic response would be the behaviour or actions taken by a majority of people in any given situation. Thus, if a client tells a counsellor of the danger she or he poses to others, or threatens suicide, reasonable behaviour would constitute telling the appropriate authorities about the danger. Reasonable behaviour means that counsellors recognize those situations in which they must break confidentiality. Reasonable behaviour also means counsellors are willing to consult with colleagues, supervisors and lawyers in cases that involve legal and ethical issues. Reasonable behaviour also implies an understanding of counsellors' skill limitations and willingness to refer clients to other specialists.

The third "R" refers to the rights and duties of informed consent. The concept of informed consent is based on all clients' freedom to make choices that directly affect them. The origins of informed consent can be traced to the rights of individuals to be free from coercion and any unwarranted interference. Informed consent, as it relates to confidentiality, refers to "the client's right to understand the limits of confidentiality at the commencement of the counselling relationship..." (Arthur & Swanson, 1993, p. 14). Not only should the limits of confidentiality be discussed before counselling begins, but several other types of information should be part of the "informed consent" discussion. Margolin (1982) listed the following:

1. An explanation of the procedures to be used and their purposes.

2. The role of the person who is providing counselling and his or her professional qualifications.

3. Discomforts or risks reasonably to be expected during counselling.

4. Benefits reasonably to be expected.

5. Alternatives to treatment that might be of similar benefit.

6. A statement that any questions about procedures used will be answered at any time.

7. A statement that the client can withdraw his or her consent and discontinue counselling at any time.

Mary DePauw (Huey & Remley, p. 41) has used a timeline to help counsellors consider ethical considerations that occur before and during counselling. This timeline has been adapted and related to the CGCA *Guidelines for Ethical Behaviour*.

1. Pre-counselling considerations:
   a) Advertising (Guidelines for Ethical Behaviour Sections A-4, A-6, D-5)
   b) Avoiding misuse of institutional affiliation (D-6)
   c) Financial arrangements (A-5)

2. Service provision issues:
   a) Adequacy of counsellor skills, experience and training (A-1, A-7, B-12)
   b) Better service option for the client (B-7)
   c) Concurrent counsellor involvement (B-13)
   d) Conflicting dual relationship (B-8)

3. Informed consent issues:
   a) Structures to educate regarding purposes, goals, and techniques (B-5)
   b) Explanation of rules of procedures and limitations (B-5)
   c) Supervision and consultation release concerns (B-6, D-4)
   d) Experimental methods of treatment (C-14), C-15)

4. Ongoing counselling issues:
   a) Confidentiality (B-2)
   b) Special issues of confidentiality with minors
   c) Consultation (B-6, D-4)
   d) Record keeping (B-4, B-11)

5. Dangerousness and Crisis Concerns:
   a) Threat to self (B-3)
   b) Threat to others (B-3)
   c) Child abuse (B-3)
   d) Gray areas, e.g., eating disorders (B-3, B-7)
6. Termination Phase Considerations:
   a) Referral if unable to assist (A-7, B-7, B-12)
   b) Professional evaluation (A-1)

This timeline approach to examining ethics helps counsellors to examine ethical considerations during the initiation phase of counselling as well as during the counselling itself.

Concluding Comments

Generally speaking, ethical behaviour consists of keeping all communications with clients confidential. Since counsellors have some limits placed on their confidentiality, it is important that clients know about these limits before or at the beginning of counselling. Counsellor informed consent statements outlining the importance of confidentiality as well as the limits of confidentiality are crucial, and have become standard practice among most members of professional counselling associations.

The principles of confidentiality that Schneiders (1963) outlined some 30 years ago still provide sound guidelines for counsellors:

1. The obligation of confidentiality is relative rather than absolute since there are conditions which can alter confidentiality.
2. Confidentiality depends on the nature of the material, so that material which is already public, or can easily become so, is not bound by confidentiality in the same way as is confidential interview material.
3. The material that is necessary for a counsellor or an agency to function effectively is often released from the bonds of confidentiality.
4. Confidentiality is always conditioned by the intrinsic right of clients to their integrity and reputation, to be secret, and to resist aggression.
5. Confidentiality is limited also by the rights of counsellors to preserve their own reputation and integrity, and to resist harm or aggression.

6. Confidentiality is determined and limited by the rights of the innocent third party and by the rights of the community.

It is the counsellor's duty to respect the counselling relationship and to keep interview material confidential. Ultimately, the success of counselling is dependent on counsellors respecting the intimate nature of client disclosures.

Bibliography

Arthur, Gibbs L., & Swanson, Carl D. (1993). *Confidentiality and privileged communication.* Alexandria, VA.: American Counseling Association.

Bok, S. (1983). *Secrets: On the ethics of concealment and revelation.* New York: Vintage Books.

Canadian Guidance and Counselling Association. (1989). *Guidelines for ethical behaviour.* Ottawa: Author.

Christiansen, Harley D. (1979). *Ethics in counseling— problem situations.* Tucson, Arizona: University of Arizona Press.

Corey, G., Corey, M., & Callanan, P. (1988). *Issues and ethics in the helping professions.* Pacific Grove, Calif.: Brooks/Cole.

Eberlein, L. (1977). Counselors Beware! Clients Have Rights! *Personnel and Guidance Journal,* 56, 219-223.

Huey, Wayne C., & Remley, Theodore P., Jr. (1988). *Ethical and legal issues in school counseling.* Alexandria, VA.: American School Counselors' Assoc.

Lakin, Martin. (1988). *Ethical issues in the psychotherapies.* New York: Oxford University Press.

Lindstrom, A. (1983). Billy, I won't forget you. *Guidepost.* February 8, pp. 2, 4.

Margolin, G. (1982). Ethical and legal considerations in marital and family therapy. *American Psychologist,* 37, 788-801.

Remley, Theodore P., Jr. (1990). *Safeguarding against ethical and legal danger points.* Presentation at the ERIC/CAPS Workshop, Ann Arbor, Michigan.

Schneiders, A.A. (1963). The Limits of Confidentiality. *Personnel and Guidance Journal,* 42, 252-253.

Slovenko, R. (1973). *Psychiatry and the law.* Boston: Little, Brown.

Tompkins, Loren, & Mehring, Teresa. (1993). Client privacy and the school counselor: Privilege, ethics, and employer policies. *The School Counselor,* 40:5, 335-342.

Whitley, Stuart J. (1992). Legal and ethical issues for school counsellors. *Education Manitoba,* March/April, pp. 20-23.

Group Counselling and Ethics

M. Westwood, N. Amundson and B. Borgen
University of British Columbia

Introduction

Counsellors often find groups to be an ideal vehicle for client learning and change in that groups provide a social context of support and opportunity to observe and learn from others. Groups also facilitate self insight and enable members to try out new behaviours. In this way groups are a very constructive counselling medium. On the other hand, counsellors need only review the literature on how groups can be misused and how members can experience coercion and threat to their integrity, to be reminded of the potentially negative influence of the group approach. At a more personal level, group facilitators can probably all recall being a member of a group or leading a group in which the dynamics occurring were far from constructive and facilitative of client development! Therefore, ensuring an ethical approach to the setting up and running of group is essential, due to the inherent power of social influence within the groups context and the potential impact these influences can have on participants.

With this awareness in mind, we have attempted to outline guidelines which are intended to insure and assist group leaders in providing sound ethical practice essential for effective group work. The guidelines have been drawn form the general "Guidelines for Ethical Behaviour" of the CGCA adopted May, 1989 and those identified by Trotzer (1989) in his book: *The Counselor and the Group: Integrating Theory, Training and Practice.*

In an attempt to operationalize these guidelines and focus their relevance to practice, we have endeavoured to link the guidelines with identified stages of group development. The model of group stage development selected is the one developed by Borgen, Pollard, Amundson and Westwood (1989).

The Stages and Relevant Guidelines

By linking the guidelines directly to specific stages of group development the reader will be able to consider what the leader and members are doing or may be concerned with at a particular point in the life of the group. The following group stages will be defined, followed by the relevant ethical guidelines: Planning, Initial, Transition, Working, Termination and Post Group. The specific guidelines from the C.G.C.A. (1989) publication are identified in parentheses.

PLANNING STAGE

This is the stage in which the leader determines what are the goals for the group members, who should be in the group, how many sessions will be needed, what materials are needed and where the group will be conducted. Screening of prospective clients is done at this time to ensure that the group is suitable for the needs of the clients.

Relevant Guidelines

In cases where the leader is working as a member of an organization, he/she should ensure that the group goals are compatible with the organization or philosophical perspective of the agency. For example, a group counselling program within an employment agency should have a direction consistent with the goals of agency i.e. career decision-making and job search. A group which focuses exclusively on self esteem development, may be of interest and help to the individual, but will not connect directly to goals of the employment agency. Members and organizations making the referrals will need to be notified in clear and precise terms as to what is the purpose of the group, the goals and for whom is it intended (B5). This will help prevent inappropriate referrals. The qualifications of the group leader(s) need be made explicit to the organization and group members at this time. Different types of groups required different levels of leader specialization (A4). Group leaders need to know the techniques and rationale for what is happening in the group and be prepared to articulate what they are doing when this requested (B5 & A7). Co-leading may be a preferred approach with certain groups. If this is the case, the leaders must determine that they have a positive relationship, and, if this is not the case, alternate arrangements must be made, including leading by a single leader (A6). Where possible, the leader should review the goals and processes involved for prospective members so they can make an informed choice on joining the group (B10). Further, group members should be reminded that their participation is voluntary and they have the right to leave the group at any time (B5 & D1). If, however, they choose to leave, they will be asked to state their reasons for leaving the group.

Finally, the leader should check early on to see if any of the members are currently involved with another counsellor or professional (B13). If this is the case, the leader will seek permission to discuss this with the member and the other professional (B6).

INITIAL STAGE

Acceptance is the primary concern of members at this point and their primary focus is on determining the extent to which they belong and are accepted by others in the group. The leader is aware that members will have a need for a sense of safety and security during this stage.

Relevant Guidelines

The objectives and the process of the group should be reviewed again so that members can seek clarification and assurance (B5). One of the actions during this stage is the development of a set of group norms which will guide the behaviour of the group (B1). Important among these norms is the establishment of a norm of confidentiality concerning member self disclosure (B2).During this stage the leader will inform members that he/she will intervene to prevent criticism of an individual and this is necessary to meet member needs of personal safety (B1). Members will be asked to adopt a set of guidelines for communicating among themselves. The leader will introduce and model guidelines for giving and receiving feedback (B1).Members are reminded they are free to participate when they wish to and have the right to refuse speaking when they feel so inclined (B1). Relevant to this stage and all the remaining stages is leader training. The leader should not attempt an intervention for which he/she has not been adequately trained (A7).

TRANSITION STAGE

This is the point of some member "ambivalence" to joining in with the group or the direction in which the group may be going. For many there is a concern with issues of control; i.e. how much control will I have and how much control will the others or the leader have. It may be a lack of commitment to the goals of the group (task) or some questions about the process of the group (maintenance). Resolution of this stage helps smooth the way into the working stage.

Relevant Guidelines

The leader will need to protect the members from feeling trauma at this stage and point out that feelings of fear and resistance are normal and may reflect an important need for some of the members to feel safer and more fully included (B1). The leader must protect the members who are showing some resistance to committing to the group from others who may attempt to unduly pressure the reluctant member to make a commitment (B1). The leader must exercise a balance between using appropriate encouragement and influence.

WORKING STAGE

This is the productive stage of the group where all members are committed to the goals and feel a sense of trust with other members. Behaviour at this point tends to be spontaneous; members can agree and disagree more freely and challenge ideas. A sense of team spirit begins to develop at this stage as the group sees change and accomplishment of member goals taking place.

Relevant Guidelines

In groups which have a personal development focus and where trust and self disclosure may be high, it is essential that the leader ensure that the confrontation and personal challenges are designed to promote learning and well being of members, rather than having them perceived as a threat or negative judgements (B1). At times the leader may need to intervene as an advocate for a member to protect him or her from feeling attacked (B1). The leader may have to limit or block certain self disclosures as being premature either for the readiness of the other members or where there may not be enough time to deal with material which has been introduced by the group member (B2). Since it is at this point that the trust and intimacy levels are often high, avoidance of excessive closeness should be maintained and sexual relationships should not be permitted among members or between the leader and the members (A8, B9). It is at this stage that member needs may be identified as exceeding those of the group, and, therefore, there will be a need to consult with other professionals for possible directions and referral sources (B6). Care must be taken to ensure that the name of the individual(s) involved not be disclosed (B2).

Also, if members are not being helped personally or their goals for joining the group are not being met, the leader may need to assist them in finding alternative situations (B7). In rare cases, it may be necessary to inform appropriate authorities about the potential danger of a member physically hurting him/herself or another person (B3). Danger to self or others takes precedence over confidentiality in such situations (B3).

TERMINATION STAGE

This is the ending of the group. Members usually have needs for closing relationships with feeling of reluctance to end the group and an eagerness to apply what they have learned to situation outside the group. Second, members usually review the achievements and goals they have attained as they move to new directions outside the group.

Relevant Guidelines

The leader is responsible for making certain that members are ready to leave the group and have a clear direction once the group has finished (B10). This frequently involves having members review their goals with the leader, the leader reinforces a sense of personal responsibility among the members. The leader is also responsible for indication that if members need to contact the leader for personal reasons arising out of the group this will be possible. This concern is one of a humanitarian nature (B5).

Time should be taken to acknowledge the feelings of loss as normal and members should be given a chance to express these feelings. This helps reduce the dependence on the group once it has finished (B10). If a member has "unfinished business" at the end of the group, the leader will indicate how he/she will assist in this process or if necessary, make an appropriate referral (B7).

POST GROUP STAGE

This is the period following the group in which members try to apply what they have learned in the group to their own lives. A follow-up session should be arranged to check to see if members are achieving their goals and if they need any additional resources.

Relevant Guidelines

Group leaders offer to help members in achieving some of their goals (B7, B10). Group leaders should conduct follow up evaluations of the members to see how they are doing and to determine the value of the group experience (B7). In this way leaders can make relevant changes. It is the ethical responsibility of the leader to determine that all the members do not have "unfinished business" which may require additional support or counselling (B10).

Conclusion

One can see that many of the guidelines apply across stages. The intention here is give direction and reminders so that counsellors are able to safeguard the standards of ethical practice particular to a variety of group counselling contexts.

References

Borgen, W., D. Pollard, Amundson, N., & Westwood, M. (1989). *Employment groups: The counselling connection.* Ottawa: Lugus.

Canadian Guidance and Counselling Association. (1989). *Guidelines for ethical behaviour.* Ottawa: Author.

Trotzer, J. (1989). *The counselor and the group: Integrating theory, training and practice.* Accelerated Development Inc. Indiana.

CHAPTER FOUR

——————— ❖ ———————

Case Studies In Testing, Research And Publication

——————— ❖ ———————

In the twenty guidelines presented in this section, members are encouraged to familiarize
themselves with proper test administration
and interpretation procedures, with ethical
behaviour when doing research with human
subjects, and with appropriate procedures for
publication.

GUIDELINES

1 In general, test results provide only one factor of a variety of pertinent data for personnel and guidance decisions. It is the responsibility of the member to supply adequate orientation and information to the examinee(s) so that the results of testing may be placed in **proper perspective** with other relevant factors. The effects of socio-economic, ethnic and cultural factors on test scores will therefore have to be recognized.

❖

2 Members have the responsibility to inform examinees about the **purposes of testing.** The criteria of the examinee's welfare and/or explicit prior understanding with them shall determine who will receive test results. The examinee has the right to know the testing results, the interpretations made, and the basis for the conclusions and recommendations made.

❖

3 Members recognize the limits of their **compe-tence** and do not offer services, administer tests or use techniques which are beyond their preparation and competence or which fail to meet professional standards established in particular fields.

❖

4 Members must consider carefully the specific **validity, reliability** and appropriateness of the test(s) before selecting them for use in a given situation or with a particular counsellee.

❖

5 When test **results are communicated** to parents, students, or other appropriate persons, they must be accompanied by an adequate interpretation or by counselling.

❖

6 Psychological test scores (as contrasted to interpreted test results) are released only to persons **qualified to interpret** and use them properly.

❖

7 When making any statements to the public about tests and testing, care will be taken to give **accurate information** and to avoid any false claims or misconceptions.

❖

8 Tests should be **administered** as prescribed in the administration manual. Departures from these procedures are permitted only when conducting research and even here must be in accord with professional standards. Any unusual behaviour or irregularities during the testing session which may affect the interpretation of the test scores, must be fully noted and reported. Unsupervised test-taking or the administration of tests through the mails is unethical. However, the use of instruments that are so designed or standardized to be self-administered and self-scored, such as some interest inventories, is permitted.

❖

9 Psychological tests and other assessment devices, whose value in part depends on their novelty to persons taking them, are limited to persons with the professional interest and compe-tence such that they will **safeguard their use.** Prior information, coaching or the reproduction of such material will not be condoned.

❖

10 Members must proceed with **caution in evaluating** and interpreting the perform-ance of minority group members or to other persons who are not represented in the norm group on which the instrument was standardized.

❖

11 Members will not appropriate, **reproduce** or modify established tests or portions thereof without the expressed permission and adequate recognition of the original author, publisher and copyright holder.

❖

12 The **principal researcher** is responsible for ethical research practice while others involved in the research activities share ethical obligations and full responsibility for their own actions.

❖

13 Participation in research must be **volun-tary.** Involuntary participation is appropriate only when it can be demonstrated that participa-tion will have no harmful effects on subjects.

❖

14 Members are responsible for the **welfare of research subjects** used. They should avoid causing injurious psychological, physical or social effects on their subjects.

❖

15 All research subjects should be **informed of the purpose** of the study except when withholding information from them is essential to the research study. In such cases the member is expected to take corrective action as soon as possible following the research.

❖

16 The **identity** of research subjects must be disguised unless otherwise authorized by the subjects when the researcher is supplying data from the research to others or in reporting the results.

❖

17 In **reporting research** results, members must publish a full report mentioning any variables and conditions that might affect the outcome of the investigation or the interpretation of the results.

❖

18 Members must give due **credit** through joint authorship, acknowledgement, footnote statements, or other appropriate means to those who have contributed significantly to the research and/or publication in accordance with such contributions.

❖

19 Members have an obligation to **collaborate with colleagues** by making available original research data to qualified others who may wish to replicate or verify the study.

❖

20 Ethical practice requires that authors not submit the same **manuscript** or one essentially similar in content for simultaneous publication consideration by two or more journals. In addition, manuscripts published in whole or in substantial part in another journal or published work should not be submitted for publication without acknowledgement and permission from the previous publication.

❖

❖ ❖ ❖ ❖ ❖ ❖ ❖ ❖ ❖ ❖ ❖ ❖ ❖ ❖

CASE STUDIES

1 In general, test results provide only one factor of a variety of pertinent data for personnel and guidance decisions. It is the responsibility of the member to supply adequate orientation and information to the examinee(s) so that the results of testing may be placed in *proper perspective* with other relevant factors. The effects of socio-economic, ethnic and cultural factors on test scores will therefore have to be recognized.

Recognizing Language Differences (+)

Mr. Richard D. is an immigrant who recently decided to leave his home in France and move to Winnipeg. He is fluent in the oral communication of English and is able to communicate well verbally. However, he has a problem in interpreting written English. He was requested to take a job evaluation test at a placement center for the unemployed. Both a written and oral form of the test were available. The counsellor, who was informed of Richard's weakness, administered the test orally to Richard and wrote exactly what Richard said for each test question.

Orientation (+)

A counsellor decided that in order to help his client, Heather, she needed a personality assessment. Before conducting the test, the counsellor held an orientation meeting with Heather. During this meeting, Heather was told the purpose of the test, ways in which the counsellor would use the test and some of the limitations of personality testing. During this meeting, the counsellor answered any questions or concerns Heather had about the test. At the end of the meeting, the counsellor felt Heather was comfortable with taking the test.

Standardized Tests For Placement (-)

An American aptitude test battery is used for the placement of students at an inner city high school. There are no Canadian, national or local norms for the tests. Based on the results of these tests, as well as school grades, students are placed in various educational streams in the school. There are large numbers of recently immigrated students in this school. Most score very low in the aptitude test and most have not achieved well in school, due to their weaknesses in English. As a result of low scores, most of these immigrant students are placed in 'high school leaving' streams.

"The Test Says..." (-)

In a private career counselling office, one counsellor regularly uses the Strong-Campbell Interest Inventory to help clients make career decisions. After clients have completed the inventory and the computer print-out of results has been returned, the counsellor tells clients, "The test says you should go into one of the following occupations..." Little or no time is taken to consider other relevant factors in career decision-making; factors such as aptitude, personality, socio-economic and job outlook.

COMMENTS AND QUESTIONS

Certain guidelines and procedures must be followed when administering a test and interpreting test results. Before a member administers a test to an examinee, the following matters should be considered:

a) the member previews in advance the language, ethnic and culture differences of examinee(s) and selects the appropriate assessment or makes necessary adjustments to ensure differences are recognized;

b) the member obtains consent from the examinee before any test is administered or information about the examinee is shared;

c) examinee(s) are informed as to the purpose of testing and confidentiality and limitations are explained;

d) examinee(s) are informed of the availability of test results, interpretations made and explanation of interpretations;

e) the member ensures the examinee understands that these test results are only one factor from a variety of data used when making a counselling or personnel decision.

1. If you were an examinee, what questions might you want to ask about the nature of the test?

2. What would you do to make an examinee feel more at ease prior to taking the test, especially if you noticed outward signs of being over-anxious?

3. How will the examinee be notified of test results? How will the test results be given to the examinee? (Written or verbal)

4. As a member who administered the test, how will the test results be used and will anybody else in your department have access to them?

2 **Members have the responsibility to inform examinees about the *purposes of testing*. The criteria of the examinees' welfare and/or explicit prior understanding with them shall determine who will receive test results. The examinee has the right to know the testing results, the interpretations made, and the basis for the conclusions and recommendations made.**

The Purpose of Testing (+)

The counsellor informs students, class by class, of the purposes of the Differential Aptitude Tests. The counsellor explains carefully the information booklet making sure all questions and information are answered. The test administration is explained by the counsellor. Students are made aware of the test's possible significance and how the results can be used in helping to make future educational and career decisions. Students are also informed that all test interpretations will be done on an individual basis so that other relevant information can be considered.

Test Orientation (+)

In this university counselling service, the counsellors organize and teach regular testing orientation sessions. Every effort is made to help clients understand the purposes and uses of any standardized tests that will be used. In addition, clear instructions are given regarding the individual interpretation that will follow.

Results For The Files (-)

Frank Newman, a high school counsellor, found out that most of the high schools were administering the Differential Aptitude Tests (DAT) to grade nine students. With administration's agreement, he scheduled two morning meetings in the gymnasium for all grade nine students to complete the DAT. Students were simply asked to complete the test in order that the school would have their scores on file.

Unstated Purpose For Testing (-)

As a regular practice, a school principal asks the teachers in her elementary school to administer the Canadian Tests of Basic Skills to all grade four and five students. One year, after the scores were known, two of the grade five teachers received very negative reports on their teaching from the principal. Upon inquiring about these negative reports, two grade five teachers were told that the students in their classes had not progressed sufficiently (one grade equivalency higher) since their testing in the previous year when the students were in grade four.

COMMENTS AND QUESTIONS

This ethical guideline requires those who are in charge of testing to delineate the purpose of testing, the criteria of the examinees' welfare and explicit prior understanding with tests, and the examinees' right to know the testing results, the interpretations made, and other aspects of the testing results. Testing provides counsellors with information so that they can make more realistic decisions, especially when the testing is carefully designed and has broad applicability.

1. How could a counsellor explore examinees' reasons for taking tests, as well as their past experience with tests?

2. What are the major purposes of testing?

3. Who should introduce the idea of standardized testing, the client or the counsellor? Why?

4. What are some ways in which the counsellor can explain beforehand how interpretations, conclusions and recommendations will be made for interest and personality inventories, intelligence tests, diagnostic tests, achievement batteries and aptitude tests?

3 **Members recognize the limits of their competence and do not offer services, administer tests or use techniques which are beyond their preparation and competence or which fail to meet professional standards established in particular fields.**

Art Therapy (+)

A beginning counsellor sees that the art work of one student consistently depicts scenes of violence involving children and adults. Recognizing that there may be psychological significance in this art work, and acknowledging the limitations of his own expertise, the counsellor hands over the collection to the guidance department head, a counsellor with many years of experience, and some knowledge of art therapy.

Staff Orientation (+)

At the beginning of a school year a counsellor at a high school holds an orientation workshop with school administration and teaching staff at which the counsellor's education background, training, experience and competencies are outlined. Participants become familiarized with the range of tests which can be accessed and ones which are beyond the competence of the counsellor to administer. The counsellor makes clear that for these situations the services of a school psychologist should be enlisted.

Score Misinterpretation (-)

A procedure of one small community high school is to administer the Canadian Test of Basic Skills to all new students entering the school with a view to determining an estimate of functional levels in language and mathematics. The school counsellor administers the tests and makes available to teachers the grade equivalent scores. No attempt is made to interpret the scores with the teachers nor to make conversions to percentile ranks. Teachers take the grade equivalent scores into account in assessing functional levels and developing individual programs often misinterpreting both the meaning and intent of grade equivalency scores.

Limited Information (-)

Art interpretation happens to be a recently discovered interest of this department head through some journal articles she has read. She has even discovered a neatly packaged technique including a test to verify the findings. She then applies the test to the client. From the test results, she concludes family violence to be the root cause of the problem. Based on her findings, she proceeds to get social workers involved to start the necessary investigations.

COMMENTS AND QUESTIONS

It is incumbent upon counselling practitioners to engage in constant self-scrutiny and self-evaluation regarding knowledge of, skills, and competence in testing.

It is both a duty and a responsibility to remain current on test availability, the latest testing techniques, the norming schemes, and the accurate interpretation of results. This can be achieved through professional reading, attendance at seminars and workshops, maintaining contact with colleagues, and enrolling in upgrading and refresher courses.

Counsellors should convey to clients the range of testing services within and outside their sphere of competence. There must be a willingness to refer to a more competent authority when cases arise requiring services outside counsellors' levels of ability or training.

1. What set of criteria might one have to determine the degree of comfort and competence in providing a testing service to clients?
2. To what extent should a practitioner attempt to upgrade and keep current on up-to-date test availability, techniques, and results interpretations?
3. What specific information about one's background and competencies should one divulge to prospective clients?
4. What guidelines might one follow in determining at which stage a referral to another authority is made?

4 Members must consider carefully the specific *validity, reliability* and appropriateness of the test(s) before selecting them for use in a given situation or with a particular counsellee.

Placement Policy (+)

A school division has a policy that all senior high students who transfer in from out-of-province must complete a standardized achievement test battery. Much time was taken by division counsellors and psychologists in selecting a test battery that was appropriate for out-of-province students. Each year the appropriateness of the test was re-evaluated.

Test Appropriateness (+)

The manager of an employment centre asks the counsellors in his office to recommend an aptitude test that will be helpful in determining the mechanical aptitude of clients. After careful examination of Buros Mental Measurement Yearbook and the examination of the technical data available on several aptitude tests, the counsellors recommend an aptitude test that appears to be appropriate, reliable and valid.

Language Deficiencies (-)

A high school student, Sophie, has recently moved from predominantly French-speaking Quebec City to an English language high school in Edmonton. Although Sophie can read and speak English, she is not at the same level as other students in her grade. When Sophie completes an aptitude test, the counsellor uses the regular normative data and makes no allowances for Sophie's language deficiencies.

Finding The Gifted Students (-)

A program for educating "gifted" children is being rushed into place by a school division that seems to be responding more to parental pressure than to any clearly defined educational goal or research to substantiate the advisability of such a program. To select students for the "gifted" program, the school superintendent asks counsellors to use a group intelligence test that measures verbal ability, numerical ability and abstract reasoning. The test is 20 years old and no data is available suggesting that the test is appropriate for the selection of "gifted" students.

COMMENTS AND QUESTIONS

This ethical guideline clearly states the importance and need to be knowledgeable and skilled in test selection and use. There must be a purpose for giving tests and standards should be followed for evaluating tests. The publication, *Standards for Educational and Psychological Tests*, is a comprehensive guide for both test developers and test users. These standards set out information that should be included in test manuals; information on technical adequacy and information on how to use the test. As well, test users will find an extensive review of tests in O.K. Buros's *Mental Measurements Yearbook*.

Several factors should be considered when selecting either norm-referenced or criterion-referenced tests. Validity is the most important factor. This means that the test must measure what it claims to measure and what the user wants it to measure. Reliability coefficients must meet acceptable standards and there should be a relatively small standard error of measurement. To make sure the test is appropriate, the population on whom the test was normed should include people like the ones to be tested. These and other considerations are to be adhered to before selecting tests for use.

1. What questions would you be prepared to discuss with your administrator if the required tests did not show evidence of sufficient validity in their test manuals?

2. If a test is a "big seller", does this imply that the test is valid? Explain.

3. How would you counter the argument, "The use of an inadequate device is better than the use of no test at all"?

4. Explain why it is realistic to demand very high standards of reliability when using tests for decision-making?

5 When test *results are communicated* to parents, students, or other appropriate persons, they must be accompanied by an adequate interpretation or by counselling.

Tests and Counselling (+)

Bob, a first year engineering student, is not enjoying his program of studies. He decided to take an interest inventory at the university counselling centre to see if his interests really were in engineering. After the results of the interest inventory were known, the counsellor discussed the results with Bob. The interest inventory scores did not support his field of study, but the counsellor pointed out that a standardized interest inventory was only one factor among many others that should influence his career decision. The counsellor and Bob then discussed some of the other factors.

Effective Test Interpretation (+)

A school counsellor telephoned the parents of one student in order to communicate a concern about the student's behavioral change over the last several months. The student appeared sullen, non-communicative with all school personnel and skipping of classes was increasing. After talking with the counsellor, the student revealed that he felt hopelessly lost in most of his subjects. The student agreed to some diagnostic testing in order to find out more specially what the major problems might be. Since the parents were very concerned and willing to help, the counsellor asked the student's permission to include them in the discussion of the test results and in future remedial learning plans.

Parental Request for Information (-)

In November of Jamie's grade six year, her parents noticed she appeared to be regressing in mathematics and not progressing in her reading ability. The parents knew that special testing was done for some students at the beginning of each year by the resource teacher and counsellor. After learning that Jamie had been tested several months earlier, the parents requested the results of the tests. The results indicated dramatic drops in performance, yet the results had not been communicated to the parents and remedial action was not implemented to correct or work with Jamie. The present classroom teachers were not informed of the child's problems or what teaching strategies might help her learning.

Inadequate Test Interpretation (-)
A counsellor is trying to do some research in the area of self concept and adolescent females. A standardized test on self concept was administered to all students in one junior high school. After test results were interpreted, the counsellor intended to meet with the students individually to discuss the test results. Due to lack of time, only half of the students were provided with this opportunity. With the rest of the students, the results were handed back to each classroom, generally to groups of thirty-five, with a short period of time made available to answer any questions students might have. As there were no questions asked, no further interpretation was provided.

COMMENTS AND QUESTIONS
This ethical guideline emphasizes that test results must be accompanied by adequate interpretation and where it is felt to be necessary, by counselling as well. Many of the tests that counsellors use are fairly easy to administer and interpret. This is true for a number of interest inventories and some aptitude tests. Nevertheless, clients will usually not be familiar with the scores provided and counsellors need to take the time to make sure that results are communicated in an understandable way. If possible, test interpretations should be provided as only one piece of information and related to other information available to the counsellor and client.

1. Is it appropriate for interpretation of test results to be done in small groups or should all interpretation be done individually?

2. Should all tests be subject to a "User Qualification Form" to ensure that only qualified people are administering the tests?

3. Who is qualified to determine whether or not a test administrator is in fact qualified to interpret the results of the test? Does a

particular degree really determine whether or not the user is qualified to interpret the results and communicate them in an ethical fashion?

4. Should test interpretation practica or workshops be required for all counsellors-in-training?

6 **Psychological test scores (as contrasted to interpreted test results) are released only to persons *qualified to interpret* and use them properly.**

Discussion of Test Results (+)

Mrs. Jones, the parent of an elementary school student, asked to know the results of the WISC-R taken by her daughter. The psychologist set up an appointment and carefully interpreted the test results so that Mrs. Jones understood the scores from the WISC-R.

Student Cumulative Files (+)

Cumulative files are kept on all students attending public schools. These cumulative files include pertinent medical data (medication, allergies, medical conditions), past grades, inventory results, and other information. Psychological test results are placed in the psychologists private files and are only released to counsellors and others who are qualified to interpret the results of each specific psychological test.

Access to Test Scores (-)

In this junior high school, all students' cumulative files can be accessed by teachers, the student, and his or her parents. When psychological assessments are sent to the school, they are also placed in the students' cumulative files.

Reporting to Outside Agencies (-)

Counsellors are in frequent contact with agencies such as Child and Family Services and Child Guidance Services regarding particular students. These outside agencies may request further information about psychological tests performed in the school. One busy counsellor gave the job of sending test results to outside agencies to the school secretary. Since the school secretary had a good friend at one of the outside agencies, she frequently reported test results verbally over the phone to her friend.

COMMENTS AND QUESTIONS

The Supreme Court of Canada has ruled that every person has the legal right to know what is written about them. This includes government documents, school files and medical records. The records must be written in such a manner that the person can understand the information, as in the case of school cumulative files. If the records are not written as such, a qualified person should be on hand to interpret the information.

1. How does one determine if the person to whom test scores are released is truly qualified to interpret and use the test scores properly?

2. What is the difference between 'psychological test' scores and 'interpreted test results'?

3. What are your organization's regulations regarding the storing of test results in clients' files?

4. Should secretaries have access to psychological test scores?

7 When making any statements to the public about tests and testing, care will be taken to give *accurate information* and to avoid any false claims or misconceptions.

Kindergarten Testing (+)
Many kindergarten students are given readiness tests when they enter school. At one particular school, the children are tested in September and then the tests and the results are discussed with parents at parent-teacher conferences. Parents are told the purpose of the standardized tests and are given a detailed explanation of the results of their child's test. The teacher also informs the parents that the tests are only used as a guide along with classroom work and teacher observations to determine areas to be practiced and students that may need extra help.

Aptitude Tests (+)
During high school, students often take an aptitude test to give them ideas as to which careers relate to their aptitudes. Before the test, the counsellor explains to the students that the test measures aptitude in areas such as verbal reasoning, mechanical, abstract reasoning and so forth. These aptitudes are later related to possible careers. It is stressed to the students that the results of the test are to be viewed as suggestions. Students are made aware that just because the aptitude test does not suggest a certain career does not mean that the student would not do well in it, or should not consider it.

Canadian or American Social Studies? (-)
A Board of Education made the decision to test the basic knowledge of middle years students in the area of social studies. A number of standardized tests were reviewed for this purpose and the one chosen was American and used American norms. When the testing was announced to the public, as well as when the results were given, teachers stated that the test was intended to measure students' knowledge of social studies, and that the students were being compared to students in the same age bracket. There was no reference to the fact that the tests were American and that many questions on the test related more to the United States than to Canada. The lack of information given would leave most, if not all, parents under the impression that the test scores reflected their child's knowledge of Canadian social studies.

New Norm Group (-)
A Canadian test publisher decides to enlarge the norm group for one popular Canadian achievement test. These changes are carefully explained in the technical manual. As a result of the new norm group, students in many school divisions score considerably higher. Since the publisher does not include the technical manual with the package of materials sent to schools, teachers and counsellors are left with the impression that students are scoring higher.

COMMENTS AND QUESTIONS
As can be seen from the two cases used to show unethical behaviour, it is easy to overlook some information and thus provide the test user with inaccurate information. It is of vital importance that test users fully understand the technical aspects of tests, the administrative aspects, and most importantly, the interpretive aspects of tests.

1. Should American standardized tests be used in Canada when no Canadian norms are available?
2. Are local norms necessary in order to provide "accurate information"?
3. What are some "statements made to the public about tests" that give misleading information?
4. What are some "statements made to the public about tests" that provide accurate information?

8 Tests should be *administered* as prescribed in the administration manual. Departures from these procedures are permitted only when conducting research and even here must be in accord with professional standards. Any unusual behaviour or irregularities during the testing session which may affect the interpretation of the test scores, must be fully noted and reported. Unsupervised test-taking or the administration of tests through the mails is unethical. However, the use of instruments that are so designed or standardized to be self-administered and self-scored, such as some interest inventories, is permitted.

Counsellor Competence (+)

A counsellor has decided to use a test designed to measure attitudes and values with a particular client. The counsellor has extensive knowledge about this type of test and about whether it is suitable and appropriate for his client. The counsellor is qualified to give this test. He carefully administers the test exactly as prescribed in the administration manual.

Irregularities Noted (+)

John Elder is qualified to administer a large number of standardized tests. During the administration of a group aptitude test, the electricity in the room goes off for three or four minutes. John carefully notes this irregularity since he feels the rest results and subsequent interpretations could be affected.

Consultant Job Placement Through the Mail (-)

A counsellor with a career consulting firm sends out brochures advertising career aptitude inventory tests which can be purchased through the mail from his firm. The advertisement claims that if you buy the test you can give yourself the test and find out what career you are best suited for. These tests have not been designed or standardized to be self-administered or self-scored.

Prescribed Material Shortage (-)

A counsellor in a high school is administering a test to a group of students. Due to budget cuts the counsellor was unable to purchase the prescribed computer answer sheets that go with the test booklets. Therefore, the counsellor has the students write out the answers on a sheet of paper and then marks and scores them himself.

COMMENTS AND QUESTIONS

This ethical guideline is a mandate for counsellors and any other qualified professionals who administer tests to do so only as prescribed in the administration manual. The only exception to changing test administration regulations would be for research, and then only if the changes are in accord with professional standards. The counsellor must note and report any unusual behaviour or irregularities during the testing session which may affect the interpretation of the test scores. Tests done through the mail are unethical, the only exceptions being those designed for self-administering and self-scoring, such as some interest inventories.

1. What qualifications would you expect to have as a counsellor before giving any tests or battery of tests?

2. Besides understanding the prescribed methods in any given administration manual, counsellors first need to be able to clarify the purposes of the test and point out any limitations for any particular client. How could this be done?

3. What are some irregularities that might occur during testing and that should be reported?

4. Why do you believe it is all right to self-administer and self-score interest inventories?

9 Psychological tests and other assessment devices, whose value in part depends on their novelty to persons taking them, are limited to persons with the professional interest and competence such that they will *safeguard their use*. Prior information, coaching or the reproduction of such material will not be condoned.

Test Security (+)

Professor Jonathan Stewart was quite concerned that many standardized tests in the Faculty of Education, where he worked, were not being properly safeguarded. He received permission from the Dean and his Department Head to draft a policy on the 'safeguarding of tests'. This policy resulted in some inventories being kept in the library and some tests in locked filing cabinets in professors' offices.

Graduate Record Examinations (+)

Joan Fisher was concerned about all the manuals that were available to help potential graduate students prepare for their Graduate Record Examinations (GRE). As well, several workshops were advertised purporting to help students score higher on their GRE. She contacted the GRE office and was reassured to find that the GRE tests were constantly being revised and that GRE Preparation Manuals and special workshops might help students somewhat, but this preparation was taken into consideration when norms were established.

Test Item Coaching (-)

In one urban school, students are placed into a "gifted" program if they have demonstrated outstanding achievement in earlier grades or if they score at the 98th percentile or above on several sub-tests of the Differential Aptitude Test (DAT). One counsellor, whose daughter attends this school, takes the DAT home and has her daughter familiarize herself with some of the test items. Not surprisingly, her daughter gets into the gifted program based on her DAT scores.

Test Reproduction (-)

One professor, who teaches a unit on John Holland's career theory, has graduate students familiarize themselves with Holland's 'hexagonal' model by having them complete Holland's interest inventory, the "Self-Directed Search." He reproduces copies of the original for each member of the class.

COMMENTS AND QUESTIONS

The first case under this guideline is used to demonstrate ethical behaviour. Test users are responsible for safeguarding the use of tests. If tests are to be valid and reliable, they must be "new" to the person taking the test. Any prior information or coaching that clients receive invalidate test results and normative data.

1. What safeguards for tests are in place in your organization?

2. Should professors or teachers be allowed to reproduce interest inventories when the inventories are only being used to explain a model? (See the last case).

3. This guideline states that psychological tests be given by persons with professional competence. What should the development of this professional competence consist of?

4. How are special manuals with sample questions and preparation for testing workshops different from the "prior information" and "coaching" mentioned in this guideline?

10 Members must proceed with *caution in evaluating* and interpreting the performance of minority group members or to other persons who are not represented in the norm group on which the instrument was standardized.

Student Placement (+)

An immigrant student who has only lived in Canada for a year recently completed several standardized tests to help school officials make placement decisions. The test results suggested placement in the stream for "slower learners." The home room teacher said she would develop other, more appropriate ways of determining this immigrant student's academic potential. She did this, and after the student performed at an above average level, the student was placed in the appropriate educational stream.

Score Adjustments (+)

Several counsellors, in a school division that has many students who are from minority groups, decided to do something about the fact that many of the minority group students did not perform well on a particular standardized test. They carefully researched the literature on this issue and learned how to adjust the scoring on their standardized test so that a more accurate score was derived for minority group students.

Miller's Analogies Test (-)

The Miller's Analogies Test was used as a major criterion for admission to one university graduate program. Many foreign students who applied did not have a strong English background and because of low scores were not admitted to the graduate program.

Non-Representative Norm Group (-)

A counsellor, working in a remote Northern community, administered tests of mental ability (I.Q.) to all the students in the school. He used an American group I.Q. test and used the American norms. When interpreting the test scores, the counsellor paid no attention to the fact that most of the students spoke English as their second language and that most of the students were not represented in the norms.

COMMENTS AND QUESTIONS

This ethical guideline states that all counsellors and researchers examine carefully the performance of minority groups on standardized tests. The following issues should be kept in mind:

a) Standardized tests provide only an estimate of an individual's performance in standard English as compared to a cross-section of American (sometimes Canadian) persons of the same age or grade.

b) Culturally diverse populations are typically under-represented in normative data.

c) Are there culturally appropriate tests available?

d) Testing is one aspect of counselling. Members must acquire competencies in multicultural counselling when interpreting tests for minority groups.

1. Since culture is not fair, can we or should we expect counsellors to use "culture-fair" tests?

2. Even though minority groups are under-represented in normative data, can we expect counsellors to develop their own norms?

3. Is what we expect of minority groups in Canada different than in the United States (cultural mosaic or melting pot)?

4. Do minority group members want special consideration?

11 Members will not appropriate, *reproduce* or modify established tests or portions thereof without the expressed permission and adequate recognition of the original author, publisher and copyright holder.

Cultural Content (+)
A member wishing to give a client a test, realized that the cultural content of the test could effect test scores, seeing the member's client had just moved to Canada from a foreign country. Keeping in mind that the purpose of this test was to obtain information to help in further decision-making, the member concluded that the content of the test had to be modified to best suit the client's cultural background. The member then contacted the original author and received permission to rewrite aspects of the test.

Copying From Masters For Markup (+)
A teacher is using tests to determine reading levels and strengths with the Alberta Diagnostic Reading Tests. In using the tests it is necessary to mark the passages to track the students' errors and miscues. If this is done on the master copy that has been purchased for use by the school, then the kit is marked and useless after its first use. To use the kit in a resource capacity with a number of students, it is necessary to make a copy of the passage the student reads to mark and track their progress as they read. Once this copy is analyzed for the students' reading level and their progress is charted the working copy is destroyed. This type of copying has been approved by the publishers of the tests since it is the only practical way to make use of the Diagnostic Reading Tests.

Ignoring Copyright (-)
A counsellor finds a copy of an interest inventory in a university library. She decides to use the inventory in her school. Rather than purchasing the inventory, the counsellor borrows the test, covers sections at the bottom of the page which state clearly "Not to be Copied", and photocopies multiple copies of the test.

Translating Without Permission (-)
A counsellor gave a written test to a client in order to receive additional information. Upon receiving the test, the client informed him that she could only read in her mother tongue, which was French. The counsellor, being bilingual, translated the test and the client completed the test in French. No permission was received from the publisher to translate the test.

COMMENTS AND QUESTIONS
This ethical guideline states that teachers and counsellors must live within the copyright laws of our country. Too many cases exist of professionals ignoring copyright legislation and making illegal copies and modifications of established tests. The fact that copyright laws are there to protect us all and to facilitate the development of better and improved tests cannot be ignored.

1. Is any modification of a standardized test permissible in order to ensure cultural equity without changing the intents, purposes, and results of the test?
2. Is a small educational faculty, with a very limited budget, justified in copying material in order to provide the best possible services for its students?
3. Does your school division or employer frown upon illegal copying and enforce copyright legislation or simply pay lip-service to the law and standards in order to save money?
4. Is borrowing and using material any different than copying?

12 The *principal researcher* is responsible for ethical research practice while others involved in the research activities share ethical obligations and full responsibility for their own actions.

Divisional Research Study (+)

The coordinator of guidance and counselling for a school division organized a task force to do research on the issue of AIDS education in junior high and senior high schools in her division. The task force consisted of parents, teachers, counsellors, administrators, and family life educators. Some of the issues discussed by the task force were age appropriateness, content, availability, and presentation of the material. Before the research on AIDS education was begun, the coordinator discussed the various ethical issues related to the study and the need for everyone to look out for the welfare of students.

Mainstreaming Research (+)

The superintendent of a large urban school division allowed a researcher and his team to study the effects of mainstreaming of students in all classrooms. Teachers were asked for their help and cooperation with the study. Before agreeing to work with the researcher, the teachers invited a professor from the university, who was very knowledgeable about research and ethics, to help them examine the ethical and practical issues related to the study.

Videotaping Interviews (-)

The head of a counselling psychology department allows all counsellor-educators in the department to have counsellors-in-training record both audio- and video-tape sessions with clients. Although clients are aware they are being taped, and that the tapes will be seen by others, no guidelines or regulations have been established by the department head regarding who has access to the tapes, where they will be stored, or when they will be erased.

Little Direction (-)

A researcher obtained a large grant to study cross-cultural counselling. Several of his graduate students were interested in doing the research. The researcher was extremely busy on several other projects he was involved in and so he gave the graduate students complete control of subject selection, interview questions and safeguards for confidentiality. He did insist on being the principal researcher.

COMMENTS AND QUESTIONS

All members involved in research have the responsibility of being familiar with ethical guidelines related to research, and the obligation of adhering to the guidelines. The principal researcher has the added responsibility of making sure that all participation in research is voluntary, that no harm will be done to research subjects, that research subjects are fully informed of the purposes of the research, and that the identity of research subjects is disguised.

1. What can the principal researcher do to ensure ethical research practice?

2. Should there be more explicit guidelines on videotaping? What might these guidelines be?

3. In the last case presented, what should the principal researcher have done?

4. What other guidelines should be included for researchers?

13 Participation in research must be *voluntary*. Involuntary participation is appropriate only when it can be demonstrated that participation will have no harmful effects on subjects.

Identity Protected (+)

A research counsellor in a large Canadian urban centre was gathering information on sexual abuse/incest obtained from records of adult survivors of such abuse. Information required was age of onset, gender, perpetrator's status in the family/community, intervention (if any), years span between last incident and seeking of help, marital history of survivor, etc.

Clients' permission was not sought for use of this information, but no identification of individuals was attached to the statistics gathered. The purpose of the research was initial information gathering on sexual abuse/incest survivors. This information was to provide a base for further study of such abuse which would hopefully lead to the development of early intervention strategies.

The long-term educational plan was the development of workshops by school counsellors for the in-servicing of school personnel division-wide on the issues/concerns of child abuse intervention strategies.

Voluntary Participation (+)

Elementary and junior high counsellors in a large Canadian urban centre where grade structure was K-6, 7-9, and 10-12, developed a longitudinal study on children with learning disabilities. The purpose of the study was to research factors which contributed to a positive or negative transition from elementary school to the junior high level.

Information gathering began at the Grade 4 level and the study continued to Grade 9. The framework was both objective and subjective. Criteria for entry into the study was established by the resource team who determined the definition of learning disability.

The study involved family (parents/siblings) and student participation. The research instruments were surveys and interviews. Partici-pants were solicited through presentation of accurate information of the study including interviews, and written explanations. Written consent from both parents and students was mandatory. In addition, participants were free to withdraw from the study at any time.

The desired outcome was (a) the development of intervention strategies which would promote successful social transitions from one school level to the next, and (b) the maintenance of this success throughout the upper level for students with their particular defined special needs.

Non-Voluntary Participation (-)

A research project on the reaction of teenagers to their parent's separation and divorce was being conducted at a university by a candidate for a Ph.D. in counselling psychology. The purpose of the study was to provide information and analysis for teachers, counsellors, and social workers who work with teenagers. The premise of the study was that the information:

a) would help to highlight individuals who are at risk from the experience,

b) would lead to intervention before crisis.

Names of prospective participants were attained randomly from the divorce dockets. Sixty teens and either one of their parents were required for the study. The committed time requested was four individual sessions of forty-five minutes over a six month period.

One interviewer, a counselling student in the Department of Counselling Psychology, became aware at a first session that one individual, a 15 year old male, was very reluctant to be in the study. He was verbally abusive to his father during the initial session, and distant and abrupt in his communications with the interviewer. She did not suggest that they consider withdrawing from the study. The reluctant behaviour continued for the remaining three sessions.

Unaware Participants (-)

A junior high school counsellor initiated a small group on the developmental issues of peer pressure relating to sexuality. The group consisted of 6 girls, ages 12-14. These students were not aware that they were being videotaped by a research counsellor. This particular researcher had requested the taping for the purpose of presenting it to counselling students who were studying adolescent sexual development.

COMMENTS AND QUESTIONS
This ethical guideline underscores that:

a) Written consent of all voluntary participants must be mandatory;

b) Written explanation of the research, including purposes of the study and techniques to be used, must be presented to all voluntary participants;

c) Voluntary participants must be clearly advised that they can choose to refuse to participate; and

d) Voluntary participants must be advised in writing that they can withdraw from the study at any time.

1. Can involuntary research participation ever be justified?

2. Should explicit rights of participants (voluntary/involuntary) be protected legally by legislation?

3. What type of consequences should be in place for researchers who:

   a) knowingly cause psychological/emotional or physical damage to participants,

   b) do not honestly inform participants about essential components of the study which could influence their consent to participate,

   d) deliberately mislead the participants?

4. In what types of counselling research would it be advantageous to have non-voluntary participants?

14 Members are responsible for the *welfare of research subjects* used. They should avoid causing injurious psychological, physical or social effects on their subjects.

Ethics Committee (+)
All graduate students and professors conducting research must submit any research proposal dealing with human beings to an ethics committee. Part of the responsibility of this ethics committee is to ensure that proper procedures are in place to safeguard the welfare of all the subjects in the research experiment.

Research on Streaming (+)
One school principal has asked the divisional researcher to study the advantages and disadvantages of streaming in the school. After observing many of the classes in the school and talking to the teachers, the researcher is convinced that the procedures needed to examine streaming will be highly disruptive to students and teachers. The researcher informs the principal that the research design that they had hoped to use will have to be changed in order to better protect students and teachers from any harmful effects.

Strenuous Exercises (-)
A physical education teacher, Butch Cassidy, was working on his Master's research thesis and gathered information for his study from students in his physical education classes. One part of his study included checking the amount of time it took students' heartbeats to return to normal after a strenuous series of exercises. No mention was made to students of the study and no precautions were taken with regards to the strenuous exercises before the study began.

Confidentiality Missing (-)
Although students enrolled in an introductory psychology course were given a detailed handout of what will be expected from them when volunteering for any experiment, there was no mention made that names of people who participated in the experiments would be included

in the results. When experiment results were released, each student was identified by first name and student number.

COMMENTS AND QUESTIONS

This ethical guideline states that subjects that participate in research experiments should not be exposed to injurious psychological, physical or social effects. This guideline needs to be considered each time a subject participates in an experiment or research situation. It should not be assumed that subjects know this guideline. The guideline needs to be discussed fully with all subjects. As well, parental permission is necessary for students to be research subjects.

Prior to participating in a research experiment, each subject should receive a detailed outline of what to expect. Some of the information contained in the outline would include:

   a) a description of the research experiment,

   b) the purpose of the research,

   c) that participation was voluntary,

   d) permission for subjects to withdraw from the research at any time,

   e) the date, time and how long the research would take,

   f) where the experiment would be held,

   g) that each student that participated in the test situation would receive results and that their names would not be identified

   h) assurances of confidentiality of all information gathered, and

   i) explanations of research results for subjects.

1. Besides presenting ethical guidelines, what are some other ways to prevent harm to research subjects?

2. What are some well-known research experiments that have caused psychological or physical harm to the subjects?

3. Should the availability of counselling for subjects after the research be part of all research designs?

4. When new counselling techniques or methods are used in research, can the psychological and social effects on clients be predicted? If not, should the research be done?

15 All research subjects should be *informed of the purpose* of the study except when withholding information from them is essential to the research study. In such cases the member is expected to take corrective action as soon as possible following the research.

New Approach to Family Life (+)

A guidance counsellor decided to use his class for a research project as a part of a university course in which he was enrolled. The project involved testing a new approach to teaching a unit in family life. The teacher and professor set up the project together.

A letter was composed to parents describing the project in general. The letter was sent home at the beginning of the family life unit and the students were informed about the project and its purpose. Parents and/or students were given the option of being part of the project. At the completion of the project, and following an analysis of the results, a summary was composed and sent to students and parents. Several parents responded with telephone calls to the counsellor and also made comments at the parent-teacher conference which followed the project. Parents were interested in the nature and results of the study.

Discipline Project (+)

A school principal and guidance counsellor set up a project in which Reality Therapy was taught to a whole school staff as a discipline approach. Teachers were informed of the purpose of the study and were given a chance as staff to opt into the program. Parents were also informed of the project and training sessions were provided for them as well. Students were taught the major tenets of Reality Therapy. Throughout the year records were kept of the discipline infractions and comparisons kept of the year before. Following the completion of the project, a summary of the results was published and circulated along with the results of a survey given to teachers, parents and students.

Self-Concept Research (-)

In a research project some guidance counsellors and parents were trained to work directly with students in the school and in the home on enhancing students' self-concept. Magic circle, active listening, and classroom meeting were some of the procedures taught. There were three groups involved. The first group of students included training for both counsellor and parents. The second group involved the training of the counsellor only. The third group was a control group in which no training was involved. A series of tests designed to measure improvement in self-concept were administered to all three groups.

No plan was in place to inform students or their parents of this research, either before or after the completion of the project. Parents of the first group were exposed to the information, but neither parents or students of the second group were aware of the project. Nothing was planned to inform the control group of the research project.

Uninformed Students (-)

A high school counsellor, John Smith, invited Grade 12 students to participate in a research project involving the research of students' backgrounds and relating this information to their academic success throughout their high school years. Students were asked to participate in this project, and were given credit in the form of term marks for participating. No mention was made of the purpose of the study to the students.

The questionnaire took from one to two hours to complete and included specific items related to family background. These items, if answered in the affirmative, would indicate criminal acts of abuse. The purpose of the project was intended to parallel research on the effects of abuse and its relationship to academic progress.

COMMENTS AND QUESTIONS

This guideline states that all research subjects should be informed of the purpose of the study or project. Researchers must take the time to explain carefully these purposes before subjects volunteer to be part of the study.

In the two positive cases presented, all parties involved were informed of the purposes of the projects. As well, results of the studies were made available. In the last case presented, the researcher, John Smith, placed himself in a very difficult position if an actual case of abuse was revealed by the questionnaire. To use marks as an incentive for participation in a project of this type is placing pressure on students to participate and reveal personal information that they might not otherwise disclose.

1. As a counsellor, how might you participate in or initiate research on abuse in your school?
2. How would the counsellor have carried out his project if family life were a controversial topic in his community?
3. How should counsellors handle resistance to research projects from other teachers?
4. What are some research projects where "withholding information" about the project is necessary?

16 The *identity* of research subjects must be disguised unless otherwise authorized by the subjects when the researcher is supplying data from the research to others or in reporting the results.

Subject Disclosure (+)

A researcher in counselling psychology is studying through direct observation and videotaping the anxiety subjects may show when asked to elaborate on traumatic childhood experiences. Before the first session with each subject begins, the researcher informs the subjects of the purpose of the research study and counselling session. The researcher makes sure that each subject fully understands the purposes and obtains written consent from each subject willing to participate and be videotaped. At the end of the study, all videotapes of sessions are erased.

Case Study Research (+)

A university researcher contacts a large child guidance centre for information on reports of child abuse. The researcher asks that these reports be given to him without any identifying material regarding the subjects.

Videotaping (-)

Gayle Jones has had second thoughts about a videotape of a session that she initially consented to and now she is asking that the researcher erase the tape of the session. Gayle is concerned about having other people see the tape and learn about her personal problems. The researcher weighs the options of erasing the tape for the subject's benefit or keeping it because it could prove useful research for the researcher's benefit. He decides to meet his own needs and keeps a copy of the subject's videotaped session. The researcher feels safe because he still has the subject's initial written consent form. The researcher allows others to see the videotape.

Subject Confidentiality (-)

A counsellor/researcher walks into the university cafeteria and overhears four of his counsellor trainees discussing counsellee subjects by name. He decides to ignore the students' conversation.

COMMENTS AND QUESTIONS

Before supplying data to others or reporting the results on specific subjects, researchers must get informed consent from the subjects involved or else disguise the identifies of these subjects. If these measures are not taken researchers can be held ethically and legally liable by their professional organization, employer, or the court system. The foremost questions researchers should ask themselves before disclosing information on specific subjects are:

a) Can the research subject be hurt in any way in this study?

b) Is the subject aware of the research and has she or he given consent to participate?

1. Should subject's identity be disguised if she or he is found to have been abused?

2. Should a subject's identity be disguised if he or she disclosed a criminal act?

3. What are some methods researchers can use to disguise subjects in qualitative research?

4. Is it ever possible to disguise the identity of subjects who are part of a study while they are "attending" an institution (prison, school, group home, etc.)?

17 In *reporting research* results, members must publish a full report mentioning any variables and conditions that might affect the outcome of the investigation or the interpretation of the results.

Ethnic Variables (+)

The school psychologist recognized the ethnic diversity of the student population at a high school he was to test as a whole. When reporting the results he included a detailed description of the school population. He described the number of recent immigrant students, the many transfer students, their ages, grade levels, and length of time living in Canada.

Sex Survey (+)

A very powerful parent committee in a small rural town of ten thousand people sought the assistance of the guidance department to survey the students at the local high school to determine their degree of sexual activity. The counsellor reported that the results were significantly lower than the national average and neighbouring towns and city. In writing his report, the counsellor explained that the results might reflect the students' awareness that the survey was prompted by the parents' committee and that the results would be given to them. Possibly, students were not entirely forthcoming due to anxiety, or possible stricter curfews, of restrictions to social functions, and of the possibility of parents finding out who was sexually active.

Superficial Study (-)

The head of a divisional counselling association has conducted a study to examine students' social values. He obtained the assistance of one counsellor from each of the high schools to help him administer the study to a number of students in each school. The results were then compiled representing the school division as a whole. The results were published in the divisional newsletter. Absent from the report were any details on the number of subjects from the vastly different high schools in this large school division. As well, no mention was made of the fact that no attempt at random selection of students was made.

'Jumping the Gun' (-)

At a 'case conference' meeting, which included all the counsellors of the high school, the school social worker and the psychologist, an 18 year old male student became the focus of attention. The student in question had become an increasing behaviour problem at school in addition to decreasing academic performance. A personality test had been administered to the student by the psychologist and the report was being shared at this meeting. The team made recommendations based on the test without consideration of the effects that the recent break up of the student's parents and death of a grandparent in a car accident might have had on the results of the personality test.

COMMENTS AND QUESTIONS

If research is to be of any real value and benefit, researchers must report any conditions or variables that may have affected the outcome or interpretation of the results. Not reporting a variable that may have affected the research results leaves the research impotent, and casts a shadow on the validity of the research findings. A few of the conditions or variables that could affect the outcome and interpretation of results are:

a) The cultural backgrounds (norms, values, beliefs) of the subjects.

b) Socio-economic influences especially if results are being grouped or compared to another social class.

c) Religious influences of the subjects, such as customs, values and beliefs.

d) The personal, social and medical histories of the subjects, where appropriate and ethical.

1. Do you feel that it is a realistic expectation that all variables and conditions that may affect results be identified?

2. Under what circumstances, if any, do you feel it is ethical to disclose a subject's medical or personal history when reporting variables and conditions that may affect results?

3. Do you feel that our own values, beliefs and biases are variables and conditions that may affect research results?

4. What are some additional variables that could affect research results?

18 Members must give due *credit* through joint authorship, acknowledgment, footnote statements, or other appropriate means to those who have contributed significantly to the research and/or publication in accordance with such contributions.

Appropriate Acknowledgment (+)

A counsellor in a relatively small high school requires additional data for a research paper she is writing. She writes to three nearby schools who can help her with the data collection. When the research is completed and the paper is written, the three schools and their counsellors are included in the acknowledgments.

Joint Authorship (+)

A counsellor is asked to write an article explaining the school's guidance program. Recently, the school principal and the counsellor had written a similar paper for another organization. After receiving the principal's approval and making some minor adjustments to the paper, the counsellor asked for permission, from the publisher of the original article, to submit this similar article. After receiving permission, the counsellor submitted the adapted manuscript for publication. Both the principal and counsellor were listed as authors.

Unethical Behaviour (-)

During a conversation with a colleague, a counsellor is given significant information pertaining to a paper he is writing. The counsellor uses the discussion as the basis for the paper and includes many of his colleague's ideas. When the paper is completed, the colleague's name is not acknowledged in any way.

Footnoting (-)

A counsellor uses an entire section of a colleague's unpublished paper within the body of a manuscript she is writing. The unpublished work is not referenced and is used as the counsellor's own ideas.

COMMENTS AND QUESTIONS

It is important to give due credit to any person or group who gives information, written or verbal, or assists significantly a researcher. Knowing where information comes from gives researchers credibility and helps to substantiate their ideas and statements. Another reason for giving due credit is to assist future researchers. It helps them to find background information and check specific data.

Major contributions to research should be given joint authorship. This includes help with writing a paper or with the actual research or testing. For example, an assistant who helps to design a test and formulates procedures should be given joint authorship. Minor contributions should be acknowledged through references or footnotes.

1. When do the ideas of others become your own? Many ideas come from someone, whether they are known or not. Where is the line between one's own idea and someone else's?

2. Is it unethical to use what you think are your own ideas if you have not checked to see whether these ideas have not been presented elsewhere?

3. If you pay someone to collect data for you, does he or she need to be acknowledged in a subsequent research article?

4. When graduate students publish parts of their theses or dissertations as articles, should they acknowledge the members of their thesis or dissertation committee?

19 Members have an obligation to *colla-borate with colleagues* by making available original research data to qualified others who may wish to replicate or verify the study.

Collaboration With Colleagues (+)

A professor in this university reports on her study that refutes some commonly held ideas regarding learning theory. The study is published in a highly regarded professional journal. A professor in Educational Psychology from another university requests to see a copy of the original data. The copy of the data is provided the following week, along with some additional comments.

Available Raw Data (+)

The department head of this Department of Educational Psychology established a policy that all the data for each thesis or dissertation published by graduate students in the department be made available to any interested faculty member or graduate student. This policy also included guidelines on confidentiality issues related to research subjects.

Non-Collegial (-)

A well-known Canadian counsellor-educator publishes an article that strongly supports a particular counselling technique that he favours. In this article he also points out how this technique is far superior to many other well-established counselling techniques. When several counsellor-educators contact him regarding the more detailed original data, he ignores their requests for more information.

Confidentiality Lacking (-)

A high school counsellor was in the process of completing her Master's thesis on teenage pregnancy and abortions. She was using the school records and her position as one of the school guidance counsellors to obtain data for her research. She had received the school administration's permission and her fellow counsellors' support in doing her study. The girls were made aware of her study and were promised complete confidentiality. She successfully de-fended her thesis and her work was made available to other university faculty and students. It was also reported in the education section of the local newspaper. Mrs. O'Shea, the chairperson of the Pro-life Council and a powerful school board member, who was trying to shut down the local abortion clinic, indicated that she wanted to examine the data some more and needed to know the names of the students. The counsellor, in fear of losing her promotion, supplied the names to Mrs. O'Shea.

COMMENTS AND QUESTIONS

This ethical guideline indicates that members have an obligation to collaborate with colleagues by making original research available to qualified others. There is no place for selfishness, secrecy and petty jealousies in the pursuit of knowledge. An open, collegial, cooperative attitude will provide the greatest benefit to the profession and to the knowledge base.

Collaboration with colleagues encourages:

a) a high level of scientifically verifiable research,

b) use of acceptable research methods,

c) honesty and accuracy in interpreting and reporting research, and

d) a faster pace of knowledge acquisition.

1. What effect does this guideline have on client confidentiality and informed consent?

2. Does cost and time factors, and a concern for the use to be made of the data, enter into the decision to make original research available?

3. Do personal feelings about your colleagues influence decisions about making research available?

4. What, if any, effect does reputation, power, position or money have on decisions to request or provide original research? Who is to be considered a qualified other?

20
Ethical practice requires that authors not submit the same *manuscript* or one essentially similar in content for simultaneous publication consideration by two or more journals. In addition, manuscripts published in whole or in substantial part in another journal or published work should not be submitted for publication without acknowledgement and permission from the previous publication.

Single Submission (+)
A graduate student in this department of counselling psychology wrote her thesis on reasonable behaviour on the part of counsellors in dealing with confidentiality in a counselling situation. After having her advisor read the thesis, she was encouraged to submit it for publication. The student obtained a list of the current journals on counselling psychology, and reviewed the most recent publications. The author chose to submit the thesis to one counselling journal that had recently published other articles related to confidentiality and other ethical issues.

Acknowledgement and Permission From Previous Publication (+)
A professor in the Department of Educational Psychology submitted a lengthy manuscript to a professional journal. The editors of the journal agreed to publish one major part of the manuscript. Various colleagues advised the professor that they found the article useful to their courses, and wished to read more about the subject. The professor was advised to submit the article in whole to another publication. He subsequently contacted the previous publisher and requested acknowledgement and permission to submit the manuscript to another publisher, in order that it might be published in whole.

Publisher Does Not Respond (-)
At this university, one professor wrote a manuscript regarding the timely issue of AIDS education in the schools. He felt that time was of the essence for publication due to the rising epi-

demic of sexually transmitted diseases among our youth. The professor was aware that it could take up to three months for a publisher to respond to a manuscript submission. Due to time constraints, the author chose not to wait for an answer to his submission, and after a six-week period, he submitted the work to another publisher.

Embarrassment Caused (-)
An author submitted the same manuscript to three publications simultaneously. Two of the three publications accepted the manuscript. The author contacted the editors of the less prestigious journal and informed them that he was withdrawing his manuscript for publication. The other journal published the manuscript.

COMMENTS AND QUESTIONS
This ethical guideline states that an author must not submit a manuscript to two or more journals simultaneously for publication consideration. As well, when an author chooses to submit for publication a manuscript which has been published in part by another publisher, it is his or her obligation to get permission from the previous publisher to allow the manuscript to be published in another journal.

Due to the costs incurred and the time required to read all the manuscripts which are submitted to a publication, there are no journal publishers who will accept a manuscript from an author, if it comes to their attention that there were multiple submissions. Counsellors and researchers should be aware of the validity of this concern by editors. It is not ethical practice to have a manuscript, or portion thereof, submitted to, or published in, more than one journal without acknowledgement. Even in the event of a time constraint, which the author may deem to be unreasonable, it would not be ethical to submit the work again at any time, without the written notification to, and the permission of, the first publisher.

1. As an author, what time period would you feel is reasonable to wait for a response from a publication?

2. Is it realistic to expect a publication to respond to you regarding acceptance or re-

fusal of your submitted manuscript within a reasonable and agreed upon time limit, for example, a period of six - eight weeks?

3. Do you believe that a letter stating "multiple submissions" should be allowed, and manuscripts could be sent to more than one publisher, if in fact, they have been so advised?

4. What are the disadvantages of allowing for multiple submissions?

❖ ❖ ❖ ❖ ❖ ❖ ❖ ❖ ❖ ❖ ❖ ❖ ❖

ESSAYS

Psychological Testing: The Counsellor's Responsibility

Beth E. Haverkamp
University of British Columbia

As the Preamble to the CGCA *Guidelines for Ethical Behavior* (CGCA, 1989) states, "the specification of ethical standards enables a professional association to clarify for its present and future members and to those served by its members, the nature of their professional and ethical responsibilities." Viewed from the client's or society's perspective, these responsibilities become the legitimate expectations that individuals have of the counseling profession. With respect to psychological testing, there are three groups which can be described as having expectations for how we practice. Our clients certainly have expectations of us, but so does the society in which we work. And, implicit in the development of an ethical code is the requirement that we have expectations of ourselves. This framework — what clients expect of us, what society expects of us, and what we must expect from ourselves — provides a way to examine the CGCA *Guidelines for Ethical Behavior* in the area of psychological testing.

What clients have a right to expect from you

Clients come into counselling expecting that their counsellor will be caring, knowledgeable, supportive and honest, and these same expectations extend to the counsellor's use of tests. As Tinsley and Bradley (1986) have noted, testing is best viewed as one component of the counselling process and not as a separate, disconnected activity. While some counsellors have held the view that testing automatically creates an impersonal, diagnosis-based approach to clients, Duckworth (1990) has described what she views as a counselling approach to the use of tests, where the goal of testing becomes empowerment of the individual. In her view, the client must be an active participant in identifying areas where testing may be helpful and in making use of the information provided by the test.

A "how to" for embedding test use within a facilitative counselling relationship is presented within the CGCA *Guidelines*, although it is not labelled as such. There are four general principles which underlie many of the specific guidelines and which describe both legitimate client expectations and the characteristics of an effective counselling relationship: (1) viewing the client as a unique individual; (2) developing a collaborative therapeutic partnership; (3) facilitating client awareness and integration of self-knowledge and (4) having client welfare as one's first priority. An understanding of how these principles are reflected in the individual guidelines can illuminate how ethical test use is also effective counselling.

One of the first responsibilities we have to our clients is to recognize and acknowledge their individuality. This mandate is reflected in Guideline C-1, which reminds us that test data is only one of many pieces of information which should be considered in decision-making and that "the effects of socioeconomic, ethnic and cultural factors (on test results) will therefore have to be recognized." Clients have a right to expect that we will help them place test information in perspective relative to other aspects of their lives and experience. Additionally, Guideline C-10 requires us to apply special caution in making use of test data for members of groups who may not be well-represented in the test's norm groups. The most carefully developed test will not apply equally well to all clients. Treating clients as unique individuals means we must ask, "What is the appropriateness of this test for this client?"

The concept of informed consent (Guideline C-2) is critical in using tests in counselling and, more generally, to developing a collaborative therapeutic relationship. However, a common misperception views this requirement as simply gaining client permission for testing and disregards the possibility of active collaboration. Collaboration becomes part of informed consent because both elements — giving consent and receiving information necessary to be an informed participant — imply that the client is a knowledgeable participant in counselling decisions that affect him or her. In addition to informing clients about the purpose of testing, who will receive results and how they will be used, we can promote client welfare (Guideline B-1) by involving the client to whatever extent is feasible in the decision-making process.

In addition to informed consent, clients have a right to the results of testing, including an interpretation that they can understand (Guideline C-2). Closely related is the requirement that an interpretation or additional counselling must accompany the communication of results to parents or other appropriate persons (Guideline C-5). There are at least two reasons why clear communication of results to the client is important. Duckworth (1990) states that tests, within a counselling approach, are "educational tools designed to stimulate insight, understanding and action"(1990). Clients cannot fully benefit from information they do not understand.

The second reason is empirically based. Goodyear (1990), in a review of research on the effects of test interpretation, found that "Clients who receive test interpretations — regardless of format or of the particular outcome criteria employed — do experience greater gains than do those in control conditions" (p. 243).

In addition to providing an understandable explanation of his or her results, a client is also entitled to an accurate interpretation. Some counsellors succumb to the temptation to "soften" descriptions of test results that they believe will be unwelcome or unpleasant. A common rationalization is that "Since tests always have an element of error, this result may be wrong...I won't threaten my client's sense of self by discussing it." The risk is that this decision may be intended to reduce the counsellor's discomfort rather than the clients; the client will receive potentially inaccurate or incomplete information about him or herself. If the test's reliability or validity is questionable, it should not be used at all. Just as it may be important to confront a client on behavior observed in an interview, it can be necessary to communicate negative test information that is relevant to the client's concern.

A final issue that impacts how counsellors and clients use tests is that tests do carry a certain mystique. Research on "bogus" personality inventories suggests that test takers may attribute credibility to results that contradict their self-perceptions (Dickson & Kelly, 1985). The perceived mystique of tests can enhance their effectiveness as interventions (Duckworth, 1990), but also heightens the responsibility we have to use them ethically. As Pipes and Davenport (1990) note, "...to many clients there is a certain amount of magic in tests; however, your specialty is psychology, not magic. Therefore, avoid describing tests in mysterious terms" (p. 122).

What society expects from testing professionals

Counsellors have approached psychological testing with attitudes ranging from enthusiasm to skepticism to distrust. As such, they reflect the attitudes of the larger society where, "tests have seemed to be powerful tools for advancing human welfare, but occasionally great concern about the real, imagined or potential abuses of tests has become a public policy issue" (Keith-Spiegel and Koocher, 1985, p.87).

The *Guidelines* outline counsellors' responsibilities to act as informed gatekeepers and caretakers of tests. The debate cited above revolves around the issue of whether or not tests are "trustworthy." The label "trustworthy" overlaps the notion of test validity, but does a better job of capturing the inescapable fact that most of the public must rely on professionals to provide the information needed to decide if a test is trustworthy. Given that most clients, parents, or newspaper reporters do not understand the technical aspects of tests, it falls to the test user to make informed decisions about appropriate test selection, use, and interpretation.

There are four guidelines which address the issue of the test user's responsibilities to the larger society; these guidelines address the ways in which counsellors are expected to use their specialized knowledge of tests to protect the public from inaccurate information and to protect the integrity of the tests themselves.

Two of the guidelines (C-6 and C-7) are both concerned with issues of accuracy. The first notes that test scores are to be "released only to persons qualified to interpret and use them properly." Inherent in this guideline is the recognition that the counsellor's responsibilities extend beyond the client-counsellor relationship where the results have been generated. This guideline also relates to the requirement that any information that identifies a client be released only with the client's express consent (B-6).

Counsellors are sometimes called upon by the general public or the media to comment on the use of tests. *Guidelines* (C-7) requires that any statements made will give accurate information and avoid any exaggerated claims of benefits or unsubstantiated criticisms. As noted above, members of the public rely on testing professionals to help them make informed decisions about whether testing is in their best interests. Irresponsible, unsubstantiated statements effectively erode the public's ability to make thoughtful decisions about testing.

The counsellor's relationship to the test development industry reflects another area of responsibility to the general public. Ultimately, test developers must rely on counsellors and other test users to protect the validity of published tests. Because the validity of some tests is seriously compromised if their items or format are revealed to test takers, Guideline C-9 forbids counsellors to provide advance information, engage in coaching test takers, or reproduce test materials.

While not stated explicitly, this guideline also protects clients. Any time the validity of a test has been compromised, the test taker is in danger of receiving false or misleading information about him or herself. For example, a student who has been coached may feel momentary pleasure at receiving a higher ability test score, but the ultimate outcome may be that inappropriate, potentially harmful decisions are made based on a distorted sense of abilities. Disclosure of protected test information that results in invalid test results is ultimately disrespectful of clients; it contradicts the norms of honesty and respect which are meant to characterize the counselling relationship.

Guideline C-11, which requires counsellors to observe copyrights by not appropriating, reproducing or modifying tests without permission, does protect the test author's or developer's interests. However, implementation of this guideline also serves clients and counsellors. In addition to conforming to public copyright laws, it helps insure that available ver-

sions of the test will represent the reliability and validity levels which were achieved in the original test development. A portion of a test, or another modification, does not have the same reliability and validity characteristics as the original. Without additional research on the modified version, you cannot be confident that the new version will produce useful, accurate information.

A second benefit of observing copyrights through the purchase of test materials is that the test developer is supported in conducting continued research and revision for the measure. The task of developing a sophisticated, well-validated test is expensive and time consuming, as are revisions that result in improvements. Respect for copyrighted material helps preserve the unspoken contract between test developer and test user, in which the test developer agrees to continue research which will make the test the best measure possible.

What should you expect from yourself?

As the Preamble to the *Guidelines for Ethical Behavior* notes, these guidelines are "intended to inspire each member to engage in professional behavior of the highest order." Like other aspects of counselling, test use requires a specialized knowledge base and ultimately, each counsellor must evaluate whether his or her breadth of knowledge constitutes competence in a given area. The willingness to monitor one's own competence, and to make responsible decisions based on that self knowledge, are among of the hallmarks of professional conduct.

For some counsellors, competence in test evaluation and use presents a challenge that differs from their sense of competence in evaluating other counselling interventions. Test evaluation does require a knowledge of psychometrics which, for some, may seem to have only a limited relationship to "the business of counselling." Many counsellors know that validity is a desirable quality for tests to have, but may not be aware that validity does not exist "in general". The counsellor must know how to evaluate this for a given situation.

Guideline C-3 mandates that counsellors not exceed the limits of their competence in using tests. Ultimately, this guideline is linked to promoting the client's welfare, as counsellors who administer or interpret tests for which they have not been trained are placing their clients at risk. Similarly, selecting tests without consideration of their established reliability and validity places clients in the position of making decisions based on faulty information.

Counsellors are directed to consider the validity, reliability and appropriateness (e.g., norms or standardization samples) of tests before using them with clients (Guideline C-4). While most counsellors are aware that these are important aspects of test quality, they must also understand how to assess reliability and validity for specific testing situations. Even a test as well-respected and carefully researched as the Strong Interest Inventory (Hansen & Campbell, 1985) is not valid or appropriate in all testing situations. Canada's multicultural society, where clients may have an ethnic heritage or language that does not match that of the test development sample, requires special caution in applying results.

Another factor that is essential to deriving valid and useful test information is the administration of the test. For many published tests, standardized administration procedures must be observed (Guideline C-9). Scores derived from casual, non-standard testing conditions are not trustworthy reflections of the client's abilities or characteristics and, again, put the client at risk for receiving false self descriptions.

When a counsellor is evaluating a traditional standardized test, the task of evaluating the test's characteristics is relatively straightforward. The test manual and test reviews by experts in the field can provide information on reliability, validity and norms. However, there are two situations where evaluation may be more difficult. The first of these is the expanding use of computerized testing; the second concerns newly developed measures for which little information exists.

Professional newsletters are filled with advertisements for computerized career choice programs and computer versions of well-known inventories. Ease of scoring and the potential savings in time make these attractive options for many agencies and schools. What is some-

times overlooked, however, is that the computerized version of an established test must meet the same criteria of reliability and validity as its paper and pencil counterpart. This is most easily seen if we considered the above discussion of standardized administration procedures (Guideline C-8). Changing from a paper and pencil to computer administration of a test has altered the standardized administration format; the psychometric properties of the new computerized version should be independently assessed. Publishers of computerized versions should provide evidence for their measures' reliability and validity.

Another area for caution is the selection or use of newly developed measures. Every year, dozens of new instruments are introduced and our mailboxes are filled with advertisements that claim to offer the 'very best way' to identify depression, sales ability, reading problems or eating disorders. The advertisement often shows how your clients or students will be classified on a multicolored chart or given a personal profile of psychological labels. Such promotional materials often look professional and convincing, and produce what can be termed the "Glossy Brochure Syndrome." It is possible to read through ten slick pages of glowing praise for a new measure without once coming across a description of research underlying the claims being made. "Used by hundred of schools!" "Praised by experienced practitioners!" The ethical counsellor's response to this should only be, "So what?" Responsible test developers conduct research as part of their test development and know that reporting on validity and reliability enhances the credibility of their measures. Responsible test publishers may use glossy brochures, too, but will include information that supports the claims being made.

What resources exist for the counsellor who wants to make informed, ethical decisions about test selection, but lacks confidence interpreting validity coefficients and factor-derived scores? In addition to test manuals, two sources that contain reviews of specific tests are the *Mental Measurements Yearbook* series and *Test Critiques*. The *Mental Measurements Yearbook* series, published by the Buros Institute of Mental Measurements, contains descriptive information about tests and critical reviews by experts in the field. *Test Critiques*, published by the Test Corporation of America, is a multi-volume series of reviews which discuss both technical and practical aspects of many tests.

The American Counseling Association (ACA), CGCA's counterpart in the United States, has published two resource books which are designed for the practising counsellor. An overview of testing practices and measures typically used in cognitive, career and personality assessment is found in Hood and Johnson's (1991) *Assessment in Counseling: A Guide to the Use of Psychological Assessment Procedures*. Kapes and Mastie (1988) have collected a series of reviews in *The Counselor's Guide to Career Assessment Instruments (2nd edition)*. This resource also contains concise guidelines for selecting tests (Womer, 1988) and a comprehensive checklist of counsellor testing competencies and responsibilities (Prediger & Garfield, 1988).

If asked what activities characterize their work with clients, few counsellors would include testing at the top of their list. However, surveys indicate that tests are widely used (Watkins, Campbell & McGregor, 1988) and that schools would increase their use of career testing if funds were available (Engen, Lamb & Prediger, 1982). The extensive use of tests can be attributed to the role they play in providing clients with information that is useful in making important life decisions. As Duckworth (1990) notes, "...People are likely to change in ways therapeutic to themselves and others if they have accurate information about themselves, their strengths and weaknesses, and the ways they are currently dealing with life. Testing is one method of getting that information and conveying it, through test interpretations, to the client" (p. 199). Our adherence to the *Guidelines for Ethical Behavior* will help insure that the information we communicate is accurate and useful, and serves our clients' best interests.

References

Canadian Guidance and Counselling Association (1981, 1989). *Guidelines for ethical behavior*. Ottawa: Author.

Dickson, D.H. & Kelly, I.W. (1985). The "Barnum Effect" in personality assessment: A review of the literature. *Psychological Reports*, *57*, 367-382.

Duckworth, J. (1990). The counseling approach to the use of testing. *The Counseling Psychologist*, *18*, 198-204.

Engen, H.B., Lamb, R.R. & Prediger, D.J. (1982). Are Secondary Schools Still Using Standardized Tests? *Personnel and Guidance Journal*, *60*, 287-290.

Goodyear, R.K. (1990). Research on the effects of test interpretation. *The Counseling Psychologist*, *18*, 240-257.

Hansen, J.C. & Campbell, D.C. (1985). *Manual for the SVIB-SCII* (4th ed.). Stanford, CA: Stanford University Press.

Hood, A.B. & Johnson, R.W. (1991). Assessment in counseling: *A guide to the use of psychological assessment procedures*. Alexandria, VA: American Association for Counseling and Development.

Kapes, J.T. & Mastie, M.M. (1988). *A counselor's guide to career assessment instruments (2nd ed.)*. Alexandria, VA: National Career Development Association, a division of the American Association of Counseling and Development.

Keith-Spiegel, P. & Koocher, G.P. (1985). *Ethics in psychology: professional standards and cases*. Hillsdale, NJ: Lawrence Erlbaum.

Keyser, D.J. & Sweetland, R.C. (Eds.). (1984-1990). *Test critiques: Volumes 1-VIII*. Kansas City, MO: Test Corporation of America.

Mitchell, J.V., Jr. (Ed.). (1985). *The ninth mental measurements yearbook*. Lincoln, NE: Buros Institute of Mental Measurements.

Pipes, R.B. & Davenport, D.S. (1990). *Introduction to psychotherapy: Common clinical wisdom*. Englewood Cliffs, NJ: Prentice-Hall.

Prediger, D.J. & Garfield, N. (1988). Testing competencies and responsibilities: A checklist for counselors. In J.T. Kapes and M.M. Mastie (Eds.), *A counselor's guide to career assessment instruments (2nd ed.)*. Alexandria, VA: National Career Development Association, a division of the American Association of Counseling and Development.

Tinsley, H.E.A. & Bradley, R.W. (1986). Test Interpretation. *Journal of Counseling and Development*, *64*, 462-466.

Watkins, C.E. Jr., Campbell, V.L., & McGregor, P. (1988). Counseling psychologists' uses of and opinions about psychological tests. A contemporary perspective. *The Counseling Psychologist*, *16*, 476-486.

Womer, F.B. (1988). Selecting an instrument: Chore or challenge? In J.T. Kapes and M.M Mastie (Eds.), *A counselor's guide to career assessment instruments (2nd ed.)*. Alexandria, VA: National Career Development Association, a division of the American Association of Counseling and Development.

The Counsellor/Researcher And The Question Of Ethics In Qualitative Research

Paul R. Madak
University of Manitoba

When the issue of research ethics is raised, the initial response given by the majority of my colleagues is that they are aware of all potential problem areas and can easily address them. However, after a short discussion with them, I usually find that while they know the basic guidelines (e.g., informed consent, no harm to the subjects, confidentiality of identity and scores/responses, and honesty in reporting the data, etc.), few have thought about these issues in any depth and fewer are clear about how to deal with those problems that fall in the "gray areas". A further complication has been the development and increasing use of the methods that fall under the general heading of qualitative research. These methods establish a much closer working relationship with the individuals under investigation. In the quantitative research models the 'subjects' are to be viewed from afar with uninvolved objectivity, while in the qualitative models 'informants' are individuals to be observed up close and interacted with (Bogdan & Biklen, 1992; Eisner, 1991; Lincoln & Guba, 1985). Therefore, the uses of qualitative research methods require a different approach to the topic of ethical behavior.

> Because qualitative methods are highly personal and interpersonal, because naturalistic inquiry takes the researcher into the real world where people live and work, and because in-depth interviewing opens up what is inside people — qualitative inquiry may be more intrusive and involves greater reactivity than surveys, tests, and other quantitative approaches. (emphasis in original, Patton, 1990, p.365).

In this article I will discuss some of the dilemmas of research ethics that can arise when the counsellor as researcher utilizes qualitative methodology. I have deliberately stated the purpose as discussing these dilemmas rather than stating I will offer solutions. The reason for this is that for many of these dilemmas there are no clear cut solutions. Each ethical dilemma will be specific to the informants under study (e.g., parents, teachers, elementary students, etc.), and the context in which information is collected (e.g., classroom, home, playground, counsellor's office, etc.). Ultimately, it is the responsibility of each researcher to weigh all the issues and to make what she/he feels are the best ethical decisions (Bogdan & Biklen, 1992; Dockrell, 1988; Palys, 1992; Patton, 1990). Therefore, in this article I will identify a number of ethical dilemmas that should be taken under consideration by the counsellor/researcher before the first piece of information is collected. It is hoped that the identification and ensuing discussion will assist in the planning process researchers go through when designing a research study.

Informed Consent.

Section C, # 14 and #15 of the *Guidelines for Ethical Behaviour* for counsellors (Canadian Guidance and Counselling Association, 1989) states that the counsellor/researcher is responsible for informing the potential participants of the purposes of the research study and for their welfare. The concept of informed consent means that the individual(s) under study not only completely understand what is expected of them, but also the possible consequences of having taken part in the study. For example, does the individual who agrees to take part in a qualitative study understand that the nature of qualitative studies is such that the researcher is always 'on'? That is, does the individual realize that the comments she/he make while having coffee, or at lunch, are considered by the qualitative researcher to be legitimate data and that this information might be included in the final report? Furthermore, was it explained to the individual that in qualitative studies the researcher acts more like a friend then a researcher, and that this 'friendship' type of relationship may result in them revealing secrets that they never intended to reveal, let alone find that they have been published for the world to see? A researcher who has good interpersonal skills can develop a client-counsellor type of trust relationship that can result in far more intimate information being provided then the informant originally antici-pated.

In short, researchers can take advantage of a quasi-therapeutic relationship because of the attractiveness of one of our most treasured gifts to others—the gift of lending serious attention and a sympathetic ear to what someone has to tell us (Eisner, 1991, p.218).

When researchers request the involvement of non-researchers in a study, we cannot as-sume that the non-researchers will understand all the subtleties of their agreement to take part. A researcher who is also a counsellor has to be particularly cautious as she/he has spe-cialized skills that could be used to take advan-tage of a trusting volunteer. However, the ma-jority of the research projects I have seen being carried out do not even attempt to ex-plain these subtleties to their informants.

A second issue regarding the concept of informed consent concerns the fact that Sec-tion C, #16 states that it is the responsibility of the counsellor/researcher to protect, "...unless otherwise authorized...", the identity of the individual who has agreed to participate in the research project. However, in qualitative re-search, researchers pay close attention to the context in which the information was col-lected and therefore provide their readers with a detailed description of the environment un-der study. Because of this detailed description, there is the real risk that someone will be able to recognize and identify the informant(s). Most researchers do not discuss this risk factor with their informants before signing them on as part of the study. This risk is especially high when a unique program, environment or indi-vidual is under investigation. For example, I served as a member of a thesis committee for a student who conducted a qualitative study on a female badminton player who was ranked third in the world. While every effort was made to hide the identity of this individual (the year of the ranking was kept secret as well as some other key factors), there was still a very strong possibility that someone would recognize her from the description provided in the study. In fact, while I did not know who this person was at the time, three years later when I was reading the sports section of the local newspaper, I came across an in-depth interview with a fe-male badminton play and from the informa-tion provided was able to identify her as the informant of the thesis. While this may be an extreme case, it points to the importance of informing our informants about the possible risks of being identified once the material is made public.

A third issue concerns the interpretation of the events as recorded by the researcher. Dockrell (1988) and Eisner (1991) suggested that the participants of a study be given the opportunity to read the material that has been written about them. The purpose of doing this is twofold. First, it allows participants to review the material for misquotes and/or misinterpre-tations of the behavior under observation. However, the degree to which the researcher is willing to make changes to the material, if it is objected to by a participant, is open for debate. That is, if the researcher feels that she/he really heard or saw what was reported, then the text should not be altered just to please the partici-pant. Altering accurate information might change the outcome of the study and thus lead the researcher to making inaccurate conclu-sions. On the other hand, if a mistake has been made in recording the raw data, then it is the responsibility of the researcher to make the requested changes in order not to make inaccu-rate conclusions. However, how does one tell the difference? There are no easy answers to this issue, it is a dilemma that must be ad-dressed by the individual researcher based on the information and contextual factors on hand.

The second point concerns allowing the informants to be the first to read material that may place them in an unfavorable light. It is much better for informants to have at least a warning that unfavorable information is about to be released about them. Lightfoot (1983) suggested that respondents go through several stages when they come face-to-face with writ-ten accounts of their actions. In the first stage there is the terror associated with having been exposed for the world to judge. The second stage is characterized by the respondents alter-nating between recognizing themselves in the description to denying that the individual be-ing described has any resemblance to them. Finally, after a period of time, respondents are able to look at the description more dispassionately and view it as a means for reflection, self criticism and personal growth. Given this process, Lightfoot's stages suggest that it is much better if respondents are allowed to view material before it becomes public information.

A number of years ago, during my tenure as a research consultant for a local school district, I was witness to a number of situations in which outside researchers reported information that did not show the district in a positive light. I found that when the district's administration and teachers had been given advanced copies of the material, the response, while not all love and warmth, was at least one of tolerance. They were able to prepare a response to the material, or to at least formulate and have ready a plan as to how they were going to alter the conditions that produced the unfavorable information. However, when the district read unflattering information in the media first, the reaction was always one of anger and total rejection of the information. In fact, in one extreme case when the district found out about negative information through phone calls from the media asking them to explain data they had never seen, the researchers involved where 'unofficially' banned from carrying out further research within their schools. Furthermore, the district totally rejected valuable information that might have assisted them in improving the quality of education. In short, the method used to inform the district of the results of the study resulted in an emotional reaction to the information. The main focus of this emotional reaction was based on their need to protect the system from outside attack.

The fourth and final issue to be discussed concerning informed consent deals with the 'innocent bystanders'. Innocent bystanders are individuals in a qualitative study who come into contact with the individual under study, but who themselves are not the focus of the study. Here the question becomes, how far should informed consent be taken? If you are observing a particular informant, do you also need the consent of the individuals who might interact with your informant? In the example of the female badminton player presented above, should the researcher have obtained permission from her husband, parents, in-laws, friends and the players she coached? Some of

my colleagues have made the case that obtaining the consent of these 'innocent bystanders' is unnecessary because they are not the direct objective of the study. On the other hand, other colleagues have argued that the intrusive nature of qualitative research demands that informed consent applies to all contacts. In the case of the female badminton player, informed consent was obtained from the husband, but not from the other individuals. It was felt by the researcher and her advisor that the privacy of the other individuals was not being invaded as their actions were not being recorded, only those of the badminton player. However, permission was obtained from the husband as the interactions between him and his wife were under direct study. That is, one of the research questions dealt with the interaction between the female athlete and her spouse. Was this a correct decision? I am not sure. This type of dilemma points to the importance of the researcher carefully weighing all the pros and cons of the situation before making a judgment.

Confidentiality

As was presented above, Section C, #16 states that it is the responsibility of the counsellor/researcher to protect, "...unless otherwise authorized...", the identity of the individual who has agreed to participate in the research project. The concept of confidentiality postulates that the individual(s) under study have a right to their privacy and thus the researcher has the responsibility to protect their identity (e.g., Bogdan & Biklen, 1992; McMillian & Schumacher, 1989; Palys, 1992; Shulman, 1990). The information collected in studies on sexual abuse or divorce may be information that respondents are willing to share with the researcher as long as their identity is not revealed to the general public. In fact, in some cases the identification of the respondents may be very costly to them in terms of placing them in physical danger (e.g., a husband who physically abuses his wife may want to punish his wife for disclosing) or putting them at risk of losing their jobs (e.g., a teacher who provides negative information about a principal/superintendent). In both of these cases the disclosure of the informant's identity can result in harm being done to them. If harm is done, then the number one ethical rule of 'no harm to the subjects' would also be violated.

However, what if the respondent does not want to remain anonymous? Section C, #18 states that it is the responsibility of the counsellor/researcher to, "...give due CREDIT through joint authorship, acknowledgment, footnote statements, or other appropriate means to those who have contributed significantly to the research and/or publication..." Unlike quantitative methods, where research subjects simply respond to surveys, questionnaires, standardized tests or other procedures that require only a response, individual(s) taking part in qualitative investigations contribute a great deal of their time, energy and personal thoughts to the researcher. They play an active role in the research process. In fact, in a qualitative design, the individuals taking part in the investigation often play an important role in the formation of the research question(s) and interpretation of the data collected. Therefore, given this added involvement, these individuals are beginning to express the desire to be publicly recognized and given credit for their accomplishments and contributions to the research study.

Shulman (1990) was the first to point out that this desire for recognition has implications for how researchers deal with the ethical requirement of confidentiality. To simply identify all those who request to be identified avoids dealing with the rights of others. For example, if a counsellor requests to be identified, what are the effects of such identification on the institution that employs her/him? Furthermore, what are the possible effects on the rights of that counsellor's colleagues and clients? What if one of the participants wants to be identified, but the other participants do not? These are serious questions that cannot be ignored because the identification of one individual may mean that the anonymity of the institution (school and/or school district, public service organization, etc.), other counsellors, and clients cannot be guaranteed. The dilemma arises in attempting to determine how the identification of one informant will affect other informants and to what extent are we obligated to protect those who are on the periphery of our study (e.g., the institution or those who make use of the institution's services).

It would appear that one possible method of handling these dilemmas is to carry out multilevel negotiations that include all the affected stakeholders. This would insure that all parties are given an opportunity for their opinions to be heard, and if a compromise can't be reached, then those who feel threatened can be given the chance to withdraw from the study. It is the responsibility of the researcher to ensure that the rights of all parties are respected. However, I agree with Shulman when she stated:

> Some colleagues have urged me to propose a set of general principles or rules of thumb for dealing with such dilemmas in the future. I do not believe that general principles are of much use in these situations. These circumstances represent a serious tangle of competing ethical obligations complicated by political realities. They are best handled on a case-by-case basis, through negotiation and deliberation among all of the relevant stakeholders (1990, p. 14-15).

Since research studies vary greatly with regards to the individuals studied, topics studied, research methods utilized, and pertinent political issues, the establishment of general principles would be of little value. Instead, what needs to happen is that all researchers must accept the obligation to carefully identify all parties who will be affected by the planned study and then to make decisions that best fit the current situation.

A second issue, or dilemma, concerns the question of whether there are any circumstances in which a researcher can ethically break the ethical requirement of confidentially. Clearly, there are such situations. For example, if a school age student discloses that she/he has been, or is currently being sexually or physically abused the researcher is required by law to file a report with the proper child protection agency or with the police. However, should the researcher file a report with the proper professional organization if he/she observes a counsellor who is inept or who is using questionable counselling techniques? Or, in the interest of gathering information on counselling which would be of benefit to the larger community of counsellors, should the researcher ignore the behavior and protect the identity of the participant? Eisner (1991) pointed out the other side of the coin by asking, what if the researcher discovers someone who is doing great work, but who's work has gone unrecognized? "In other words, is the obligation, if it is an obligation, to commend as important as to give negative criticism?" (Eisner, 1991, p.219). These are question for which there are no easy answers, but which require the researcher's careful attention. Patton (1990) has stated that the researcher should develop a personal ethical framework for dealing with the possible occurrence of these events before beginning the research process. Waiting until an event or dilemma arises may place the researcher in the difficult situation of trying to make a complex decision quickly without the luxury of having time to completely think out all the possible consequences of a particular option. Furthermore, by having a pre-established ethical framework the researcher is more likely to have completely informed the participants of what their involvement in the research project might entail.

Finally Patton (1990) warned researchers that they do not have the same legal protection that clergy and lawyers have and therefore we can be summoned to testify in court. Knowledge about activities such as the use and selling of illegal chemicals may be behaviors that local law enforcement agencies may request or demand. In these situations, the researcher is required to testify in court regardless of a promise to keep such information confidential.

Participation as a Positive Experience

While taking part in a research study should be a positive experience for both the counsellor/researcher and the selected participants, there are many situations where this is not the case. Currently, I am working with two students who are doing thesis work in the area of sexual abuse. In the design stages of both of these research projects, we had to be aware of the likelihood that the process of interviewing female volunteers would touch on, not only very personal and sensitive information, but also emotionally painful memories. Therefore, as part of the overall research designs, a debriefing session had to be added to the research

process. These debriefing sessions allowed the informants to make closure and provided them with a list of available counselling services. Furthermore, a process was developed which allowed for the termination of any interview session that was becoming too stressful for the informant. This later provision was, for the most part, a judgment call for the researchers to make. That is, what is too stressful for one individual might not be too stressful for another. It places the researcher in the awkward situation of being part interviewer and part counsellor. This situation is awkward because the respondents are already in a counselling relationship, and thus, entering into a second counselling situation could lead to a violation of ethical practice (see Section B, #13, Canadian Guidance and Counselling Association, 1989). While collecting information that might help other victims of sexual abuse, we believed that is was not important enough to place the informant in an unreasonably stressful situation. How much stress was reasonable and when did the interview stop being an interview and turn into a counselling session? This was a question that each of these two student-researchers had to asked and answer during every interview session. While we spent a great deal of time talking about this issues amongst ourselves and with other colleagues, the bottom line was that each student-researcher had to make this judgment for each informant. While, both student-researchers stated that the pre-data collection discussions helped them make the necessary decisions, it did not make the decisions easier.

Discussions were also held with the student-researchers to talk about how they would deal with questions they received. That is, what if one of the respondents asked for advice concerning reporting the sexual abuse to the police? Or, what if the respondent asked for advice concerning whether their current counsellor was providing them with quality treatment? It is very easy for the respondent to turn the interview around and make the researcher the interviewee. The problem of how to deal ethically with the questions of the respondent needs to be worked out carefully before the first interview takes place. Once in the field, it is too late to say 'time-out, while I go and get advice'.

The process of being taken through a directed, reflective process affects the persons being interviewed and leaves them knowing things about themselves that they didn't know — or least were not aware of — before the interviews. Two hours or more of thoughtfully reflecting on an experience, a program, or one's life can be change-inducing (Patton, 1990, p.353-354).

This 'change-inducing' process applies not only to the respondent, but also to the researcher who is collecting the information and playing the role of empathic listener. In addition to the above procedure that was developed for the respondents of the study, the design also included debriefing and support for the student-researchers. As was recommended by Patton (1990), a process was needed so that the student-researchers could deal with the things they heard. Given the atmosphere for negative information concerning the women they were listening to, the student-researchers in the above example needed to have a support network in place to deal with the pain and suffering they were hearing about.

In the example presented above, it is relatively easy to see the need for debriefing sessions, but there are other situations where the researcher may not have predicted a need for such sessions, but for which they are needed, or should at least be planned for just in case. For example, a researcher could be interviewing counsellors about their work experiences and in the process of the interview discover that some of them are suffering from 'burn out' or from some other emotional problem. This disclosure can happen because of the intimate and trusting relationship that is desirable and fostered in interviewing situations. In order to obtain the most reliable and valid data, interviewers are trained in much the same way as counsellors are in terms of questioning and listening techniques. Another situation can arise in which the interviewee asks the interviewer for advice. For example, in an evaluation study of a program for young children (ages 4-6) that I was conducting, the parents being interviewed would often ask interviewers for advice on discipline problems or problems concerning older children not included in the project. In short, it is difficult to predict

what will happen in an interview situation, and, therefore, the researcher must always be prepared to handle the unexpected.

Handling Raw Data

Dockrell (1988, p.184) stated that "Research data are not private property. They are an individual's contribution to a common wealth of knowledge and understanding." A research issue has consistently been that researchers make their raw data available for at least five years after the publication of the article in which they have been published. This will allow others to examine the original data set and to either re-analyze the data or to carry out further analyses.

When dealing with quantitative data, it is fairly easy to keep the original data that was used in the data analysis process without fear of giving away who the individual subjects were. All the researcher has to do is to provide a code number for each individual in the data set. However, when using the qualitative methods, it is much more difficult to hide the identities of the informants. The field notes and interviews will contain a great deal more specific information about individuals and environmental information which will make it all but impossible to keep the identities of the participants confidential. Going through the material and removing all identifying information (e.g., names of individuals, places, etc.) is time consuming and may, in some cases, change the data. Therefore, the requirement by many university ethics committees for researchers to destroy original documents containing subject names and other personal information is no longer valid. Furthermore, the extent to which the researcher 'blackens out' or replaces information with codes, abbrevations or letter designates will be an individual one made according to characteristics of each specific situation. Again, it comes down to the fact that it is the responsibility of the researcher to review carefully all the possible ethical dilemmas and to make the best possible decisions based on the specific characteristics of the situation.

Conclusions

The purpose of this article was to review some of the more common ethical dilemmas associated with conducting qualitative research. Specifically, the purpose was to indicate that the rules of ethics originally developed for the quantitative methodologies can not be directly applied to qualitative methodologies. It should be noted, however, that the ethical dilemmas discussed above are not meant to be all inclusive. However, the major dilemmas of informed consent, confidentiality, positive experience and data handling were discussed.

The basic conclusion that can be reached from the material presented is that it is extremely difficult to propose a general set of guidelines or principles that would cover the full range of research methodologies and research situations. In the long run, it is the responsibility of each researcher to carefully review her/his research procedures to ensure those participants/subjects are not harmed either purposefully or accidentally (Eisner, 1991; McMillian & Schumacher, 1989; Palys, 1992; Patton, 1990; Shulman, 1990). While all researchers agree that we should be guided by ethical principles, deciding what those principles should be for every situation can be a difficult, if not impossible task. In order to help keep us honest, researchers can seek the advice of colleagues, ethics committees (at the university, professional organization, school district, etc.) and the potential participants/subjects themselves.

> But there are few right and wrong answers; the process is always one of weighing advantages and disadvantages. On the one hand, we have the contribution that a given piece of research might directly or indirectly make to knowledge and human welfare. On the other hand, there is the cost that doing this research entails to the human research participant. The general ethical question is thus always *whether there is a negative upon the dignity and welfare of the participants that the importance of research does not warrant.* Stated in other terms, any prospect of harm to research participants had better have a strong and explicit justification (emphasis in original, Palys, 1992, p.96).

References

Bogdan, R. C. & Biklen, S. K. (1992). *Qualitative research for education: An introduction to theory and methods* (2nd. ed.). Toronto: Allyn and Bacon.

Canadian Guidance and Counselling Association (1989). *Guidelines for ethical behaviour.* Ottawa: Author.

Dockrell, W. B. (1988). Ethical considerations in research. In J. P. Keeves (Eds.), *Educational research methodology, and measurement: An international handbook* (pp. 180-185). Toronto: Pergamon Press.

Eisner, E. W. (1991). *The enlightened eye: Qualitative inquiry and the enhancement of educational practice.* Toronto: Collier Macmillan Canada, Inc.

Lightfoot, S.L. (1983). *The good high school: Portraits of character and culture.* New York: Basic Books.

Lincoln, Y. S. & Guba, E. G. (1985). *Naturalistic inquiry.* Beverly Hills: Sage Publications.

McMillian, J.H. & Schumacher, S. (1989). *Research in education: A conceptual introduction.* (2nd. ed.). Glenview: Scott, Foresman and Company.

Palys, T. (1992). *Research decisions: Quantitative and qualitative perspectives.* Toronto: Harcourt Brace Jovanovich Canada Inc.

Patton, M. Q. (1990). *Qualitative evaluation and research methods* (2nd. ed.). Newbury Park: Sage Publications, Inc.

Shulman, J. H. (1990). Now you see them, now you don't: Anonymity versus visibility in case studies of teachers. *Educational Researcher, 19*(6), 11-15.

CHAPTER FIVE

—————— ❖ ——————

Case Studies In
Consulting And
Private Practice

—————— ❖ ——————

Consulting is a business and as such is governed by legal and ethical regulations and guidelines. Counsellors, both in private practice and as part-time consultants, need to be aware of their additional responsibilities in relationship to advertising, contracts and business.

❖ ❖ ❖ ❖ ❖ ❖ ❖ ❖ ❖ ❖ ❖ ❖ ❖

GUIDELINES

1 Members acting as consultants must recognize that consultation is a **voluntary relationship** between a counsellor and a help-seeking individual, group or organization.

❖

2 Members working as consultants must have a high degree of **self-awareness** of their values, knowledge, skills and limitations. The focus of the consulting relationship should be on the issues or problems to be resolved and not on the person(s) presenting the problem.

❖

3 Members must be reasonably certain of their **competencies and resources** for giving consultative help and that appropriate referral resources are available to the consultant.

❖

4 There must be understanding and agreement between the consultant and client regarding the definition of the problem, the goals and interventions selected. This consulting relationship must foster the **growth and self-direction** of the client.

❖

5 In advertising services as private practitioners, members must **advertise** their services in a manner that accurately informs the public of their services, expertise and techniques of counselling. Members may list the following: highest relevant degree, type and level of certification, address, telephone number, office hours, description of services, and other relevant information. Such information must not contain false, inaccurate, misleading, partial, out-of-context, or deceptive material or statements.

❖

6 Members do not present their affiliation with any organization in such a way that would imply **inaccurate sponsorship** or certification by that organization. It is unethical to use one's institutional affiliation to recruit clients for one's private practice.

❖

❖ ❖ ❖ ❖ ❖ ❖ ❖ ❖ ❖ ❖ ❖ ❖ ❖ ❖

CASE STUDIES

1 Members acting as consultants must recognize that consultation is a *voluntary relationship* between a counsellor and a help-seeking individual, group or organization.

Best Proposal (+)

A counsellor-educator with a great deal of expertise in cross-cultural counselling was asked to put forward a consulting proposal for a large organization involved in numerous cross-cultural activities. The counsellor-educator was informed that two other individuals and a small consulting firm had also been asked for proposals. All the consultants were aware of this "tendering" process.

"Miles Apart" (+)

After working together for several months, a consultant and the firm that was paying her for her expertise realized that they were "miles apart" regarding possible solutions to a long-term problem that the firm's management had with its employees. The consultant, realizing that she could not be of further help, voluntarily resigned from the job.

Outside Consultant Not Wanted (-)

A recommendation was made by an external evaluator that a consultant, from outside the university, be hired to mediate differences among professors in one university department. The professors, almost unanimously, favoured appointing an internal team to help resolve matters. Nevertheless, the outside consultant was brought in to help reconcile departmental differences.

Resistance (-)

Soon after a consultant began working for a government department, he realized that management had been forced by the owners to obtain consultative services. Management felt it was a "slap in the face" not to be allowed to work out their own problems. After all, they were the managers and they should be left to manage. In spite of almost universal resistance, the consultant took the job believing that he could win over the reluctant managers.

COMMENTS AND QUESTIONS

This guideline stresses the importance of people within an organization or group voluntarily agreeing to consultative services. Owners or management, at times, use consultants to avoid taking responsibility for decisions, or lending support for decisions they plan to make. It is very important that consultants spend time with all those concerned to build a relationship where everyone voluntarily agrees to work together with the consultant.

1. Can consultants hope to get reliable information for management who hired them, when the employees, who need to be interviewed for information, are opposed to management bringing in consultants?

2. Should consultants take on a consulting project if the people they will be working with are not in favour of using the services of a consultant?

3. Should consultants accept projects where they know they are basically being asked to lend support to a decision management plans to make?

4. Should counsellor/consultants accept consulting projects where they know they will be asked to exert influence on others?

2 Members working as consultants must have a high degree of *self-awareness* of their values, knowledge, skills and limitations. The focus of the consulting relationship should be on the issues or problems to be resolved and not on the person(s) presenting the problem.

Consultant's Planning (+)

A professor in counsellor education has considerable expertise in the area of employment counselling. As well, he has worked with a large number of different ethnic and socio-economic groups. The professor is contacted by the regional headquarters of Employment Canada regarding the difficulties that employment counsellors are having placing workers with several large mining companies. The professor agrees to work with the employment counsellors on the condition that she be allowed to meet with the counsellors and the directors from the mines separately to find out first hand what each group sees as the major problems.

Values Awareness (+)

Joseph Overland, a consultant in a large Canadian city, was approached to help a provincial agency make decisions regarding funding for several pregnancy information organizations. Joseph was very aware of his values regarding abortion and other issues, and felt his strong "Pro Life" stance would get in the way of his being fair to organizations appealing for funds for abortion counselling. He did not take the job.

Expertise Lacking (-)

A consultant who has just started his own two-person consulting firm, was anxious to attract business to his firm. He competed for a big contract related to work in an employee assistance program. Much of the work was related to establishing programs for employees abusing drugs and alcohol. Neither of the consultants in this firm had training in the area of drug or alcohol abuse counselling, but the consultant felt his background in counselling would provide him with the necessary skills and knowledge.

The Wrong Issue (-)

Management of a large company, with many employees, has hired a consultant to help smooth relationships between management and the many union workers. After some preliminary work, the consultant realizes that many of the problems between management and the union members relate to lack of worker input on decision-making rather than on the small pay increase union members are seeking. The consultant senses that it will be difficult to get the two groups together to discuss how workers can be more involved in management decisions. He knows he has two other consulting jobs that he must complete. As a result, the consultant opts for the quicker approach; namely, to settle for higher wages. He tells the union workers to push for a pay increase and encourages management to accept the workers' wage demands.

COMMENTS AND QUESTIONS

One of the most difficult things for consultants to do (particularly beginning consultants) is to refuse a consulting project because of insufficient skills or knowledge. Consultants often assume that they will be able to learn quickly what is needed to do the consulting project and take on projects for which they lack the knowledge and skills. Or, the consultants have an exaggerated opinion of their skills; that is, they do not have a high degree of self-awareness. This self-awareness also implies that consultants be aware of the divided loyalties of their work. What if the consultant sees some "bending of the rules" within the organization? Does the consultant follow his/her conscience or strictly adhere to the job guidelines? Self-awareness of values is crucial!

1. To what degree is it possible to focus on the problem and not the people presenting the problem?
2. Is it realistic to expect beginning consultants to give up lucrative contracts because they may lack some knowledge or skills?
3. In the second case presented, the consultant, knowing that he is "Pro Life", refuses a

consulting job. What would you have done in a similar situation?

4. Is it ethical to take on consulting jobs for which consultants may lack the expertise, if they inform the people who are hiring them of their limitations?

3 Members must be reasonably certain of their *competencies and resources* for giving consultative help and that appropriate referral resources are available to the consultant.

Referral Resources (+)

John Smith, a member of a small consulting firm, was asked to help a large electrical and electronics wholesaler with a research project that demanded both a knowledge of complex statistical procedures and an understanding of a number of standardized group tests. John Smith, who is quite knowledgeable in the area of testing, accepted the job, with the provision that he would be using the statistical expertise and computer software of another consulting firm.

Skill Awareness (+)

Joan Sutherland, a career consultant, has many contacts in business and industry. She has been asked to be a consultant for a firm owned by a good friend of hers. The work is mainly in conflict management. Ms. Sutherland informs her friend that although her knowledge of career counselling and consulting has made her familiar with conflict management, she does not feel she has enough expertise in the area to take on this job.

Mediation Services (-)

A counsellor-educator at a university accepted a consulting contract to work with a large insurance company to help management and workers establish a program for mediation of disagreements. The counsellor-educator has very little knowledge about mediation services.

Lacking Resource Knowledge (-)

A counsellor/consultant moved to a new city and opened a one-person counselling and consulting firm. Because of past associations with several national firms, he was able to obtain a lucrative consulting contract from one of the firms. Much of the work consisted of community liaison, and a knowledge of community resources was a definite asset to any consultant taking on this job. The consultant, although new to the city, felt he would quickly learn about available resources and made no mention of his limited knowledge of the city's community resources.

COMMENTS AND QUESTIONS

The first case illustrating this ethical guideline shows a consultant who is aware of his own competencies (in this case, a knowledge of tests), who is not at all reluctant to admit to his limited resources in computer software for statistical analysis, and who is willing to use the expertise of another firm that has the appropriate resources.

1. Is 'on the job' training acceptable for consultants?
2. Is it appropriate for consultants to accept contracts from former employers?
3. How should consultants advertise their skills or competencies?
4. Will it be seen as a shortcoming if and when a consultant uses other resources?

4 **There must be understanding and agreement between the consultant and client regarding the definition of the problem, the goals and interventions selected. This consulting relationship must foster the *growth and self-direction* of the client.**

Collaborative Action (+)

A guidance and counselling coordinator in a British Columbia school district has been asked by the principal in another school division to help the counsellors in his school reorganize a guidance and counselling program that will meet the needs of students, teachers, parents and administrators. The coordinator meets with students, teachers, parents and administrators and then verifies the goals and techniques with the principal in order to affirm continuing support. He then begins the work of reorganizing the program, making sure that counsellors, parents, teachers, administrators and students are consulted.

Group Leadership Skills (+)

A few years ago Canada Employment and Immigration decided to begin a program whereby all their employment counsellors would be trained in group leadership skills. Several university counsellor-educators were hired as consultants to work with Canada Employment to get the project under way and to provide the initial group leadership training. After a few years, the training program was well established and the consultants were no longer directly involved.

Further Consulting Offered (-)

A counsellor/consultant was hired to help prepare counsellors to organize and train students in their schools for peer-helper programs. After a two-week program, the consultant indicated that his services were available to each of the participants in the program to help them actually start peer-helper programs in the schools. The consultant explained that his years of experience were needed to start the programs effectively. The counsellors had been led to believe that the two-week program would prepare them to do the organizing of the peer-helper programs by themselves.

Ready For Self-Direction (-)

A consultant is hired by an Employment Agency to help employment counsellors with the skills of conflict management. The counsellors are eager and skillful counsellors and after a few days of professional development appear ready to use their newly developed skills. The consultant, knowing she is being paid a per diem of $500 per day, decided to spend another five days of professional development with the employment counsellors, going over much of the same material once more.

COMMENTS AND QUESTIONS

There can be a temptation on the part of consultants to "want to be wanted." That is, skilled consultants with many answers are reluctant to let clients 'fly on their own.' In this guideline, the member is reminded that the goal of consultation is to foster "growth and self-direction" in clients. The last two cases show a reluctance on the part of the consultant to let the clients begin work on their own. This is particularly unacceptable when the motivation for continuing the consultative service is to generate more business or money.

1. How could the problems in the last two cases have been avoided?
2. This guideline suggests that the client agree to the interventions selected. Are there any problems with this requirement?
3. How does a consultant know when a client is ready for "self-direction"?
4. What happens when the client and consultant do not have agreement regarding "the problem, the goals and interventions"?

5 In advertising services as private practitioners, members must *advertise* their services in a manner that accurately informs the public of their services, expertise and techniques of counselling. Members may list the following: highest relevant degree, type and level of certification, address, telephone number, office hours, description of services, and other relevant information. Such information must not contain false, inaccurate, misleading, partial, out-of-context, or deceptive material or statements.

Business Card (+)

A recent graduate from a doctoral program in general and family counselling established his own private counselling service. After joining CGCA, he applied for Canadian Counsellor Certification and was accepted. His business card read as follows:

John Smith, Ph.D.
Certified Counsellor (CGCA)
111 Chestnut Road (204) 123-4567 (residence)
Winnipeg, Manitoba (204) 765-4321 (business)
— personal counselling
— family counselling

Private Practitioner (+)

A private practitioner had received a Master's degree in counselling psychology, and had specialized in family counselling. Both in his advertising and his informed consent forms, he carefully pointed out that typical counselling sessions would consist of relationship building, discussion of concerns, decision-making, and formulating plans of action.

False Advertising (-)

A counsellor in private practice had received her Master's degree from a Faculty of Education, in the Department of Educational Psychology. Many of the courses she had taken in her Master's program were in school counselling. In her advertising for her private counselling services in the Yellow Pages, she indicated that her degree was in "Counselling Psychology". The Faculty of Education that she graduated from offered no degree in counselling psychology.

Deceptive Advertising (-)

A recent advertisement in a paper read, in part, as follows:

> ....trained counsellor specializing
> in family counselling....

This counsellor had received a degree in theology from a non-accredited university and his total counsellor training consisted of a weekend workshop on "family reconstruction."

COMMENTS AND QUESTIONS

The gist of this ethical guideline is that members accurately inform the public of their "services, expertise and techniques of counselling." Too often the expertise of the member is glowingly described or implied through the listing of paper credentials, but the detailed description of services and techniques are neglected.

Members are implored not to advertise information that is "false, inaccurate, misleading, partial, out-of-context, or deceptive." In the last two cases presented, the members presented either false or misleading advertising.

1. What are some examples of misleading advertising of counsellor services that you are aware of?
2. What is your responsibility once you become aware of misleading or false advertising of counsellor services?
3. How should counsellors advertise their "techniques of counselling"?
4. Since so much of advertising exaggerates positives, can we expect counsellors to inform accurately or realistically?

6 **Members do not present their affiliation with any organization in such a way that would imply *inaccurate sponsorship* or certification by that organization. It is unethical to use one's institutional affiliation to recruit clients for one's private practice.**

Non-Faculty Member (+)

A counselling consultant, who has a four-person consulting firm, frequently teaches courses at a nearby university. Even though the consultant is frequently introduced as teaching at the university, she quickly clarifies by saying she has her own consulting firm, has on occasion taught a course for the university, but is not a faculty member at the university.

CGCA Member Only (+)

Bob Reynolds, a counsellor in a rural high school, recently became a member of the Canadian Guidance and Counselling Association. At a divisional meeting of counsellors, where counsellor certification is being discussed, most of the counsellors assume Bob is certified since he has been accepted for membership by CGCA. Bob points out that he is only a member of CGCA and has not applied for counsellor certification through CGCA.

Recruiting Clients (-)

A part-time instructor at a university was hired to offer a counselling practicum in the Continuing Education Division of a university. Students were strongly encouraged to seek their own counselling in order to experience the feelings clients might have. The part-time instructor was also a partner in a private counselling service and suggested that the practicum students might wish to receive counselling at his counselling service. He would see to it that his partners would offer students favourable counselling fees.

Misleading Business Cards (-)

Tom Anderson, a counsellor in a high school, was hired by the university in his city to teach a summer school course for beginning counsellors. While at the university, he had 1000 business cards made up with the university logo. He felt this university affiliation would help him in future consulting and counselling work.

COMMENTS AND QUESTIONS

In 1993, the American Counseling Association (See ACA Legal series) made the following observations regarding the advertising of professional counselling services:

1. The advertisement should conform both in form and content to lawful licensing board regulations and ethical standards published by professional associations, national certifying boards and regulatory boards.

2. The advertisement should both be truthful and accurate, and make no unverifiable claims as to quality of service.

3. The advertisement should be reviewed by an attorney experienced in both mass media law and the law of mental health regulations.

It is obvious that in the case of Tom Anderson and his "Misleading Business Cards", little or no attention was paid to the above advertising guidelines. As this guideline suggests, members must not imply inaccurate sponsorship.

1. Can you provide some examples of inaccurate sponsorship?

2. Is there a "fine line" between being a member of a university and recruiting clients for private practice?

3. Should counsellor-educators at universities involved in practicum supervision have their own private counselling practice?

4. How can consultants best avoid any implied affiliation with a professional organization or an institution?

❖ ❖ ❖ ❖ ❖ ❖ ❖ ❖ ❖ ❖ ❖ ❖ ❖

ESSAYS

You've Got to Accentuate the Ethical: Enhancing Ethical Awareness and Action With Comic Consciousness

David Zinger
Vital Balance Consulting
Winnipeg, Manitoba

Herscovitch (1985) provided the following update of the American Psychological Association's ethical guidelines:

Principle 1: It is unethical to inquire about whether you are in the will of a suicidal patient.

Principle 2: It is unethical to refer to impotent patients as "noodle city."

Principle 7: It is unethical to interpret missed sessions due to death as resistance.

Principle 11: It is unethical to raise your rates during the bargaining phase of terminal illness (p. 9).

Ethical principles are not jokes but I believe we can keep our ethical actions centered and alive by maintaining a sense of humour about ourselves and our profession. Ethics are much more than a superficial understanding of the CGCA *Guidelines for Ethical Behaviour*. I feel that it is too easy to lose sight of ethics in private practice and consulting when we take ourselves and our work too seriously or we get too caught up in the financial requirements and desires in operating a private practice. Balancing the freedom and flexibility of consulting must be a focus on ethical actions.

The purpose in writing this article is to explain how humour and ethics contribute to professional behaviour in private practice and consulting. I have taken a personal approach to this piece. I hope that my reflections go beyond counselling/business belly-button gazing to providing you with an opportunity to reflect upon your own ethical practices.

I take ethical conduct seriously while taking myself lightly. Yet, I will also step back from our ethical guidelines, as I did at the start of the article and at times see the lighter side of ethics. The absurd update of ethical principles caused me to laugh while also reminding me that I conduct my counselling/consulting from a much more ethical point of view. I want my ethical base to be alive and lively. Too often in the past I viewed ethics as a narrow focused academic pursuit of some dour faced ethicist dwelling in a basement office in a philosophy department at a large impersonal university.

A sense of humour keeps my limitations and humility in focus. As Blanchard and Peale (1988), in a book on the power of ethical management, stated: "people with humility don't think less of themselves...they just think about themselves less" (p. 49). Ethics takes me outside of myself and my practice to a wider consideration of important issues in how I provide assistance to clients. Our code of ethics provides a foundation for conduct. It helps to steer us in the right direction and to let us know where we stand. There is an old aphorism that states: "If you don't stand for something you'll fall for anything."

Section D on consulting and private practice assists me in determining where I stand on: voluntary relationships, self-awareness, competencies, resources, growth, and self-direction.

In my work in an employee assistance program in Manitoba, I have had two clients who were mandatory referrals. I was very uncomfortable with the whole idea of mandatory referrals when I first started working with employees eight years ago. When I receive a mandatory referral I take strong steps to ensure that the client is aware that they still have a choice in entering a counselling relationship with me. Although the referral is mandatory, the relationship is voluntary. During the first session I always explore options and consequences. Balancing the ethical concern, I am also aware that the mandatory referral part of the program has been instrumental in helping a few troubled employees that would not have been helped in any other way and could have potentially lost their jobs and families.

I strive to maintain a high degree of self-awareness. I continually monitor my working relationships with clients and seek feedback from them. To heighten my self-awareness at the end of each counselling or consulting session I ask myself two key questions: What did I like about what I did? What would I do differently if I was to do the same session again? I find these two questions help me to build my foundation of strengths while also helping me to consider future changes or adjustments. I continually read the professional journals to reflect upon my work. I also teach a lot of counselling courses at the University of Manitoba and my work with students keeps my self-awareness fresh, alive and challenged.

Coinciding with my self-awareness is an awareness of my competencies and resources. I do not hesitate to make referrals and I am very careful not to tackle a project that is beyond my competencies. For instance, I encourage female clients to consider the option of working with a female counsellor and I have made this type of referral in the past. My obligation is much more to my client than to myself.

Beyond the ethical principle, counselling has always implied working towards client growth and self-direction. I frequently tell my clients that I see my job as putting myself out of business as they develop increased skills and confidence in defining their own problems, choosing goals and selecting interventions. One of the biggest compliments I have received in this work is to hear a client terminate a counselling relationship by saying that although they appreciated my assistance they really felt they did it on their own!

I have never done any advertising as most of my clients find me by word of mouth. It seems that Manitoba is small enough that people will seek you out if you do a good job. I do a lot of speaking and make a copy of my brochure available that lists my professional highlights.

I do not use any false, inaccurate or misleading information yet problems still arise. For instance, many organizations and people make the assumption that I am a professor, hold a doctorate degree or refer to me as a psychologist. At the earliest possible time I correct them in the error. I have had to begin a few speeches thanking the organization for granting me a doctorate but having to tell them that I do not hold this advance degree even though I did enjoy playing doctor when I was 4 and 5 years old. I add the humour so the person who misrepresented me does not feel too bad. I am not a psychologist and I have had to phone the media on a few occasions to correct their inaccurate referral to me as a psychologist. I take pride in what I have achieved and what I do; I do not have any desire to take credit for what I have not done.

In addition to consulting, I teach a lot of counselling courses at the university. I always take time to go over the code of ethics with my students. I also make them aware that I cannot function as their counsellor and I keep an updated list of possible referrals for students who are seeking counselling assistance.

Because of my ethical balance, I have refused lucrative contracts on three separate occasions. Although it hurt financially at the time, I believed it was the right thing to do. As Blanchard and Peale (1988) stated: "there is no right way to do a wrong thing" (p.9). Paradoxically, one of the clients I initially had to turn down because of an ethical conflict has become one of my most frequent consulting clients. He stated that my initial conduct set a basis for trust and professionalism in our relationship. I do not believe we should conduct ourselves ethically for some external reward, but I think our ethical behaviour does not go unrecognized by the people we work with.

The Vital Balance, a book by Karl Menninger on the life process in mental illness and health, is a reminder to keep balance and perspective on what I do. I balance the serious side of counselling with humour. I help clients make sense of themselves, others and situations while also making new sense and nonsense of the same things. In addition, I keep a vital balance between my work and my home and I use the code of ethics to balance the financial and personal requirements of my business.

Along with our code of ethics I rely on good judgement, combined with respect for the dignity and integrity of my clients. Like a parent who gives their children roots and wings, the ethical guidelines give me a part of my counselling roots while humour gives me some feathers in my counselling wings. Although I make no claims to be an angel and I have a fondness for life as a human being, I appreciate C.K. Chesterson's line: "Angels can fly because they take themselves lightly."

Our eagerness to follow ethical principles and laugh in this profession are two key ways to ensure that we last in this profession.

References

Blanchard, K., & Peale, N.V. (1988). *The power of ethical management.* New York: William Morrow.

Herscovitch, J. (1985). Ethical principles of psychologists: An update. *Journal of Polymorphous Perversity, 2,* 9.

Menninger, K. (1963). *The vital balance.* New York: Penguin Books.

Consulting and Ethics

Bryan Hiebert
University of Calgary

There are two mentions of consultation in the *Guidelines For Ethical Behaviour*. In section D:1, consultation is defined as "a VOLUNTARY RELATIONSHIP between a counsellor and a help-seeking individual, group, or organization." Section D then goes on to elaborate the nature of the collaboration and the role of the consultant. Consultation also is referred to in Section B:6, where the *Guidelines For Ethical Behaviour* states that a "member reserves the right to CONSULT with any other professionally competent person about the counsellee." Although consultation and counselling might have overlapping domains, these two references to consultation convey some important differences between counselling and consultation.

First, the voluntary nature of consultation is important. Although counselling often represents a voluntary interaction, it frequently is the case that people enter counselling reluctantly, as in the case when court legislation dictates that a person seek counselling or a supervisor stipulates that an employee seek counselling as a condition of continuing employment. In such cases a counsellor must first of all deal with the inevitable resistance and resentment that the reluctant client brings to the counselling enterprise. When consultation is viewed as a voluntary endeavor, such resentment typically is not encountered and the client of the consultant (i.e., the consultee) typically is eager to obtain the consultant's input.

Second, in counselling there is an expectation, either implicit or explicit, that clients come into counselling to change some aspect of their lives and that the counsellor has some responsibility for making that change occur. Depending on the counsellor's orientation, words like facilitate, guide, enable, or invite may be used to describe the process, but the implication remains that client change is an expected outcome of counselling and the counsellor has some important part to play in the change process. In consultation, the expectation for consultee change and the expectation that the consultant has responsibility for consultee change, is far less. The assumption in consultation is that the consultant simply provides expertise. There is little expectation, either implicit or explicit, that the consultee necessarily will follow the consultants suggestions (Gladding, 1988). In counselling, there always is the expectation that some form of client change will occur and that the counsellor has some degree of responsibility for that change.

There is beginning to be a literature base on consulting, addressing theoretical background, research, skills and practices, and future directions. However, counsellor training programs often do not expose students to this literature even though some consultation activity likely will be part of most counsellors' role descriptions. Therefore, the literature will be reviewed briefly in an attempt to provide a frame of reference for counsellors to use when engaging in consultation activities.

The Nature of Consulting

Kurpris (1978) points out that consultation is by nature triadic, i.e., it involves an interaction between a consultant and a consultee, for the purpose of addressing the client group that the consultee services. The ultimate goal of consultation is the client group that the consultee services, not the consultee him or her self (Bacon & Dougherty, 1992; Kurpuis, 1986). The need to consult may occur when a counsellor experiences difficulty working with a specific client problem, when a counsellor wishes to expand areas of service and seeks advice from someone with greater expertise in the new area, or when an organization wishes to provide service or staff training in areas where it currently does not have expertise. In all of these cases, the substantive or procedural knowledge of the consultant is requested by the consultee, in order to provide better or more extensive service to the client group the consultee serves. Thus, as Gallessich (1985) points out, consultation is most often content based (supported by a recognized body of knowledge) and goal oriented (it has a specific objective).

Focus Of Consulting

Elaborating the above perspective, Gladding (1988) mentions three levels of consultation, individual, group, and organizational. In *individual consultation* an individual, usually a counsellor, wants advice and asks a consultant. There is no expectation that the consultant will help the consultee's client change, only that the consultant will provide accurate information. Typically, the information request is substantive or procedural in nature. Substantively, the consultee may be requesting information about matters like different organizational interaction patterns, factors involved in particular client problem areas like anger management or career planning, or special considerations pertinent to particular client groups like natives, abused young people, or women in transition. Procedural requests usually focus on ways to approach skill training, for example teaching clients relaxation, assertiveness, or self-management skills, or suggestions for working with difficult clients, for example when a counsellor "has tried everything" to get a client motivated to change and wants some further suggestions that might be more effective. Although there is some overlap between substantive and procedural domains, it is useful to conceptualize the procedural domain as addressing the training (i.e., practice & feedback) component of working with clients in addition to merely the knowledge about the nature of the client problem or the characteristics of a particular client group.

Group consultation is similar in nature to individual consultation, except that it is to a group of people. The group may be composed of several counsellors wishing input on a common problem, for example new developments in ways to approach career planning. Alternatively, group consultation can sometimes take the form of training workshops where a group of clients contract with a consultant to provide instruction in a particular problem area, like assertiveness training or stress management. The focus can be on the individuals in the group, for example, teaching time management in a group setting, or it can be on the group itself, as when a consultant is hired to conduct conflict resolution sessions with a group that is in conflict. With group consulta-

tion it is perhaps easier to see that client change is not the goal of consultation. The consultant's role is to present the information and each group member, or the group as a whole, is free to adopt or reject the consultant's information.

Organizational or community consultation is similar to group consultation except it has a broader context. Consultants may be asked to examine and comment on different aspects of an organization, for example communication channels, hiring practices, or performance appraisal procedures. Additionally, consultants may be asked to do staff training in any number of a wide variety of areas, such as time management, career planning, or stress management. Finally, consultants may be asked to provide direct service to employees in areas where a firm does not have sufficient staff to address area itself, for example in areas like out-placement or employee assistance programs. In this last area, the boundary between consulting and counselling becomes fuzzy because in such cases there usually is an expectation that the "consultant" will be instrumental in fostering change in those receiving service.

Approaches To Consulting

Bacon and Dougherty (1992) describe three models of consultation, the educational-training model, the collaborative model, and the advocacy model. The *Educational-Training Model* deals primarily with skill or knowledge focused staff training and the focus for the consultant's intervention is the professional development of the consultee(s). In educational settings this might address areas such as child-rearing practices, instructional methods, classroom management, stress management, communication skills, or how to use prepared programs like DUSO or Magic Circle. In organizations the focus might be on training supervisory skills, explaining new software packages, or briefing employees on new management practices. In all of these cases, the consultant has primarily an instructional role and the consultee's role is that of learner or applyer. The consultant approaches his or her task by doing a needs assessment to determine the nature of the skills needed, designing the training experience (content, process, outcomes, delivery methods), delivering the training experience, and evaluating the training.

The educational-training model has the advantage of being very cost effective, for the consultant can influence large numbers of people at the same time, but one drawback is that it is easy to overlook individual needs due to the focus on group delivery and group needs. Herein lie several potential ethical dilemmas. In some staff training workshops the focus is so entirely on the issue to be addressed or the skills to be learned that the consultant seems to forget that there are individual people in the group and that there is some responsibility on the part of the consultant to make sure the training addresses the needs of the group participants. In such cases, consultants may end up delivering "canned packages" rather than assessing the needs of the group participants and tailoring the training program to their needs. Moreover, there have been cases where group activities have increased participant awareness of problem areas or sensitized group members to problems that otherwise would not have existed. For example, one of my students recently told me of an organization who hired a consultant to do some stress management training with its workers. The thrust in the workshop was on identifying the stressors in people's lives, sharing the nature of people's experience stress, and describing the health risks associated with stress. Many of the participants in the group ended up feeling more stressed at the end of the workshop than before. Clearly in such cases, the consultant has an ethical responsibility to follow-up with the individuals concerned and assist them in resolving the issues that the training precipitated.

Another potential ethical dilemma arises from training demands made on consultants. Sometimes when a consultant is a good trainer, there is pressure to provide service in areas that are not squarely within the consultant's area of expertise. For example, a person offering stress management training might be asked to provide some consultation in time management. In such cases, it might be easy for a consultant to be "seduced" into offering training in areas where realistically speaking he or she does not really have the expertise.

In the *Collaborative Model*, consultant and consultee work together, combining resources to solve a particular problem. This approach is most effective in situations requiring frequent modification of process, where only the underling principles can be outlined clearly and ongoing coaching is necessary to be effective in operationalizing the principles. In educational settings, a collaborative approach is most frequently used in response to situations like working with children who have learning, emotional, or behavioural problems or teachers and administrators mobilize the support of parents in various school endeavours. In organizations, a collaborative approach works well in helping supervisors deal with problem employees or helping companies design and implement a down-sizing program. In a collaborative approach, the consultant typically approaches his or her task by establishing rapport (gaining entry), diagnosing the problem and the stakeholder's areas of expertise, designing and implementing the game plan for approaching the problem, and withdrawal or disengagement.

A collaborative approach is useful in helping organizations deal with seldom occurring problems or areas that are beyond the expertise of its staff members. This poses several potential ethical dilemmas for consultants. The first lies in loosing sight of the triadic nature of consulting, i.e., forgetting that the ultimate goal of the consultative process is improvement of service to the client that the consultee is working with. In a very real sense, the consultant is working the consultee to change the consultee's way of interacting with clients. This may violate the expectation that the consultee is free to adopt or not adopt the consultant's suggestions and may in fact be moving the consultant away from the accepted consultant role of simply providing expertise.

A second danger is that consultees may tend to perceive the consultant's expertise as extending beyond realistic limits, creating the impression that the consultant is the "expert" on everything. Some consultants resolve this problem by focusing on process and leaving the content to the other collaborator. Other consultants resolve the issue by admitting their limited expertise in a given area, pointing out that others have similarly limited amounts of expertise, and that they at least are willing to work sincerely on the problem. Clearly, the line between objective reality and self-delusion is often fuzzy in this area and one where the consultant must be ever vigilant.

In the *Advocacy Model*, the consultant's main focus is on protecting the rights of clients or lobbying on behalf of particular client groups. This model emphasizes the consultant's preventive role as a proactive initiator of self-chosen goals rather than a retroactive crisis-resolver. Important areas for this type of consultative endeavour include suspected child abuse, child neglect, special services for disabled clients, family legal rights, etc. In such cases, consultants may serve primarily a mediating role, helping to coordinate existing services, or an advocacy role, creating an alternative plan for service delivery.

Sometimes, consultants may overlook their advocacy roles in the process of meeting the more direct service-related needs stemming from their educative and collaborative roles. Consultants can play a powerful advocacy role and provide an effective catalyst for change in an organization for they are seen as the "outside experts" without the vested interest of those involved in primary service. However, this may potentially place the consultant in a double bind where clients become more self-empowered and service delivery increases to the point where there is a reduced demand for the consultant's services. This situation has the potential for another form of ethical dilemma for the consultant.

Consulting Skills

Consultation skills and counselling skills overlap considerably, therefore it is easy to assume that because one is a good counsellor, one also will be a good consultant. However, the third-party nature of consultation requires some additional skills in order to work effectively within the system of the consultee to effect change in the system of the consultee's clients. The purpose of the paper is not to elaborate the skill differences between counselling and consulting. My purpose for raising this issue is simply to point to the existence of those differences and to caution counsellors against auto-

matically assuming that effectiveness in providing direct service to clients implies that one can be successful in the triadic context of helping consultees provide better service to their clients.

Issues

Following directly from the above point, one of the biggest temptations for private practice consultants is to extend their areas of claimed expertise beyond reasonable limits or, putting it more bluntly, pretending to have expertise where they don't. This is seldom done as a deliberate, planned charlatan act. More often it happens as a result of success in one area and a request for further consulting input in a related area that actually lies at the periphery of the consultant's expertise. In other cases, it might come as a result of a request for consultant service at a time when the consultant is experiencing a business slump and is vulnerable to over-estimating the extent of professional expertise. However, readers are reminded that Section D of the *Guidelines for Ethical Behaviour* emphasizes that consultants must have a high degree of SELF-AWARENESS, in order to be aware of their COMPETENCIES AND RESOURCES, i.e., their skills, knowledge, and limitations. Of course many people reading this paper may draw on their reserve of self-righteous indignation and claim emphatically that they never extend themselves beyond their limits. However, our assurance that we are blameless is probably one of the best early warning signals that perhaps we are not keeping very close tabs on this situation for ourselves.

A related problem arises from the fact that consultants often operate in areas where there is not an abundance of expertise to begin with. That lack of available expertise in a particular area means that it is not necessary to know very much in order to be ahead of the average practitioner. There is the potential for someone to attend a workshop, read a book or two, and start offering workshops in a designated area. In such cases, a consultant may learn the jargon associated with a particular area, be able to talk a good line on that content area, and appear to be the expert, but in actual fact know very little about the area. I have encountered this situation with some consultants working in areas like: sexual abuse, suicide, classroom management, communication skills, and stress control.

A final ethical issue stems from the triadic nature of consultation and involves loosing sight of the ultimate client in the consultative process, i.e., the client the consultee is servicing. Section D of the *Guidelines for Ethical Behaviour* emphasizes that the focus in consulting should be on the issue or problem to be resolved (not the person presenting the problem), there must be agreement between the consultant and client on the problem definition, the goal of consultation, and the chosen intervention. Thus, the overall goal in consulting is to "foster the GROWTH AND SELF-DIRECTION of the client (i.e., the consultee), but the consultant may sometimes end up focusing more on the interests of the third party, not the consultee.

Conclusion

Consulting is in its infancy as a professional practice and much work is needed to map out the accepted domains of consulting endeavour and accepted practices for consultants. In other contexts, the profession of counselling under-took to establish meaning in its existence, the counsellors took it upon themselves to map out the domain and expertises of counselling. It is hoped that consulting may travel a similar path and as research and principles of practice become more extensive, the guidelines for conduct will become more clear. However at its present stage consultation presents may temptations and ethical pitfalls for counsellors wanting to branch out into consultation as a part of their scope of practice.

References

Bacon, E. H., & Dougherty, A. M. (1992). Consultation and coordination services for prekindergarten children. *Elementary School Guidance & Counseling, 27*, 24-32.

Gallessich, J. (1985). Toward a meta-theory of consultation. *The Counseling Psychologist, 13*, 36-354.

Gladding, S. T. (1988). *Counseling: A comprehensive profession.* Columbus, OH: Merrill

Kurpuis, D. J. (1978). Consultation theory and process: an integrated model. *Professional Psychology, 56*, 335-338.

Kurpuis, D. J. (1986). Consultation: An Important Human and Organizational Intervention. *Journal of Counseling and Human Service Professions, 1*, 58-66.

CHAPTER SIX

--- ❖ ---

Case Studies
In Counsellor
Preparation
Standards

--- ❖ ---

Counsellor-educators are in a unique position of not only teaching and discussing ethical guidelines, but also modelling ethical responsibilities. These ethical responsibilities are presented in the cases, discussions, questions and essays in this chapter.

❖ ❖ ❖ ❖ ❖ ❖ ❖ ❖ ❖ ❖ ❖ ❖ ❖ ❖

GUIDELINES

1 Members responsible for **training others** must be guided by the preparation guidelines provided in the C.G.C.A. Position Paper on counsellor preparation.

❖

2 Members must **orient students** to program expectations, basic skills development, and employment prospects prior to admission to the program.

❖

3 Members in charge of learning experiences must establish programs that **integrate** academic study and supervised practice.

❖

4 Members must establish a program directed toward developing students' skills, knowledge, and self-understanding, stated whenever possible in competency or **performance terms**.

❖

5 Members, through continual student **evaluation and appraisal**, must be aware of the personal limitations of the learner that might impede future performance. The instructor must not only assist the learner in securing remedial assistance but also screen from the program those individuals who are unable to provide competent services.

❖

6 Members must provide a program that includes **training in research** commensurate with levels of role functioning. Paraprofessional and technician-level personnel must be trained as consumers of research. In addition, personnel must learn how to evaluate their own and their program's effectiveness. Graduate training, especially at the doctoral level, would include preparation for original research by the member.

❖

7 Members must make students aware of the **ethical responsibilities** and standards of the profession.

❖

8 Preparatory programs must encourage students to value the **ideas of service** to individuals and to society. In this regard, direct financial remuneration or lack thereof must not influence the quality of service rendered. Monetary considerations must not be allowed to over-shadow professional and humanitarian needs.

❖

9 Members responsible for educational pro-grams must be skilled as **teachers and practitioners**.

❖

10 Members must present thoroughly **varied theoretical positions** so that students may make comparisons and have the opportunity to select a position.

❖

11 Members must develop clear policies within their educational institutions regard-ing **field placement** and the roles of the student and the instructor in such placement.

❖

12 Members must ensure that forms of learning focusing on self-understanding or growth are **voluntary**, or if required as part of the educational program, are made known to prospec-tive students prior to entering the program.

❖

◆ ◆ ◆ ◆ ◆ ◆ ◆ ◆ ◆ ◆ ◆ ◆ ◆ ◆

CASE STUDIES

1 Members responsible for *training others* must be guided by the preparation guidelines provided in the C.G.C.A. Position Paper on counsellor preparation.

C.G.C.A. Position Paper (+)

A counsellor-educator phoned the C.G.C.A. headquarters in Ottawa indicating that her department was reorganizing their counsellor education program and they wanted to have the latest position of C.G.C.A. on training. The counsellor-educator was informed that the C.G.C.A. *Position Paper for the Provision of Counselling Services* would be mailed to her. She also pointed out that Canadian Counsellor Certification requirements consisted of a graduate degree in counselling, a counselling theories course, a supervised counselling practicum and graduate course work in any six of the following areas: communication and relationship skills, group counselling, career development, assessment and testing, research and evaluation, consultation methods, learning and human development, psychological education, counselling intervention strategies, counselling girls and women, multi-cultural counselling and counselling in specialized settings.

C.G.C.A. Accreditation (+)

At a meeting of the C.G.C.A. Board of Directors, several counsellor-educators presented their proposal for accreditation of university counsellor training programs.

These accreditation principles and guidelines were based on the C.G.C.A. position paper on counsellor preparation. When asking for volunteers to pilot the accreditation procedures, four counsellor-educators from different Canadian universities offer to have their counsellor education program go through the pilot accreditation process.

Counselling Practicum (-)

One university with a small number of counsellor-educators admits many graduate students to its counselling program. Nearly all the students are teachers or counsellors who plan to take all the courses during the summer months when they have vacation. Since a counselling field experience is not offered during the summer, these counsellors complete their program of studies without ever being supervised in an actual counselling situation.

Program Philosophy (-)

A school counsellor, interested in further graduate studies, phoned the department head of a counsellor education program in a neighbouring province regarding the philosophy, admission requirements and other program specifics. The department head provided some information regarding admission and courses, but when asked whether their program followed the guidelines for training suggested by C.G.C.A., the department head indicated he was not familiar with the C.G.C.A. Position Paper or certification regulations.

COMMENTS AND QUESTIONS

The purpose of the 1989 C.G.C.A. *Position Paper for the Provision of Counselling Services in Canada* is "to provide a statement of the basic needs of Canadians and the services which should be provided through C.G.C.A. members in order to meet these needs..." Within a developmental perspective, Van Hestern and Pawlovich, the authors of the C.G.C.A. Position Paper, identify human needs from infancy through middle childhood, adolescence, early adulthood, middle age and later maturity. They feel it is the challenge of all counsellors to become more developmentally focused in their counselling orientation.

The C.G.C.A. Position Paper also identifies people in Canadian society with particular needs. These groups include: female clients, single persons, exceptional clients and the handicapped, Native peoples, prison inmates, unemployed people, apprentices, and immigrants.

Finally, Van Hestern and Pawlovich set a challenge for all counsellors; namely, to acquire "cultural awareness and to develop a critical consciousness of the social, economic, political, and technological factors and processes which either facilitate or impede optimal human development."

1. Should all university departments offering degree programs in counsellor education

offer programs that reflect the course work and practica suggested in the C.G.C.A. Position Paper and certification regulations?

2. What are your opinions regarding accreditation of counsellor training programs in Canada?

3. Is the C.G.C.A. Position Paper too general? Does it help clarify the position for specific groups of counsellors such as family and marriage counsellors, school counsellors or career counsellors?

4. Do you agree with the C.G.C.A. certification requirements for counsellors; namely, practicum, a counselling theories course and course work in six additional counselling-related areas?

2 Members must *orient students* to program expectations, basic skills development, and employment prospects prior to admission to the program.

Student Information (+)

This department of counselling psychology sends a very detailed booklet to each graduate student applicant in counselling. Included in the booklet is material on admission requirements, programs of study, course expectations, student expectations and typical jobs received by graduates from this counselling psychology department.

Orientation (+)

Several weeks before class registration the department head of this department of counsellor education organizes an extensive orientation program. Various professors discuss the advantages and disadvantages of the thesis versus the practicum route; other professors give detailed outlines of the core courses in counselling as well as the elective courses; and former graduate students comment on their present jobs and field questions regarding their former programs of study at this university.

Professor Leaves (-)

At one small department of educational psychology (which included counsellor education) several good courses in consulting had been developed by a professor who specialized in the area of consultation. Several graduate students were attracted to this university and department because of their desire to learn a great deal about counselling and consulting. When registration for courses began, the graduate students learned that the professor teaching the consulting courses had moved to another university and the consulting courses had been cancelled.

No Graduate Follow-Up (-)

Although the university department of counsellor education did spell out the basic program expectations, no attempt was made to link the skills of counselling to specific courses or even the total program. At no time in the last 10 years had any efforts been made to follow-up graduates of the program in order to give prospective students some idea of the employment prospects.

COMMENTS AND QUESTIONS

This ethical guideline suggests that counsellor education departments clearly delineate their program expectations, the basic counselling skills that must be developed and the job prospects for graduates. This has not always been done, but in recent years more and more counselling departments are developing not only detailed brochures and other materials, but are offering extensive, in-person orientation programs to students prior to registration.

As a minimum, the orientation materials that prospective students receive should contain information on the following:

a) Admission requirements, including not only minimum admission requirements, but the typical grades and other criteria that recently admitted students obtained;

b) Complete descriptions of program and course expectations. This would include detailed course outlines for all courses. These outlines would indicate the nature of the course, teaching format, assignments and a grading system;

c) The skills and attitudes that students are expected to develop; and

d) The employment prospects for graduates, including data on recent graduates.

1. What questions would you ask a department head if you were considering a graduate program in counselling in her/his department?

2. Is it realistic to expect counsellor education departments to know and report on employment prospects of counselling graduates?

3. What would you include in an in-person orientation session prior to registration?

4. What materials would you include in the materials you would send to students who were interested in your counsellor education program?

3 Members in charge of learning experiences must establish programs that *integrate* academic study and supervised practice.

Supervised Practicum (+)

One counsellor-educator feels it is extremely important for students to have a good understanding of counselling philosophy, counselling theory, psychological assessment and counselling techniques before students are placed in a supervised counselling practice situation. To make sure that he will have time to do intensive supervision of counselling practice, he arranges for all these aforementioned academic subjects to be scheduled in the first semester so that he can devote most of his time in the second semester for on-site supervision of students. He arranges weekly meetings for each student as well as a seminar, for the whole practicum group, where students can discuss their philosophies and theories in light of the realities of their practice.

Integrated Program (+)

This Canadian university offers a two-year, full-time study Master's program in counselling. Students are required to have a background in psychology before beginning the program. Courses in theories of counselling and counselling techniques are completed before students begin their supervised counselling practica. During the supervised field experience, students are encouraged to try out and integrate the counselling theories and techniques they have studied or practised in earlier courses.

"Smorgasbord" (-)

In one university the administration changed the program-centered graduate training to a totally flexible format, where students were allowed to take whatever courses they wanted to take or were being offered. After completing any six full courses, students graduated. The advising of students was left to clerical staff in the administrative office, and few, if any, attempts were made to integrate courses into a specific program of study.

"Get-Wet-All-Over" (-)

The course offered in group counselling was a very practical, 'hands-on' course. During the first weeks of classes, the instructor of this course told students that they were required to "run a group" with some of the clients they had in their counselling practicum setting. This group was to begin within two weeks and meet a minimum of 8 times. Although the counselling students valued the chance to have actual experience with a group, they were hesitant about beginning since they had not studied any material related to group leadership, group dynamics or group member needs and roles.

COMMENTS AND QUESTIONS

Counsellor-educators in charge of the learning experiences of students in counsellor training need to integrate academic training with supervised practice in counselling. The Canadian Counsellor Certification regulations provide the framework and the possibility for this type of integration.

The revised certification criteria (January 27, 1990) indicate the following:

A. C.G.C.A. Membership

All persons who are members in good standing of the Canadian Guidance and Counselling Association are eligible for certification.

B. Graduate Training

A graduate degree, or equivalent, in counselling or related field from a C.G.C.A. recognized higher education institution is required, showing evidence of GRADUATE work in:

1. *Counselling Theory*
   A study of basic counselling theories, models of counselling, principles and techniques of counselling.

2. *Supervised Counselling Practicum*
   A supervised counselling experience in an appropriate work setting of at least 120 hours should be spent in direct client contact.

and GRADUATE course work in *six* of the following areas:

3. *Communication and Relationship Skills*
   A study of counsellor/client relationship skills.

4. *Group Counselling*
   A study of group leadership, types of groups, group practices, group methods and techniques, and group dynamics.

5. *Career Development*
   A study of areas such as career development theory, career choice and lifestyle, educational, and career information and decision-making.

6. *Assessment and Testing*
   A study of individual and group assessment and testing, case study approaches, individual differences, and methods of data collection and interpretation.

7. *Research and Evaluation*
   A study of research design, statistics, evaluation, and types of research.

8. *Consultation Methods*
   A study of consultation theory research and practice. Topics include the process or stages of consultation, ethical issues, and approaches to consultation.

9. *Learning and Human Development*
   A study of the nature and needs of individuals at all developmental levels. Included would be topics such as learning theory, human behaviour, studies of change, and personality theory.

10. *Psychological Education*
    A study of topics in psychology such as personality, growth, development, attitude formation, and socialization.

11. *Counselling Intervention Strategies*
    Theory and practice in planning and implementing client change interventions in counselling.

12. *Counselling Girls and Women*
    A study of sex role development, stereotyping and social roles, and corresponding counselling theories and counselling approaches.

13. *Multi-Cultural Counselling*
    An examination of cross cultural issues in counselling, influence of social and cultural contexts on client problems, and relevant counselling theories and counselling approaches.

14. *Counselling in Specialized Settings*
    A study of issues, applied theory, and rel-

evant counselling approaches pertaining to a special client population or setting, e.g., families, rehabilitation, schools, disabled clients, etc.

1. This particular ethical guideline suggests that academic study should be integrated with supervised practice. How can this best be done?

2. What areas of graduate course work would you add or delete from the list of 14 course areas?

3. Do you believe more of the areas should be compulsory? For example, should all counsellors have compulsory course work in group counselling, research and evaluation and communication skills?

4. Is it realistic to require 120 hours of "direct client contact" during a counselling practicum?

4 **Members must establish a program directed toward developing students' skills, knowledge, and self-understanding, stated whenever possible in competency or *performance terms.***

Performance Objectives (+)

Soon after two new members joined a small department of five counsellor-educators, the chairperson saw this as an opportune time to get all members involved in evaluating and modifying their counsellor education program. At the end, course objectives were written for all courses and performance standards for counsellors were presented in clear, measurable terms.

Group Leadership Skills (+)

In a group counselling course offered in a Master's program in counselling, the course instructor requires all course members to lead a group to demonstrate interaction skills such as linking, process observing and limiting. At the end of the practice session, each student leader receives feedback on the specific leadership skills from the course instructor.

Research Emphases (-)

A potential graduate student sought information from six different Canadian universities regarding their Master's programs in counsellor education. After studying the written materials from each of the universities, he applied and was accepted into one university program that seemed to promise training both in research and in counselling skills. Too late, the graduate student was disappointed to learn that the practicum was cancelled for that year, but he was allowed to substitute additional courses in research and statistics. He graduated with his Master's degree without having taken a counselling practicum.

Practicum Supervision (-)

One professor is assigned to teach and supervise a counselling practicum for eight graduate students. This practicum course has been described in the university calendar as consisting of practice and supervision of counselling skills for participants. The professor assigns each practicum student to a school and his 'supervision' consists of the occasional phone call to the school. No directions are given as to the counselling skills that are to be practised or supervised. At the end of the course, all eight practicum students are awarded grades of "A".

COMMENTS AND QUESTIONS

Detailing the skills and knowledge for all counselling courses and experiences in performance objectives can be a long, difficult task. The task is, however, very worth doing. The following few examples provide some notion of how counsellor skills and knowledge can be described in behavioral, performance terms:

a) the student can describe three basic theories of learning and evaluate the theories in terms of importance, operationalization, parsimony, precision, empiricism and research possibilities;

b) the student is able to demonstrate ability to administer, score and utilize results in counselling of selected individual tests and inventories.

1. Is it possible to delineate trainee competencies in performance terms, knowing that counsellor attitudes are as important as counsellor skills?

2. Many counsellor-educators believe that the attitudes of counsellors are more important than specific counselling skills. What do you think? How does this effect the need to delineate specific skills in performance terms?

3. Stating counsellor training objectives in performance terms may suggest a microcounselling skills approach to training. Is this limiting?

4. What skills, knowledge and self-understanding would you include in a counsellor education program?

5 Members, through continual student *evaluation and appraisal*, must be aware of the personal limitations of the learner that might impede future performance. The instructor must not only assist the learner in securing remedial assistance but also screen from the program those individuals who are unable to provide competent services.

Relationship Skills Lacking (+)

In a counselling practicum situation, co-taught and co-supervised by two counsellor-educators, one of the counsellors-in-training does not appear to relate very well to clients. Both counsellor-educators observe her in videotaped counselling situations and are not satisfied with her progress. Helpful suggestions are given to the trainee, but a month later her relationships with clients remain cool and distant. The counsellor-educators clearly tell the trainee that her skills in relating with clients must improve if she hopes to be a counsellor.

Pre-Practicum (+)

During the first semester of a counsellor training program, all counselling students are required to take a pre-practicum, laboratory course, designed to help students develop their communication skills, but also to help staff determine whether or not a student should be recommended for the counselling practicum. At least two supervisors observe each student and write detailed evaluations of each student's communication and relationship skills.

Screening Students (-)

At this university many students took their graduate training in counselling as part-time students, doing the course work and other requirements during the summer months. Frequently, their study was spread over five or six years. Many of these students took the counselling practicum as their last course. The summer practicum was intensive, and only six weeks in length. Most students did not receive specific feedback on their counselling skills till about the third or even the fourth week of the practicum.

In one particular practicum group, the counselling supervisor realized that two students needed to be "screened from the program" since they were just not capable of establishing a meaningful counselling relationship. The instructor, realizing that a "pass" in the practicum was all that the students needed in order to get their Master's degree, decided to pass the students so they could get a degree and a subsequent salary increase.

Counselling Suitability (-)

A graduate program in counselling makes no attempts at evaluating or appraising students' ability to counsel or to relate to people. The program consists of 10 half courses in counselling, and a counselling practicum is optional, though highly recommended.

COMMENTS AND QUESTIONS

The first two cases presented demonstrate ethical behaviour on the part of counsellor-educators. They are evaluating the performance of counsellors-in-training, and are prepared to make helpful suggestions. In the last two cases no attempt is made, as this guideline suggests, to "screen from the program those individuals who are unable to provide competent service".

1. What would you have done in the case entitled "Screening Students"?
2. In the last case, what should be done to a counsellor training program that makes a supervised practicum optional?
3. What criterion should be established to determine which students in counselling do not "provide competent service"?
4. What are the preferred methods of evaluation and appraisal for students in counselling?

6 Members must provide a program that includes *training in research* commensurate with levels of role functioning. Paraprofessional and technician-level personnel must be trained as consumers of research. In addition, personnel must learn how to evaluate their own and their program's effectiveness. Graduate training, especially at the doctoral level, would include preparation for original research by the member.

Research and Evaluation Courses (+)

A faculty of education at one Canadian university requires all teachers and counsellors to complete a research course, designed to help teachers and counsellors understand research in the literature; and a measurement and evaluation course, designed to help the student prepare to use measurement instruments and to evaluate course and program effectiveness.

Research Workshops (+)

Every year this university department offers a lecture and workshop series on research for theses and dissertations. This series is in addition to required research courses for all graduate students in Master's or Doctoral programs.

No Research and Statistics (-)

One department of counselling psychology that offers a Ph.D. program no longer requires students to take courses in research and statistics. Many graduate students complained of the difficulty they were having with research and statistics and as a result the research and statistic courses were made optional to students.

Waiving Research Requirements (-)

A professor learned that one of his doctoral advisees was having a great deal of difficulty in an advanced research course. He asked the research instructor to make sure his student got a good grade. Not being offered any such assurances, he advised the doctoral student to withdraw from the research course, and he then waived the research requirements for the student.

COMMENTS AND QUESTIONS

Research is an important part of any profession, and particularly so for a relatively new profession like counselling. This guideline emphasizes the importance of research not only for master's and doctoral students, but also for paraprofessional and technician personnel in counselling.

1. Why is it that research and statistics courses are avoided, if possible, by many students?
2. Should research courses be compulsory for students in counselling?
3. What should be the major focus of an initial course in research for counselling students?
4. One part of this guideline refers to the need for members to have skills in program evaluation. Is "evaluation" taught in most research courses? Should an evaluation course be required of all graduate students in counselling?

7 Members must make students aware of the *ethical responsibilities* and standards of the profession.

Course in Ethics (+)

This university has introduced a new course entitled "Legal and Ethical Issues in Counselling." The course is compulsory for all students in counselling. The course is taught by an acknowledged expert in the area of legal and ethical counselling issues.

Ethics Workshop (+)

One university provides all students with the C.G.C.A. *Guidelines for Ethical Behaviour* during the first class of its compulsory introductory course in counselling. As well, a three-hour workshop is provided which includes small group discussion on such issues as `confidentiality' and `danger' to self and others, an opportunity to discuss other guidelines in the C.G.C.A. *Guidelines for Ethical Behaviour* and a chance to examine ethical cases of interest to the students.

Ethics Deemphasized (-)

The counselling program at one Canadian university does not have any course on ethical issues in counselling. Nor is the topic of ethics discussed or presented in any of the other counselling and related courses. Students are encouraged, however, to read the chapter on ethics in their introductory counselling course— "although", says the professor, "it will not be on your final test."

Practicum Experience (-)

A graduate student in a counselling practicum informs her practicum supervisor at the university of some of the practices of the counsellor she is working with in a high school. The male school counsellor at times gives female students back and neck massages in his office. The practicum supervisor does not discuss this with the graduate student and dismisses the issue by saying it is the school's business.

COMMENTS AND QUESTIONS

Stated in the preamble to the C.G.C.A. *Guidelines for Ethical Behaviour* is the following: "The Guidelines for Ethical Behaviour are intended to inspire each member to engage in professional behaviour of the highest order. The basic principles underlying these Guidelines are the respect for the dignity and integrity of persons, responsible caring in counselling relationships, and responsibility to society."

Counsellors must consider carefully basic principles such as the following:

a) telling the truth,

b) generally treating everyone equally,

c) safeguarding the rights of others,

d) keeping promises of confidentiality, and

e) respecting people's rights to make their own decisions.

1. Should all counsellor education programs offer a required course or courses in ethics?

2. What are the best ways of educating students regarding their ethical responsibilities and the standards of the counselling profession?

3. What values would you wish to maximize in any given situation?

4. Can we, or should we, priorize values and principles in ethical decision-making?

8 Preparatory programs must encourage students to value the *ideas of service* to individuals and to society. In this regard, direct financial remuneration or lack thereof must not influence the quality of service rendered. Monetary considerations must not be allowed to overshadow professional and humanitarian needs.

Volunteer Work (+)

Recently, all the counsellor-educators of one faculty met to discuss ways in which they could encourage students to value the "ideas of service" to individuals and the community. As a result of these discussions, the counsellor-educators initiated two major services:

a) Counselling graduate students in their final semester of study voluntarily devoted their time to an educational and career service for undergraduate students in their faculty; and

b) Arranged speakers from several volunteer organizations to talk to graduate students in counselling, encouraging them to devote some time to providing volunteer service in the community.

Counselling the Elderly (+)

One professor has always stressed to counselling students the notion of "helping others" as the cornerstone of counselling. She not only talks about the importance of caring and helping but practices what she talks about. Every week she devotes either one or two evenings to counselling the elderly in a neighbourhood senior citizens' apartment block.

Summer Counselling Courses (-)

Most of the Canadian universities offer summer school counselling courses for the many teachers and counsellors who can attend university during July and August. One Canadian university had a large number of courses, including a counselling techniques course. In this course, students had an opportunity to learn and practice their skills in a laboratory situation. As well, arrangements were made with a high school near the university, allowing counsellors in this counselling techniques course, to counsel any summer high school students who might wish to talk to them. It was expected that the two instructors teaching this course would spend some time after the scheduled laboratory portion of the course, reviewing tapes of interviews with high school students. Both instructors, however, gave little or no time for tape review, but spent most of the time enjoying personal recreational activities.

Counsellor Availability (-)
Modelling to counselling students the value and importance of service is probably one of the best ways to encourage students to value these ideas of service for themselves. In a short-term certificate program in counsellor preparation, one full-time instructor posts no office hours and is seldom available for students. He does not provide students with either his office or home phone number.

COMMENTS AND QUESTIONS
Several of the cases presented here and elsewhere indicate the importance of counsellor-educators modelling "service to others".

A number of questions remain:

1. Can the ideas of service be "taught" in a program?
2. What can be done during the selection process of trainees to assure that service-oriented people enter the counselling program?
3. If ideas of service can be "taught", what are some ways of teaching counsellors responsibility to individuals and society?
4. Should a service component be compulsory for all counselling students?

9 Members responsible for educational programs must be skilled as *teachers and practitioners.*

Improved Teaching (+)
Because of complaints of poor teaching in this department of counselling psychology, the department head invited several professors from different departments (known to be excellent teachers), to offer a series of lectures and demonstrations on 'effective college teaching.'

Counselling Skills (+)
A professor had just been granted a year-long sabbatical leave. In applying for this leave, he had had some difficulty convincing the university administration that he wanted to devote time during this year not only to research and publication, but also to improving his skills as a counselling practitioner. He was convinced that if he improved his counselling skills by becoming involved in counselling others and receiving feedback on his counselling, he would be in a better position to help students in subsequent years when he taught the counselling skills courses.

Out-Dated (-)
A professor in counsellor education regularly teaches an introductory course on the role, function and services of high school counsellors. Since this professor has seldom been in a high school after she left her high school counselling position 20 years ago, she continues to talk about the role and function of counsellors in the sixties and early seventies. All her examples are drawn from what she did in her high school 20 years ago.

Teaching De-valued (-)
In a 1991 study by Stuart Smith's Commission of Inquiry on Canadian University Education, Smith claimed that "the best teacher in the world given a poor or non-existent research record, has little or no chance of promotion at most of the research-intensive universities." On the other hand, Smith added, "a truly terrible teacher" with an excellent research

record will be promoted. Many professors agreed with this report saying that there was no personal payoff to spend time on teaching well. In addition, several professors indicated that in spite of the fact that they had received only fair teaching evaluations, and their university had a service where they could receive help in improving their teaching, they would not take advantage of this service, feeling that the time was better spent on "writing another article."

COMMENTS AND QUESTIONS

Unfortunately, the attitudes of some counsellor-educators are expressed in this last case, where university administrators still favour research over teaching. Nevertheless, it is of vital importance that counsellor-educators not only become competent teachers, but that they are successful practitioners who can demonstrate their counselling skills and can give personal examples of counselling effectiveness. Research/Study leaves for counsellor-educators are readily available in most Canadian universities, but typically counsellor-educators decide, during their leaves, to do research rather than improve their teaching or practitioner skills.

1. What should universities do to encourage better teaching?
2. What recommendations would you make regarding the improvement of the practitioner skills of counsellor-educators?
3. Should counsellor-educators be required to be practitioners as well?
4. When hiring new counsellor-educators, what can the search committees do to ensure that they are getting skilled teachers and practitioners?

10 Members must present thoroughly varied *theoretical positions* so that students may make comparisons and have the opportunity to select a position.

Personal Theory of Counselling (+)

One professor of a counselling theories course briefly stated the purpose of her course as follows: "A study of various approaches to counselling, so that each student will have an opportunity to not only see the philosophical concepts, theoretical bases and techniques of a variety of well-established theories of counselling, but also to examine these counselling models in light of personal values, interests and skills." One of the major assignments of the course was for students to examine those models that especially appealed to them and to write a paper on their personal theory of counselling.

Guest Speakers (+)

In order to give counsellors-in-training a chance to see first hand various counselling approaches, a counsellor-educator invites practitioners, representing a wide variety of counselling positions, to speak about and demonstrate their approach to counselling.

Past Experiences (-)

One counsellor-educator had been a student of one of the leading counselling theorists in the United States. His experiences with this theorist were so negative that he refused to present this well-recognized theory of counselling in any of the counselling theories courses that he taught.

Non-Adlerian (-)

An instructor in a counsellor training program for elementary school counsellors does not include any study of Adlerian counselling. The instructor admits his own limited understanding of the model, but acknowledges to one of his Adlerian colleagues that the Adlerians seem to have made a considerable contribution to both counselling and consultation.

COMMENTS AND QUESTIONS

In the 1960s and 1970s it was common practice for counsellor education departments to indicate that in their training they followed one theoretical position and that they expected counselling students to adhere to this stated theoretical view. Fortunately, this is seldom the case today. Most graduate training programs in counselling encourage students to examine themselves and a wide variety of counselling models in order to integrate their own personality into their own theoretical position and counselling practice.

1. If counsellor-educators at a specific university all agree on one model of training and inform students, is this acceptable?
2. Does "academic freedom" of professors mean they can freely choose the theoretical positions they wish to emphasize?
3. Is the expression "jack of all trades, master of none" relevant to this guideline?
4. Is the trend toward integrative, multi-modal counselling one you endorse?

11 Members must develop clear policies within their educational institutions regarding *field placement* and the roles of the student and the instructor in such placement.

Counselling Internship (+)

It is the practice of one university to offer several counselling internships to doctoral students in the university's counselling centre. A great deal of planning has gone into making this field placement a positive learning experience for the counselling interns. At the beginning of the year a meeting is held with the interns, the counselling director and all the counsellors in the centre. All are made aware of the goals and expectations of the interns. As well, the counsellors are all encouraged to help provide counsellees for the interns and to arrange some discussion time with the interns. A schedule of supervision is also presented at this meeting.

Teamwork Supervision (+)

One counselling practicum supervisor sees the real need for cooperation among the students in training the cooperating counsellors in the field and the university counsellor education department. The supervisor meets with all cooperating counsellors before the field placements are made. Not only does she determine their willingness to supervise student counsellors, but she develops a contract specifying the goals and objectives for the cooperating counsellor and the student in training.

Residence Hall Counsellors (-)

One practicum supervisor arranges for all the doctoral students in his practicum to spend one semester counselling undergraduate students in residence halls. The doctoral students are told to spend five hours a week at the residence hall and attempt to "drum-up some business." No suggestions are given as to how to get potential student clients involved in counselling and no guidelines are given as to interview structure or feedback. Furthermore, the doctoral students are not allowed to tape their interviews.

Supervisory Overload (-)

In 1990, one college counsellor training department doubled its enrolment. Instead of 20 students requiring field placements in counselling, the college now needed 40 counselling sites. Many of the new cooperating counsellors had little idea of what their role and responsibilities were in supervising the student counsellors. Since the two counsellor supervisors from the college were now responsible for supervising twice as many students, they felt they did not have enough time to meet with all the cooperating counsellors beforehand to discuss their roles and responsibilities for supervision.

COMMENTS AND QUESTIONS

As indicated in this guideline, there is a need for college and university counsellor training departments to state clearly the expectations and roles of the counsellors-in-training, the cooperating counsellors in the field and the supervisor from the college or university. Trainees need to know the amount of time or number of clients they must see. Clear instructions on record keeping and taping must be provided. Evaluation criterion should be stated in measurable terms. Also, the amount and type of supervision by the cooperating counsellor and university supervisor must be specified clearly.

1. What should be the role of cooperating counsellors?
2. Should cooperating counsellors assign grades to counsellors-in-training?
3. What should be stated in a field placement policy guide?
4. What should be the supervisor's role in the field?

12 Members must ensure that forms of learning focusing on self-understanding or growth are *voluntary*, or if required as part of the educational program, are made known to prospective students prior to entering the program.

Dealing With Group Pressure (+)

In a counselling practicum class, all the students are required to practice their counselling skills for one day per week at a school or agency. In addition, the students in this class meet for three hours weekly with their practicum instructor to discuss counselling issues, their counselling experiences and their own personal development as counsellors. During one class seven of the eight students in the class had shared some of their personal development as counsellors. There was a silence as the class members waited for the last member to say something. The practicum instructor, sensing the reluctance of this last person to say something at this time, interjected and pointed out that all disclosures were completely voluntary and she did not want anyone to feel any pressure to say something simply because everyone else had. The instructor then introduced a new topic for discussion.

Informing Graduate Student Applicants (+)

At a university in Western Canada, all graduate students, before admission, are provided with detailed brochures and statements from the counsellor education department regarding the expectations and challenges that are part of the training program. These materials contain comments on ethical standards, non-sexist language, involvement in personal growth group experience, and personal counselling expectations.

Group Counselling (-)

Prior to students beginning an advanced group counselling course, they were unaware of the fact that they would be required to become part of a growth group where they would be under both group leader and group member pressure to reveal personal aspects of their lives. Furthermore, they were given a grade for this 'growth group assignment' portion of the course.

Personal Counselling (-)

During their first counselling practicum seminar, students learn for the first time that one requirement of their practicum is for each of them to receive counselling by one of the counsellors at the university counselling centre. No substitute for this "assignment" is allowed.

COMMENTS AND QUESTIONS

It has been my experience that many Canadian universities pay some attention to this guideline, but may not be going far enough. Most universities ask professors for detailed course outlines including teaching approaches, assignments and student expectations. In group counselling courses and practica, students are informed that they will be expected to roleplay clients, they will be asked to disclose personal information, and that they will be part of a personal growth group.

In most Canadian universities, students are not informed of these types of expectations prior to admission, although many, probably most, graduate students welcome the opportunity to be involved in personal counselling and part of a growth group experience.

1. Are students given enough information if they are informed of the need for personal disclosures at the beginning of the course?

2. How legitimate are the personal disclosure activities as part of counsellor training?

3. Will counsellor-educators allow personal growth activities to be voluntary.

4. Should all personal growth activities be voluntary?

❖ ❖ ❖ ❖ ❖ ❖ ❖ ❖ ❖ ❖ ❖ ❖ ❖ ❖

ESSAYS

Ethics and Professional Education in Counselling Psychology

Max R. Uhlemann,
University of Victoria

John C. Gawthrop,
Shoreline Community School Association,
Victoria, B.C.

In response to concerns within the psychology profession and pressures from consumers of psychological services, there has been increased attention to ethics education in graduate programs in recent years (DePalma & Drake, 1956; Newmark & Hutchins, 1981; Pettifor & Pitcher, 1982). The issue has changed from whether to include ethics education in applied programs to how best to teach ethics (Pettifor & Pitcher, 1982).[1]

Despite the growing consensus that theory-based moral reasoning, ethical decision-making models, and values should be the foundation of ethics education for helping professionals (Eberlein, 1987), the gap between theory and practice has been bridged very slowly, as shown by surveys of training programs (DePalma & Drake, 1956; Handelsman, 1986a; Newmark & Hutchins, 1981; Pettifor & Pitcher, 1982; Tymchuk et al., 1979). These surveys revealed how the informal teaching of ethics (in the context of another course or during clinical supervision) has declined and yet persisted at the graduate level of training for counsellors and psychologists. [Canadian graduate schools offering master's and doctoral degrees in psychology were surveyed by Pettifor and Pitcher (1982), and they found that 55% of the programs reported offering formal courses in ethics, while 29% reported offering ethics informally, such as in clinical supervision.] Most recently, [in a study based on a United States sample,] Handelsman (1986a) found that, although 87% of the 289 graduate psychology programs [offering a terminal master's degree in professional psychology] in his survey offered ethics education in some form, [29% had formal courses,] 47% covered ethics as a component of another course, and 11% still dealt

with ethics only through discussions during practicum and internship supervision. Handelsman (1986b) has deplored such [informal training in ethics as] training by "osmosis," arguing that the ability to generalize from one situation to others may not be adequately developed if a general conceptualization of ethical issues is not taught.[2]

The literature on the effect of current ethics education (Haas, Malouf, & Mayerson, 1985, 1986, 1988; Shertzer & Morris, 1972; Tymchuk et al., 1982) indicates wide variability among counsellors and psychologists on how to deal with hypothetical ethical dilemmas. Consensus on how to respond to ethical vignettes varies across studies (all other demographic variables being equal) as a function of whether the ethical issues encountered are of a high- or low-profile nature (Haas et al., 1985, 1986; Tymchuk, 1982). Even practitioners who agree on how to respond still vary widely in their reasons for choosing their responses (Haas et al., 1988).[3] These data are less than reassuring for those seeking psychological services. It appears that the unsystematic nature of much of ethics education is matched only by the unsystematic ethical decision-making processes used by practitioners.

The recent increased emphasis placed on education of counsellors and psychologists in ethics, concern expressed in the literature about lack of rigor in ethics education that still exists, and professionals' apparent weakness in demonstrating consistent ethical decision-making abilities in hypothetical situations have implications for all counsellors and counsellor-educators, especially those who belong to the Canadian Guidance and Counselling Association (CGCA). The revised CGCA *Guidelines for Ethical Behaviour* (1989) include a new section on counsellor preparation standards which includes the following statement: "Members must make students aware of the ETHICAL RESPONSIBILITIES and standards of the profession" (p. 11). For the first time the CGCA code states specifically the responsibility of faculty to educate counsellors-in-training in the application of their code of ethics.

The purpose of this paper is to provide counsellor-educators and counsellors in the field with a summary of the professional literature dealing with ethics education in the areas of evaluation of formal ethics education programs and reports describing models for teaching ethics education. Also, a description is presented of a course on professional issues in counselling psychology with a primary focus on ethics and legal education.

Impact of Formal Ethics Education

The research that has been undertaken on the impact of formal ethics education is an attempt to deal with the lack of clarity on how to educate students in ethics and ethical decision-making. Only four studies are reported in the literature up to 1980 that attempted to assess the effects of a formal learning experience with an ethics component (Baldick, 1980; Granum & Erickson, 1976; Morrison & Teta, 1979; Paradise, 1976). Not until 1991 do other studies (Elliot, 1991; Gawthrop & Uhlemann, 1992) begin to appear in the literature that examine the quality of ethics education.

Utilizing a posttest only, control group design, Paradise (1976) found that master's level counselling students who had participated in small group discussion of general moral dilemmas (experimental condition) scored higher on a test instrument measuring ethical judgement than other counselling students who did not receive the exposure (control condition). The results supported the hypothesis that ethical judgement could be influenced by academic training. The test instrument, the Ethical Judgement Scale (Van Hoose & Paradise, 1979), has since been the focus of considerable debate over validity and reliability (Doromal, 1987; Post, 1989; Welfel & Lipsitz, 1984). However, the Paradise study was a significant contribution to the literature, since it was the first to examine counsellor performance on an ethics-related task based on previous exposure to ethics-related discussion.

Granum and Erickson (1976) presented master's and doctoral level counselling students with a self-paced, seven-hour, independent learning module on confidentiality. A paper-and-pencil test containing 36 case vignettes measured students' retention of confidential information presented in each vignette. Pre- and posttest change scores on the test showed that, compared with a no-treatment control group, subjects studying alone or in pairs became significantly less willing to compromise confidential information. This study contributed to the literature by showing that ethical decision-making can be affected by pertinent instruction.

Morrison and Teta (1979) studied graduate students in nursing, education, and social service work who were enrolled in a course in humanistic psychology. A significant component of the course was discussion of ethical conflicts in the clinical field. One of the self-report instruments used in the study was a questionnaire which presented 20 items describing situations which would cause clinicians to experience some ethical conflict, which would be indicated somewhere on a seven-point scale. Pre-test, posttest and three-month follow-up scores on this instrument showed a significant increase in ethical conflict scores among students. Students had therefore become more aware of ethical issues during the course, and were more sensitive to situations which would present an ethical dilemma.

A survey by Baldick (1980) focused directly on the efficacy of previous formal education in ethics. Clinical psychology interns were sent the Ethical Discrimination Inventory (EDI), an instrument consisting of 12 hypothetical clinical situations containing a variety of hidden ethical issues. Respondents were asked to determine and list, in a two- to five-word phrase, as many ethical issues present in the situations as possible. After returned questionnaires were scored, results showed that subjects who had either received a formal ethics course during their training or at least five hours of ethics discussion (details of which were not provided) were able to discriminate ethical issues better on the EDI and thus scored significantly higher than subjects who had received less or no ethics instruction during training. Exposure to ethics at the graduate level apparently resulted in greater ability to discriminate ethical problems in given situations.

In a pilot study involving a treatment group only, Elliot (1991) reported the pre- to posttest effects of an ethics education module of a course for Masters' students in educational psychology at the University of Alberta on actions in ethical dilemma resolution and level of ethical orientation. Thirty-seven graduates students participated in a three-week module including 15 1/2 hours of class time devoted to increasing awareness of ethical problems and to teaching problem-solving skills to deal with ethical dilemmas. The course focused on a case study and problem-solving approach to ethical, legal and professional issues described by Eberlein (1987; in press). Scores on the Haas Ethical Dilemma Questionnaire (Haas, Malouf, & Mayerson, 1986; 1988) across the two administrations indicated that in four of the ten dilemmas the students' awareness of alternate options and actions appeared to increase. Scores on the Ethical Orientation Checklist, an application of Van Hoose and Paradise's (1979) five stage model of assessing ethical reasoning, indicated that student level of ethical orientation increased significantly on two of the ten ethical dilemmas. These results suggest that the ethics learning component did have an effect on some aspects of the students' ethical orientation.

Gawthrop and Uhlemann (1992) examined the effects of a workshop on ethical decision-making using a case study and problem-solving approach (CPA, 1986; Eberlein, 1987, 1988a; Tymchuk, 1986) to ethics education. The study included three participant conditions composed of undergraduate students randomly assigned from child and youth care, social work and counselling psychology courses. The treatment group received a three-hour ethical decision-making workshop involving discussion of prepared and self-generated case vignettes, and demonstrations of the application of the CGCA *Code of Ethics* (1981) with the Canadian Psychological Association (1986) decision-making model in dealing with the vignettes, and responded to a case vignette containing ethical dilemmas. The informed control group began their workshop by working on the standardized case vignette with the aid of the CGCA (1981) code sections and the CPA (1986) ethical decision-making model. The uninformed control group began their workshop by completing the case vignette unaided by the CGCA (1981) code sections and the CPA (1986) ethical decision-making model, but they were given brief written instructions to indicate in writing what they would do if they were the counsellor

in the vignette and why. Written responses were scored for decision-making quality on the Tymchuk Rating Scale (Tymchuk, Ouslander, Rahber, & Fitten, 1988; Ouslander, Tymchuk, & Rahbar, 1989). The treatment group scored significantly higher than did either of the control groups on decision-making quality; there was no significant difference between the scores of the control groups. These findings suggest that even when it is not possible to devote a full course to ethics education, counsellors can learn content and decision-making skills for improving their response to ethical dilemmas, especially when a well-defined teaching model is used.

In summary, the literature on the impact of formal ethics instruction is surprisingly small, with various methods and subject samples among the few studies that have been undertaken. Most of these studies showed weaknesses, including lack of standardized measurement and frequent failure to clarify the nature of ethics instruction in the independent variable. However, each of these studies contributes to the literature by at least attempting to account for differences in counsellor performance on ethical and moral tasks based on extent of prior academic or non-academic exposure to philosophical material. Some evidence for the efficacy of formal ethics education has been demonstrated, however qualified. Of note are the studies by Elliot (1991) and Gawthrop and Uhlemann (1992) which acknowledge the importance of models in ethics education and the need to assess the efficacy of those models under controlled conditions. The second of these studies is the first in the literature to investigate the efficacy of a specific model in a rigorous experimental context and to clarify the content and process of the model under investigation. That model of ethics education and several others which are found in the literature are examined below.

Models for Teaching Moral Reasoning and Ethics

An early example of an ethics teaching model was a ten-week graduate seminar designed and taught by Abeles (1980). Students were presented with ethical dilemmas and selected readings. During class discussions the students were challenged on their values and beliefs in the process of dealing with the dilemmas. Lack of formal evaluation was a drawback of this course, but there was at least some movement beyond sole reliance on ethical codes as course content.

An unusual approach was introduced by McMinn (1988), who designed a generic case-study simulation program for use with computers. When integrated into McMinn's ethics course, this tool provided students with the opportunity to select from dichotomous responses in each of two case studies, to be presented with results based on their choices, and to repeat the process through a series of text screens toward one of 16 possible case outcomes per case study. After each decision was made, the program requested the reason for the decision. Student responses were accessed afterwards for analysis in class. Following the case outcome, the program evaluated the student's decisions based on ethical guidelines which were written into the software. This software was used as a springboard for discussion on moral issues and ethical decision-making (McMinn, 1988). This unusual contribution to ethics education has so far not been evaluated elsewhere in the literature.

A course designed by McGovern (1988) provided a semester-long examination of numerous issues such as moral behaviour, competence, professional relationships, critical thinking, case studies and values. All topics are structured around APA ethical principles (APA, 1981). The process of the course moved from early attention to information and content toward analysis and philosophical understanding in order to foster increasing complexity in student thinking.

A strength of this course lay in its use of evaluation. Students were subject to pre- and post-course testing and self-evaluation. They were given three essay examinations during the course, and produced five position papers on case studies for critique by instructor and peers. Finally, they provided post-course evaluation of the instructor. A weakness of the course lay in the failure to provide an ethical decision-making tool with which to assist students who, by the final exam, were struggling to reconcile conflicts between their own values, ethical guidelines and societal norms (McGovern, 1988).

Kitchener's (1986) proposed curriculum for ethics education is based on the following four goals: a) sensitizing students to ethical issues in the profession; b) improving ethical reasoning; c) developing moral responsibility and the ego strength to act ethically; and d) teaching tolerance of ambiguity in ethical decision-making. Suggestions for achieving these goals in ethics courses include the following: a) reading and discussion of ethical codes and case vignettes; b) self-generation of ethical cases from experience; c) study of Kitchener's (1984) model for levels of ethical decision-making and ways it can be applied in specific cases; d) generating and justifying ethical decisions about specific cases; e) role playing; and f) utilizing professional resource people in seminars. Although Kitchener's model is theory-based and shows much attention to content and process, no suggestions for evaluation are included.

Eberlein (1987) has described another teaching approach which evolved out of work on the new Canadian Psychological Association *Code of Ethics* (CPA, 1986). This code contains a decision-making model based on work by Tymchuk (1981, 1986). Ethics teaching which uses this approach involves the study of ethical guidelines but includes a consideration of personal values and consultation around case vignettes. In addition, a decision-making model is used to assist in the weighing of alternatives and to foster a move away from simplistic conceptualizations of ethical dilemmas. The decision-making model used in the problem-solving approach (CPA, 1986, 1988; Eberlein, 1987; Tymchuk, 1986) includes a final step calling upon the practitioner to remain accountable during the consequences of a decision.

Eberlein (1987) has used this model in the ethics component of the regular graduate clinical and counselling course at the University of Alberta. Course content and process include the following: a) written statements outlining students' policies with clients on the issues of confidentiality, competence and informed consent; b) preparation and discussion of case dilemmas with use of the CPA code and its ethical decision-making model; and c) a final exam which tests knowledge of the code and its ethical decision-making model. The exam is graded on "the appropriateness of a student's choice of ethical principles and [italics added] on the quality and completeness of the rationale for the decision chosen" (Eberlein, 1987, p. 357). Throughout the course, "critical-evaluative" moral reasoning (Kitchener, 1984) is fostered (Eberlein, 1988a). This course, with its combining of an ethical code and a decision-making model, was the only one of its kind to be reported in the literature.

Another feature of Eberlein's (1987) examination of the current nature of ethics education was noteworthy. Eberlein distinguished between two approaches which seemed to describe most teaching models: the "Correct Answer" approach and the "Problem Solving" approach. The former was characterized by reliance on codified ethical principles and guidelines as providing solutions to ethical problems. The latter also used ethical principles but added consideration of personal values, consultation, the weighing of alternatives and the use of decision-making models in the search for solutions to ethical problems.

More recently, Eberlein (in press) provides the reader with an excellent update and elaboration of his experience in the education of psychologists in ethics and professional conduct. He proposes that ethics education courses consider the following "issues and goals:" a) students must become sensitive to when an ethical problem exists; b) they need to learn to "cope with the anxiety associated with 'moral ambiguity and uncertainty' in ethical dilemmas" (p. 2) where more than one acceptable alternative exists or where no alternative seems desirable; c) they should realize that the "values and moral principles" vary among the codes of ethics of different professional associations and rules of the law and policies of institutions and agencies; d) it is important for students to develop a decision-making procedure that leads to "moral judgement" and to "a 'moral responsibility' to act" (p.3); e) students need to learn about "professional norms" that are included in ethical decision-making that address the professional and business aspects of the profession; and f) the professional needs "to be aware at all times, consultation is impor-

tant when making decisions that can have serious legal or ethical consequences" (p. 3). As well, a listing of professional issues to be covered in a graduate course on professional issues is presented for consideration. Counsellor-educators are encouraged to read this comprehensive and thought-provoking examination of the issues in ethics education.

Fine and Ulrich (1988) reported a fifteen-week formal course in ethics which integrated the perspectives of psychology and philosophy. The course was offered in small-group format to graduate clinical psychology students, and was team taught by two instructors with academic and professional backgrounds in philosophy, counselling and clinical psychology. Based on the ideas of Kitchener (1984), Eberlein (1987), Keith-Spiegel and Koocher (1985), and others, the course included didactic instruction, case presentations, discussion and student presentation of cases. Course evaluation included a mid-term exam, a written case presentation to the class by each student, and a thorough written case analysis from each student's own clinical experience. A three-month follow-up was conducted with former students who were working in clinical settings. Returned questionnaires showed that students still perceived the course as having had a strong impact on them. The authors recommended clinical supervision in practicum settings as a future part of an ethics course, as well as more attention to process in ethical decision-making.

In summary, the courses and curricula presented in this section indicate that the formalization of ethics education has increased in recent years. They show that the underlying rationale for content and process of ethics instruction has been considered, articulated and incorporated into classroom instruction. There has also been progress made in the area of formal evaluation, in keeping with the assumption that ethics is an academic subject requiring normal evaluation procedures like other subjects.

A Course on Professional Issues In Counselling Psychology

The first author has had the opportunity to teach a graduate course on professional issues in counselling psychology for a number of years, first at the University of Western Ontario and more recently at the University of Victoria. Through the years, the author's thinking on the teaching of professional issues has been particularly influenced by the work of several writers. One of the writers, Tymchuk (1981, 1982, 1986), was among the earliest writers to discuss ethical decision-making in values issues. Corey, Corey and Callanan (1979) wrote one of the earliest texts in the area of ethics education. The textbook is comprehensive and challenging in its examination of counsellor and client issues. This text, which is now in its fourth edition (Corey, Corey, & Callanan, 1993), is the one I have used as the basic reading in my course since I discovered it. Also, the work of Eberlein (1987, 1988a, 1988b, in press) enunciates the importance of education in values and moral reasoning in ethics education and stresses the importance of teaching students how to deal effectively with ethical dilemmas in professional pracitice. Out of the work of these writers and others, the first author presents in Table 1 the 11 content areas covered last year in his course on professional issues in counselling psychology with students at the master's and doctoral level.

The content of the course includes an examination of professional, ethical, and legal issues relevant to counselling psychology (Uhlemann, 1992). It is proposed that a trained counsellor must be well-versed with the many issues involved in working with clients in a helping interaction, being a member of a helping agency or institution, being in private practice, or responding to societal and professional organization expectations. As well, the helping professional must be aware of his/her personal beliefs, values, biases, and moral structure when in the helping role. The primary purpose of the course is to identify professional issues and to study their impact on the student as a professional in training. Emphasis is given to learning through the use of case studies and the decision-making approach found originally in the CPA (1986, 1991) *Code of Ethics* and now also present in the CGCA (1989) *Guidelines.*

The format of the course is a series of 13 weekly three-hour seminars. The instructor

---

TABLE 1

Content Areas for A Course on Professional Issues in Counselling Psychology

---

Class 1. History of ethics education, what is a code of ethics and its key components, need for a decision-making model, and clients' rights.

Class 2. Conditions that lead to ethical dilemmas, ideal conditions for decision-making, who violates ethical sanctions, preventive actions for making ethical decisions under pressure.

Class 3. Malpractice, negligence law, civil and criminal issues, reasonable standard of care.

Class 4. Counsellor's roles as a person and professional, self-awareness, transference and counter transference, stress and burnout.

Class 5. Values and value conflicts in life style and philosophy.

Class 6. Competence, licensure, training, supervision, and continuing education.

Class 7. Components of informed consent in counselling and research; records.

Class 8. Privacy, privilege, confidentiality, duty to warn and protect.

Class 9. Dual role relationships with clients, students, colleagues, agencies, and institutions.

Class 10. Gender issues in counselling.

Class 11. Ethical issues in couple and family counselling.

---

conducts the first four seminars to build a basis of knowledge and process to be used by students throughout the course. Teams of two or three students take responsibility for subsequent class sessions in which they are to study widely in the topic areas to be covered during the class of their responsibility, select addi-

TABLE 2

Resources on Ethics and Legal Issues in Counselling Psychology

1. Ethics in the Practice of Psychology by Carroll, Schneider & Wesley, (Prentice-Hall), 1985.

2. Keeping Up the Good Work: A Practitioner's Guide to Mental Health Ethics by Haas & Malouf (Professional Resource Exchange), 1989.

3. Dual Relationships in Counseling by Herlihy & Corey, (Association for Counseling and Development), 1992.

4. Ethical Standards Casebook by Herlihy & Golden (Association for Counseling and Development), 1990.

5. Ethical & Legal Issues in School Counseling by Huey & Remly (American School Counselor Association), 1988.

6. Ethics in Psychology: Professional Standards and Cases by Keith-Spiegel & Koocher (Random House), 1985.

9. Children, Ethics and the Law by Koocher & Keith-Spiegel (University of Nebraska Press), 1990.

10. Ethics in Psychotherapy and Counseling: A Practical Guide for Psychologists by Pope & Vasquez (Jossey-Bass), 1991.

11. A Legal Handbook for the Helping Professional by Turner & Uhlemann (Sedgewick Society for Consumer and Public Education), 1991.

12. Canadian Code of Ethics for Psychologists: Companion Manual(Rev. ed.). (Canadian Psychological Association), 1992.

tional readings for the class to study and conduct a two-hour workshop which educates the class through planned didactic, experiential and discussion activities in the areas of focus for the seminar. The remaining hour of each class is devoted to class members working through a case dilemma related to the topic of

study for the week. Evaluation in the course is based on the quality of seminars presented and a final, take home examination which involves applying a form of the decision-making process found in the CGCA and CPA codes of ethics taught during the course to dilemmas collected from colleagues and developed by the instructor.

Ten years ago the number of resources available for teaching such a course was relatively small compared to today. In recent years an increasing number of texts and other resources have become available to inform the student and the practising professionals on the range of professional issues that face practitioners in their daily client contacts. Presented in Table 2 is a short list of some of the most useful resources in the literature.

The counselling program at the University of Victoria has been fortunate to be able to include a separate course on professional issues with the entire focus on ethical and legal issues in the practice of counselling psychology. This outline of course content and resources is presented only as an example for others to expand upon and develop to meet their needs. The number and range of professional issues to be covered in such a course are obviously extensive and variable depending on the interests of the instructor, the graduate program, and the students. (In the first author's course, for example, two or three seminar topics are usually selected in consultation with the students.) As well, the range of quality resource material is much more extensive than can be listed here, so the reader is encouraged to go beyond the list presented in Table 2. These topics and resources can be adapted for use in formats other than an independent course, such as a designated segment of a larger course or as a series of professional development sessions in the applied settings.

Conclusion

Expectations mount from within the counselling profession and from the outside through increased consumer advocacy for professional accountability in counselling practice. One of the most important areas that the counsellor-educator and practitioner can be proactive in responding to these demands is in the area of increased knowledge and skill in dealing with the daily ethical dilemmas that counsellors encounter. The time for learning ethical descision-making by "osmosis" (Handelsman (1986b) is quickly becoming a part of the past. The literature provides the counsellor-educator and the counsellor in the field with the rationale, teaching models, and content material for developing sensitive and informed decision-making ability in the complex world of professional issues. It is hoped that the content of this paper will assist counsellors to further their thinking in this area and encourage them to further refine academic and professional development curricula in the area.

References

Abeles, N. (1980). Teaching ethical principles by means of value confrontations. *Psychotherapy: Theory, Research and Practice, 17*(4), 384-391.

American Psychological Association (1981). Ethical principles of psychologists. *American Psychologist, 36,* 633-638.

American Psychological Association, Ethics Committee. (1988). Trends in ethics cases, common pitfalls, and published resources. *American Psychologist, 43*(7), 564-572.

Baldick, T. (1980). Ethical discrimination ability of intern psychologists: A function of training in ethics. *Professional Psychology, 11,* 276-282.

Bernard, J., & Jara, C. (1986). The failure of clinical psychology graduate students to apply understood ethical principles. *Professional Psychology: Research and Practice, 17*(4), 313-315.

Canadian Guidance and Counselling Association, (1981). *Guidelines for Ethical Behaviour.* Ottawa, Ontario: Author.

Canadian Guidance and Counselling Association (1989). *Guidelines for Ethical Behaviour* (Rev. ed.). Ottawa, Ontario: Author.

Canadian Psychological Association, Committee on Ethics. (1986). Code of Ethics. *Highlights, 8*(1), 6E-12E.

Canadian Psychological Association (1991). *Canadian Code of Ethics for Psychologists* (Rev. ed.). Old Chelsea, Quebec: Author.

Canadian Psychological Association, Committee on Ethics (1988). *Canadian Code of Ethics for Psychologists: Companion Manual.* Old Chelsea, Quebec: Author.

Canadian Psychological Association (1992). *Canadian Code of Ethics for Psychologists: Companion Manual* (2nd ed.). Old Chelsea, Quebec: Author.

Corey, G., Corey, M.S., & Callanan, P. (1979). *Issues and ethics in the helping professions.* Pacific Grove, Calif: Brooks/Cole.

Corey, G., Corey, M. S., & Callanan, P. (1993). *Issues and ethics in the helping professions.* Pacific Grove, Calif.: Brooks/Cole.

DePalma, N., & Drake, R. (1956). Professional ethics for graduate students in psychology. *American Psychologist, 11,* 554-557.

Doromal, Q. S. (1987). An evaluation of selected psychometric characteristics of the Ethical Judgement Scale (Doctoral dissertation, Virginia Polytechnic Institute and State University, 1986). *Dissertation Abstracts International, 47*(7), 2456A.

Eberlein, L. (1987). Introducing ethics to beginning psychologists: A problem solving approach. *Professional Psychology: Research and Practice, 18*(4), 353-359.

Eberlein, L. (1988a). The new CPA code of ethics for Canadian psychologists: An education and training perspective. *Canadian Psychology, 29*(2), 206-212.

Eberlein, L. (1988b). The use of the Ethical Judgement Scale for ethics education. *Canadian Journal of Counselling, 22,* 242-245.

Eberlein, L. (in press). The eduction of psychologists in ethical and professional conduct. In Dobson, K. S., & Dobson, D. J. (Eds.), *The practice of psychology* in Canada. Toronto: Hogrefe & Huber.

Elliot, M. M. (1991). *Ethical decision making and judgements of psychologists: An exploratory study.* Unpublished doctoral dissertation, University of Alberta, Edmonton.

Fine, M., & Ulrich, L. (1988). Integrating psychology and philosophy in teaching a graduate course in ethics. *Professional Psychology: Research and Practice, 19*(5), 542-546.

Gawthrop, J., & Uhlemann, M. (1992). Effects of the problem-solving approach in ethics training. *Professional Psychology: Research and Practice, 23,* (1), 38-42.

Granum, R., & Erickson, R. (1976). How a learning module can affect confidential decision making. *Counselor Education and Supervision, 15*(4), 276-284.

Haas, L., & Malouf, J. (1989). *Keeping up the good work: A practitioner's guide to mental health ethics.* Sarasota, FL: Professional Resource Exchange, Inc.

Haas, L., Malouf, J., & Mayerson, N. (1985, August). *Ethics training and professional characteristics of practicing psychologists: Are they related to ethical decision making?* Paper presented at the annual convention of the American Psychological Association, Los Angeles, CA.

Haas, L., Malouf, J., & Mayerson, N. (1986). Ethical dilemmas in psychological practice: Results of a national survey. *Professional Psychology: Research and Practice, 17*(4), 316-321.

Haas, L., Malouf, J., & Mayerson, N. (1988). Personal and professional characteristics as factors in psychologists' ethical decision making. *Professional Psychology: Research and Practice, 19*(1), 35-42.

Handelsman, M. (1986a). Ethics training at the master's level: A national survey. *Professional Psychology: Research and Practice, 17*, 24-26.

Handelsman, M. (1986b). Problems with ethics training by "osmosis". *Professional Psychology: Research and Practice, 17*(4), 371-372.

Keith-Spiegel, P., & Koocher, G. P. (1985). *Ethics in Psychology: Professional standards and cases.* New York: Random House.

Kitchener, K. (1984). Intuition, critical evaluation and ethical principles: the foundation for ethical decisions in counseling psychology. *Counseling Psychologist, 12*(3), 43-55.

Kitchener, K. (1986). Teaching Applied Ethics in Counselor Education: An Integration of Psychological Processes and Philosophical Analysis. *Journal of Counseling and Development, 64*(5), 306-310.

McGovern, T. (1988). Teaching the ethical principles of psychology. *Teaching of Psychology, 15*(1), 22-26.

McMinn, M. (1988). Ethics case-study simulation: a generic tool for psychology teachers. *Teaching of Psychology, 15*(2), 100-101.

Morrison, J., & Teta, D. (1979). Impact of a humanistic approach on students' attitudes, attributions, and ethical conflicts. *Psychological Reports, 45*, 863-866.

Newmark, C., & Hutchins, T. (1981). Survey of professional education in ethics in clinical psychology internship programs. *Journal of Clinical Psychology, 37*(3), 681-683.

Ouslander, J., Tymchuk, A., & Rahbar, B. (1989). Health care decisions among elderly long-term care residents and their potential proxies. *Archives of Internal Medicine, 149*(June), 1367-1372.

Paradise, L. (1976). Towards a theory on the ethical behaviour of counselors (Doctoral dissertation, University of Virginia). *Dissertation Abstracts International,* 1977, *37,* 4140A-4141A. (University Microfilms No. 77-204)

Pettifor, J., & Pitcher, S. (1982). Ethics training in canadian graduate schools of psychology. *Canadian Psychology, 23*(4), 235-242.

Post, P. (1989). The use of the Ethical Judgement Scale in counselor education. *Counselor Education and supervision, 28*(3), 229-233.

Shertzer, B., & Morris, K. (1972). APGA members' ethical discriminatory ability. *Counselor Education and Supervision, 11*(3), 200-206.

Tennyson, W., & Strom, S. (1986). Beyond professional standards: Developing responsibleness. *Journal of Counseling and Development, 64*(5), 298-302. (used in Appendix G)

Tymchuk, A. (1981). Ethical decision making and psychological treatment. *Journal of Psychiatric Treatment and Evaluation, 3*, 507-513.

Tymchuk, A. (1982). Strategies for resolving value dilemmas. *American Behavioral Scientist, 26*(2), 159-175.

Tymchuk, A. (1985a). *Effective decision making for the developmentally disabled.* Portland, OR: Ednick Communications.

Tymchuk, A. (1985b). Ethical decision making and psychology students' attitudes toward training in ethics. *Professional Practice of Psychology, 6*(2), 219-232.

Tymchuk, A. (1986). Guidelines for ethical decision making. *Canadian Psychology, 27*(1), 36-43.

Tymchuk, A., Andron, L., & Rahbar, B. (1988a). Effective decision making/problem solving training with mothers who have mental retardation. *American Journal on Mental Retardation, 92*(6), 510-516.

Tymchuk, A., Drapkin, R., Ackerman, A., Major, S., Coffman, E., & Baum, M. (1979). Survey of training in ethics in APA-approved clinical psychology programs. *American Psychologist, 34*, 1168-1170.

Tymchuk, A., Drapkin, R., Major-Lingsley, S., Ackerman, A., Coffman, E., & Baum, M. (1982). Ethical decision making and psychologists' attitudes toward training in ethics. *Professional Psychology, 13*(3), 412-421.

Tymchuk, A., Ouslander, J., Rahbar, B., & Fitten, J. (1988). Medical decision making among elderly people in long term care. *The Gerontologist, 28*(Suppl.), 59-63.

Uhlemann, M. (1992). Course outline for ED-D 519C Professional Issues in Counselling Psychology. Victoria: University of Victoria.Van Hoose, W., & Paradise, L. (1979). *Ethics in counseling and psychotherapy.* Cranston, R. I.: Carroll Press.

Welfel, E., & Lipsitz, N. (1984). The ethical behaviour of psychologists: A critical analysis of the research. *The Counseling Psychologist, 12*(3), 31-42.

Footnotes

[1] From "Effects of the Problem-Solving Approach in Ethics Training"
by J. C. Gawthrop and M. R. Uhlemann, 1992, *Professional Psychology: Research and Practice, 23*, 38-42.

[2] From "Effects of the Problem-Solving Approach in Ethics Training"
by J. C. Gawthrop and M. R. Uhlemann, 1992, *Professional Psychology: Research and Practice, 23*, 38-42.

[3] From "Effects of the Problem-Solving Approach in Ethics Training"
by J.C. Gawthrop and M. R. Uhlemann, 1992, *Professional Psychology: Research and Practice, 23*, 38-42.

Teaching Ethics: Linking Abstract Principles to Actual Practice

Beth E. Haverkamp
University of British Columbia

When a counselling student encounters an ethical dilemma, supervisors will often refer him or her to a set of ethical standards. The student, however, often returns with the lament "...but it doesn't tell me what to *DO!*" Paradoxically, that frustrating realization is the beginning of ethical awareness because learning about ethics means learning how to deal with ambiguity, how to discern underlying principles in a complex situation. Experienced practitioners know that even well intentioned efforts to follow ethical codes do not insure ethical consequences, and that one's actions can benefit one client yet introduce the risk of harm to others.

The goal of ethics instruction is to help trainees develop an ethical stance toward counselling which they will carry into their professional lives. Kitchener's (1986) listing of the goals of ethics training captures the expectations we have for ourselves and our students: to create sensitivity to ethical issues and to the implications of our actions, to acquire the ability to reason about ethical dilemmas, to promote moral responsibility and an innate determination to act in an ethical manner, and to acquire a tolerance for the ambiguity inherent in ethical reasoning.

The developers of the *Guidelines for Ethical Behavior* (CGCA, 1989) have recognized this complexity and have provided a useful tool to guide counsellors in handling ethical dilemmas. The section of the *Guidelines* on "Resolving Ethical Conflicts" is a valuable resource for both beginners and experienced professionals. Its practical guidelines for decision-making can effectively promote the awareness and reasoning ability that Kitchener has identified as important. The purpose of this essay is to offer additional suggestions for the counsellor-educator who is engaged in the teaching of ethics.

As Schmidt and Meara (1984) note, "Trust in the professional is the foundation of therapeutic relationships" (p. 59). Our counselling trainees readily understand that developing trust and rapport with a client is essential to effective counselling. One of the goals of teaching ethics is to help the trainee understand how the *Guidelines for Ethical Behavior* provide a framework of conduct within which trust can be established. The *Guidelines* are not just a series of "rules" which the profession has imposed; their effective implementation depends on the individual counsellor understanding the link between the guidelines and the client's ability to trust. How to promote this understanding is the challenge facing the counsellor-educator.

It is my belief that the preparation of ethical counsellors requires specific course work or seminars on this subject. Handelsman (1986) reports that only 27% of terminal master's programs in psychology offer a formal, separate course in ethics, while a significant number incorporate the teaching of ethics within practicum or clinic settings. While the latter approach has the advantage of demonstrating real-life application of the issues, it is difficult to be comprehensive. Material on ethical issues in research, in consultation or teaching may not be covered. Finally, some supervisors are unwilling to point out ethical issues which arise in the context of supervision they are currently conducting.

The discussion that follows outlines suggestions for teaching ethics and covers both recommended content areas and ideas for experiential learning. Just as the skill of establishing rapport requires that the trainee both acquire knowledge about the dynamics of a counselling relationship and then have opportunities to practice applying this knowledge, ethical conduct has both knowledge and application components. Each program will undoubtedly need to make revisions to meet the needs of its students and the settings in which they are most likely to practice, but these suggestions may provide a starting point for your own creative approaches to teaching in this important area.

Content areas:

Kitchener (1984) has made the point that our individual, intuitive sense about ethical and moral questions is an important part of ethical reasoning, but is inadequate on its own. She draws on contemporary ethicists (Beauchamp & Childress, 1979) in noting that a "critical-evaluative" level of moral reasoning is needed to direct and refine our informal judgments. The critical-evaluative level is composed of three increasingly abstract domains which we can use in evaluating ethical decisions: rules and professional codes; general ethical principles; and abstract ethical theory.

While a thorough discussion of Kitchener's (1984) thoughtful contribution is beyond the scope of this essay, the first two levels of her model are immediately applicable to teaching ethics. The first of these, our professional codes, represent a consensus among counsellors about those behaviors which characterize ethical practice. Second are the more general principles which ethicists have identified as useful standards for decision-making in ambiguous circumstances.

Our professional code, the *Guidelines for Ethical Behavior*, is important in directing counsellors to take certain actions and avoid others, and also provides a basis for reprimands to members whose behavior transgresses these standards. The *Guidelines* are likely to be consistent with most trainees' intuitive ethical sense, but this does not substitute for the necessity of learning the explicit content of the code. The ethical requirement of confidentiality (Guideline B-2) surprises few trainees, but the requirement to consider a client's financial status in setting fees (Guideline A-5) is less apparent to some. Formal instruction which covers the complete content of the *Guidelines* also increases the likelihood that issues which rarely arise during training will not be overlooked. For example, advertising one's services (Guideline D-5) is of limited relevance for students, but becomes important when entering private practice.

The *Guidelines* are the first resource to consult when faced with ethical dilemmas, but many writers have noted that ethical codes often provide ambiguous and contradictory direction. Kitchener (1984) recommends that counsellors become familiar with broader, more general ethical principles as a means of deciding which elements of an ethical code take precedence in a given situation. For example, a number of ethicists (Beauchamp & Childress, 1979; Kitchener, 1984) contend that the concept of nonmaleficence ("above all, do no harm") generally overrides the mandate to promote client welfare, or "do good". Kitchener (1984) and Thompson (1990) provide useful overviews of core ethical principles which are relevant to counselling. Similarly, the *Guidelines for Ethical Behavior* includes a series of questions and listing of principles (e.g., telling the truth; keeping promises) and suggests that counsellors ask themselves which principles are paramount in a given situation.

Classroom use of these resources and others are effective ways to introduce students to the specifics of the *Guidelines* and to broader principles which can underly development of more sophisticated ethical reasoning. However, the ambiguity and complexity of the subject area makes it unlikely that students will benefit from simply reading a list of mandates or principles. It is necessary to consider how the *Guidelines* apply in various situations and to illustrate the links between the guidelines and more general principles. For example, "Promoting client welfare" (Guideline B-1) can become ambiguous when dealing with two members of a couple in marital counselling; whose welfare is promoted? The concept of safeguarding psychological tests (Guideline C-9) becomes more meaningful when students consider that "coaching" or otherwise breaching test security will result in clients receiving false information about themselves, in contradiction of several guidelines and the general principle of truthfulness.

Table 1 presents a suggested topical outlines for a course or series of seminars on ethics is counselling. The outline is an alternative way of presenting the *Guidelines* and can provide a first step in linking them to specific elements of practice. The learning experiences described in the next section can provide additional links between the *Guidelines* and real life, and can help students develop and internalize their own mode of ethical decision-making.

TABLE 1

Suggested topical outline for a course on ethics in counselling

1. Understanding the role of ethical standards
   a) distinctions between ethical, legal, and moral guidelines
   b) metaethical principles (autonomy, fidelity, justice, beneficence, nonmaleficence).
   c) characteristics of violators (i.e. unaware, impaired)

2. Confidentiality and privacy
   a) distinctions between confidentiality, privacy, privilege
   b) legal issues and limits to confidentiality (i.e. duty to warn, mandated reporting requirements; court subpoenas)
   c) release of information

3. Counselling practice and client welfare
   a) the therapeutic contract and informed consent
   b) evaluating the ethics of specific interventions
   c) clients who are not benefitting; timely termination
   d) burnout and self-care as ethical issues

4. Competence
   a) training issues
   b) recognizing the need to refer
   c) ongoing professional development

5. Dual relationships
   a) sexual boundaries: ethical prohibitions; dealing with sexual feelings; seeking consultation
   b) non-sexual boundaries: teacher/student; friendship; the difficulties of working in rural areas or small communities

6. Business issues
   a) record keeping: retention and disposal
   b) fees, advertising and billing
   c) informed consent re: releasing information to third parties

7. Relationships with colleagues
   a) consultation
   b) making referrals
   c) informal peer monitoring and ethical violations by colleagues

8. Special settings and populations
   a) group and family counselling
   b) issues unique to schools, businesses, or residential treatment
   d) stereotyping and discrimination

9. Supervision and teaching
   a) dual relationships
   b) counsellor preparation standards
   c) responsibilities of teachers (i.e. methods, student evaluation)

10. Scholarship
    a) research methods
    b) research participants
    c) authorship (i.e., joint authorship; plagiarism)

11. Testing
    a) selection, administration and interpretation of tests
    b) test security
    c) computerized testing

12. Ethical review committees
    a) common complaints
    b) grievance procedures
    c) assisting clients with a grievance

Structured Learning Experiences

As noted above, an understanding of ethics rests on both a knowledge base that has been assembled by professionals in the field and on experiential learning, which provides opportunities to debate and reflect upon the subtleties of ethical decision-making. A series of activities which have proved useful in generating discussion and self reflection among counselling trainees are described below.

1. Discussion of ethical vignettes

Vignettes describing actual or hypothetical situations that present ethical dilemmas can provide vivid, memorable examples of the guidelines. Feedback from students indicates that discussion of case vignettes can be an effective way to teach decision-making skills (Corey, Corey & Callahan, 1988). Hypothetical situations may be most useful with beginning students, as they can be written to provide clear illustrations of a single guideline, whereas actual situations (with names and other identifying information altered or deleted) can stimulate discussion of the complexity that exists in many ethical decisions. The American Association for Counseling and Development (AACD, 1982) and the American Psychological Association (APA, 1987) have published ethics casebooks which describe cases that have been adjudicated by these organizations' ethical review committees. Both the case and the outcome of the adjudication, and the rationale underlying the decision, are described.

2. Interviews of professionals in varied practice settings

Professional organizations try to write guidelines that will be applicable to members who practice in different settings. However, it is instructive for students to learn about the unique ethical dilemmas and legal requirements that various practitioners regularly encounter. A useful exercise is to ask students to interview practitioners in a variety of settings, asking what ethical issues they encounter most frequently, or how different principles (e.g., confidentially, dual relationships) are most likely to emerge in their setting.

Students who have participated in this exercise have found, for example, that school counsellors are more likely than career counsellors to wrestle with administrative requests for private client information. Counsellors working in small towns or rural areas face special challenges in the areas of dual relationships, as when one's dentist comes in for couple's counselling. Marriage and family counsellors face dilemmas in promoting client welfare when the needs or goals of individual family members are contradictory. The value of this exercise for students is the opportunity to see that an ethical principle such as "confidentiality" or "competence" can carry different nuances in different settings.

3. Program review and development

A program development exercise that has been used effectively, is for an ethics class, at the program's request, to become involved in some aspect of the program's current policies and procedures for ethical grievances. The activity can take the form of reviewing current policies and procedures to determine if they conform to the CGCA guidelines. Or, if no written policy currently exists, the class may be asked to make suggestions for a draft policy. Alternatively, the class could take on responsibility for preparing an information sheet for students that outlines student rights and procedures for filing a grievance, or be given responsibility for conducting a workshop on these issues during new student orientation. If the department currently has a faculty ethics committee, the students' interaction with this group can be invigorating for both.

4. Client Rights and Responsibilities

An effective way of helping a class understand the ethical issues that surround informed consent and confidentiality is to assign development of a handout on "Client Rights and Responsibilities." The class, or small groups, work together to produce a document that a practitioner could hand to all clients who come to him or her for counselling.

One university counselling centre (Univ. of Minnesota, 1984) uses a similar document, and listed client rights such as "You have a right to be treated with respect and consideration," "You have a right to see a second counsellor if you wish to obtain an additional opinion or believe you would work better with another person." Client responsibilities described the role the client was expected to play to contribute to successful counselling (e.g., asking questions when the experience is not clear, keeping appointments). The section on confidentiality spells out how confidentiality is assured, its limits, and the procedures for retention and elimination of records.

A variation on this assignment that will accomplish many of the same objectives would be to ask students to compile a list of questions that clients have a right to ask counsellors. Handelsman and Galvin (1988) have developed a client handout titled "Information you have a right to know," which presents a comprehensive series of questions that clients might want to ask their counsellors (e.g., "What should I do if I feel therapy isn't working?" "Do I need to pay for missed sessions?"). While the Handelsman and Galvin (1988) model would be useful for the instructor to consult, the primary value of the exercise for students derives from identifying, debating and writing the questions themselves.

Conclusion

As Mark Twain once said, "To be good is noble, but to teach others to be good is nobler — and less trouble." While Twain's humor will bring a smile to many faces, the counsellor familiar with social learning theory will also recall that modelling is one of the most potent forms of learning. It seems appropriate, therefore, to end a discussion of teaching ethics with a reminder that as educators, our most potent form of instruction is the model that we, our programs and curricula provide for our students. Ethical dilemmas abound as soon as one moves away from the textbook and into relationships with others, whether as client, supervisee or colleague. Allowing our students to see how we grapple with these issues, and to learn from each other as we resolve them, will surely contribute to the trust our clients have in our profession.

Resources for teaching ethics

Corey, G., Gorey, M.S. & Callahan, P. (1988). *Issues and ethics in the helping professions* (3rd ed.). Pacific Grove, CA: Brooks-Cole.

Keith-Spiegel, P. & Koocher, G.P. (1985). *Ethics in psychology: Professional standards and cases*. Hillsdale, NJ: Erlbaum.

Koocher, G.P (Ed.) (1991). *Ethics & behavior*. Hillsdale, NJ: Erlbaum.

Thompson, A. (1990). *Guide to ethical practice in psychotherapy*. New York: Wiley and Sons.

References

American Association for Counseling and Development (AACD). (1982). *Ethical standards casebook*. Alexandria, VA: Author.

American Psychological Association (APA). (1987). *Casebook on ethical principles of psychologists*. Washington, DC: Author.

Beauchamp, T.L. & Childress, J.G. (1979). *Principles of biomedical ethics*. Oxford: Oxford University Press.

Canadian Guidance and Counselling Association (CGCA) (1981, 1989). *Guidelines for ethical behavior*. Ottawa: Author.

Corey, G., Corey, M.S. & Callahan, P. (1988). *Issues and ethics in the helping professions*. (3rd ed.). Pacific Grove, CA: Brooks-Cole.

Handelsman, M.M. (1986). Ethics training at the master's level: A national survey. *Professional Psychology: Research and Practice, 17*, 24-26.

Handelsman, M.M. & Galvin, M.D. (1988). Facilitating informed consent for outpatient psychotherapy: A suggested written format. *Professional Psychology: Research and Practice, 19*, 223-225.

Kitchener, K.S. (1984). Intuition, critical evaluation and ethical principles: The foundation for ethical decisions in counseling psychology. *The Counseling Psychologist, 12*, 43-55.

Kitchener, K.S. (1986). Teaching Applied Ethics in Counselor Education: An Integration of Psychological Processes and Philosophical Analysis. *Journal of Counseling and Development, 64*, 306-310.

Schmidt, L.D. & Meara, N.M. (1984). Ethical, professional and legal issues in counseling psychology. In S.D. Brown & R.W. Lent (Eds.), *Handbook of counseling psychology*. NY: Wiley & Sons.

University of Minnesota Student Counseling Bureau (1984). *Handout on client and counselor rights and responsibilities*. Unpublished document. Minneapolis: Office of Student Affairs, Univ. of Minnesota.

Appendices

❖ ❖ ❖ ❖ ❖ ❖ ❖ ❖ ❖ ❖ ❖ ❖ ❖

APPENDIX A

Standards For The Clinical Practice Of Mental Health Counseling

American Mental Health Counselors Association

A. Standards of the Profession

Mental health counselors who deliver clinical services shall comply with established standards of the profession.

COMMENT: National standards for the clinical practice of mental health counseling require the counselor to have a minimum of a master's degree and a total of 60 graduate semester hours consisting of a 48-hour core curriculum, with 12 hours in mental health counseling; clinical counseling practicum; and clinical counseling internship.

Mental health counselors who deliver clinical services must document a minimum of 3,000 hours of supervised post-graduate clinical experience over at least a two-year period including a minimum of 200 hours of face-to-face supervision. Clinical experience is defined as the direct delivery of counseling to clients as clients, involving the presence of a diagnosed mental disorder as defined by the current edition of the *Diagnostic and Statistical Manual*, or *International Classification of Diseases, Clinical Modification*.

In addition, they must adhere to ethical standards established by the profession, submit an acceptable clinical work sample, pass the national clinical mental health counselor examination, adhere to the profession's standards for clinical practice, and where available, be licensed by the state licensing board at the clinical level of practice.

B. Statutory Regulations

Mental health counselors who deliver clinical services shall comply with local statutory regulations which govern the practice of clinical mental health counseling.

COMMENT: Mental health counselors who deliver clinical services must be aware of and adhere to all state laws governing the practice of clinical mental health counseling. In addition, they must be aware of and adhere to all administrative rules and regulations, ethical standards, and other requirements of state clinical mental health counseling or related regulatory boards. Counselors must obtain competent legal advice concerning interpretation of and compliance with all relevant statutes and regulations.

In the absence of state laws governing the practice of counseling, mental health counselors who wish to deliver clinical services must adhere strictly to the American Mental Health Counselors Association's *Standards for the Clinical Practice of Mental Health Counseling*. Counselors must obtain competent legal advice concerning interpretation of and compliance with these standards.

C. Codes of Ethics

Mental health counselors who deliver clinical services shall comply with the established codes of ethics for the specific practice of clinical mental health counseling.

COMMENT: Mental health counselors who deliver clinical services are responsible first to society, second to consumers, third to the profession, and last, to themselves. Clinical mental health counselors identify themselves as members of the counseling profession. They must adhere to the codes of ethics of the American Counseling Association, American Mental Health Counselors Association, the Clinical Mental Health Academy of the National Board of Certified Counselors. They also must adhere to ethical standards endorsed by state boards regulating counseling, and cooperate fully with the adjudication procedures of ethics committees, peer review teams, and appropriate state boards.

All clinical mental health counselors must willingly participate in a formal review of their clinical work, as needed. They will provide to clients appropriate information on filing complaints alleging unethical behavior.

D. Continuing Education

Mental health counselors who deliver clinical services shall have and maintain a repertoire of specialized counseling skills and participate in a continuing education program to enhance specialized knowledge of the practice of clinical mental health counseling.

COMMENT: Mental health counselors who deliver clinical services must have knowledge of human behavior necessary for effective diagnosis and treatment of individuals, families, and groups. Competencies in the following areas are necessary:

- **Counseling theory**, including counseling processes, theories of psychotherapy and counseling, and marriage and family counseling;
- **Human growth and development**, including human development through the life span, theories of personality development, and abnormal psychology;
- **Social and cultural foundations**, including multicultural issues and trends, social and cultural foundations of mental health counseling, human sexuality, sociology and anthropology;
- **Helping relationships**, including counseling techniques, and consultation skills and procedures;
- **Groups**, including applied group dynamics, group processes, and group counseling;
- **Lifestyle and career development**, including facilitating career development, lifespan career development, and informational services;
- **Appraisal**, including testing and assessment, appraisal techniques, assessment techniques, and psychological assessment;
- **Research and evaluation**, including research methodology, outcome research, intensive case design, survey research, educational research, and statistics;
- **Professional orientation**, including introduction to counseling and ethics for counselors;
- **Foundations of mental health counseling**, including an introduction to mental health counseling;

- **Mental health counselors and the mental health care system**, including mental deviance and mental health institutions and counselors in the mental health care system;
- **Clinical services in mental health counseling**, including a supervised clinical practicum and internship, and courses related to assessment and treatment procedures in mental health counseling, psychopharmacology, addictions and chemical dependence, abuse (sexual, emotional, domestic) and psychopathology.

Clinical mental health counselors must be skilled in a variety of counseling modalities and be able to use those techniques selectively in order to meet clients' treatment needs.

To maintain and enhance skills, and acquire additional knowledge, mental health counselors who deliver clinical services must actively participate in a formal professional development and continuing education program. A minimum of 25 contact hours per year must be documented.

E. Responsiveness

Mental health counselors who deliver clinical services shall respond in a professional manner to all who seek their services.

COMMENT: Clinical mental health counselors must provide services to each client requesting services regardless of lifestyle, origin, race, color, age, handicap, sex, religion, or sexual orientation. They must be knowledgeable and sensitive to cultural diversity and the multicultural issues of clients.

However, clinical mental health counselors must limit their services to clients whom they have the knowledge, skills, and resources to assist. When they cannot meet the needs of a particular client for any reason, clinical mental health counselors must do what is necessary to ensure the client is put in contact with an appropriate mental health resource.

Timely appointments must be available to all clients. Mental health counselors who deliver clinical services must determine the urgency of the client's situation and be available to see the client when needed to ensure the welfare of the client. If counselors are not available to see clients when needed, it is their responsibility to assist clients in finding an appropriate and timely resource.

Clinical mental health counselors must honor the wishes of their clients to terminate, even when clinical judgment indicates further treatment is needed. It is the responsibility of counselors to refer clients to other appropriate resources prior to termination. When clients elect not to be referred, counselors must terminate the relationship in a manner that allows clients the opportunity to return to treatment as needed.

When clients elect to terminate treatment and seek help elsewhere, counselors must facilitate continuity of care by providing records, upon written request, to new counselors or therapists without delay. Counselors will cooperate fully in completing the transition.

Clinical mental health counselors must not disparage the qualifications of colleagues. Neither may they claim skills superior to those of colleagues for any reason.

F. Accessibility

Mental health counselors who deliver clinical services shall be accessible to clients.

COMMENT: Mental health counselors who deliver clinical services must be available to clients at all times. The unscheduled needs of clients will be handled through personal answering services or by answering machines. Telephone calls must be checked on a regular basis and returned promptly, accurately, and in a respectful manner. When out of town, on vacation, ill or otherwise unavailable, mental health counselors who deliver clinical services must make arrangement for coverage by competent professionals.

Offices of clinical mental health counselors must be accessible by public transportation, where available. Their office space must be easily accessible to the handicapped.

G. Accurate Representation

Mental health counselors who deliver clinical services shall accurately represent themselves to consumers.

COMMENT: All information concerning clinical mental health counselors, services available, and related activities must be truthful, accurate, and complete, to assist prospective clients in making informed judgments and choices on matters of concern.

Mental health counselors who deliver clinical services must limit personal information to name; highest relevant degree conferred from a regionally accredited institution of higher learning; state licensure, certification or registration, including number; address, telephone number, office hours; brief explanation of types of services offered, types of problems dealt with, and cost of services.

Clinical mental health counselors must not refer to degrees earned from non-regionally accredited colleges and universities, or outside the field of counseling, that is, in administration, physical education, or other unrelated fields. Neither may they for any reason fail to state the relevant terminal degree designation after their name.

Clinical mental health counselors must indicate clearly their clinical certification status, and not imply endorsement by an clinical certification body unless in possession of a formal document attesting to full clinical certification, eligibility, or equivalency.

When advertising services, clinical mental health counselors must not imply endorsement of services by professional organizations, associations, agencies, or the like, unless services are actually provided by or under the direct supervision and control of such groups.

Clinical mental health counselors may announce membership in or affiliation with professional organizations, associations, and agencies. For example, clinical mental health counselors may choose to announce professional membership in the American Counseling Association, the American Mental Health Counselors Association, and the International Society for the Study of Multiple Personality Association. However, clinical mental health counselors *may not imply endorsement* of personal professional services by any professional entities.

Mental health counselors who deliver clinical services must not announce or imply possession of unique skills beyond those available to others in the profession. Neither may announcements contain evaluative statements, testimonials or quotations regarding professional services available. Announcements and advertisements must be factual and not make false promises of treatment outcomes.

Clinical mental health counselors must make available to clients written professional disclosure statements, keeping in mind the above variables, the Standards of Clinical Practice, ethical codes and where available, applicable regulations. Statements must contain information about themselves, available treatments, office practices and the address and phone number of applicable regulatory boards.

H. Confidentiality

Mental health counselors who deliver clinical services shall protect the confidentiality of clients.

COMMENT: Trust between clinical mental health counselors and their clients is an essential ingredient of the counseling process. Therefore, except when explicit, overriding circumstances require, mental health counselors who deliver clinical services must not share relevant information concerning clients without their written and informed consent. In situations where reporting is required by law, clinical mental health counselors must fully inform clients of the exceptions to confidentiality, advise them fully of information that will be shared, and handle the feelings evoked. Such situations include suspected child sexual abuse and disclosures necessary for the safety and personal well-being of the client, such as a child's self-destructive behavior or an adult's overt threat to kill someone.

All soft and hard copy materials related to clients must be considered official records and maintained so as to be useful to mental health counselors treating clients. They also must be handled so as to ensure the privacy and confidentiality of clients and the integrity of all counseling materials. Information concerning clients is not available to anyone without clients' fully informed and written consent. Provision must be made for destruction of all or parts of official records when the data is no longer useful. No part of official records may be destroyed after clients request data or courts request information concerning clients.

I. Office Procedures

Mental health counselors who deliver clinical services shall develop and adhere to consistent office procedures.

COMMENT: Clinical mental health counselors must establish and adhere to consistent office policies and procedures. They should obtain a legal opinion on them and refer to such opinion, as needed.

Professional disclosure material must be created and regularly updated.

Standard procedures for collecting and maintaining data on clients must be established and followed. All records must be maintained accurately, without bias or prejudice, and handled in a safe and secure manner. Records must be made available to clients upon request. Clinical mental health counselors must discuss with clients the implications of the materials before they are shared.

Clinical mental health counselors must maintain appropriate professional liability insurance, premises accident liability insurance, and any other insurance appropriate for protection of both counselors and clients.

Fee schedules, billing procedures, and collection procedures must be established and followed throughout the course of treatment. Should changes be necessary, clients must be informed of such changes in advance.

Clinical mental health counselors must not refuse to serve clients solely on the absence of health insurance. Neither must clinical mental health counselors be prohibited from providing services on a pro bono basis.

J. Peer Review, Supervision and Consultation

Mental health counselors who deliver clinical services shall maintain a program of peer review, supervision and consultation.

COMMENT: Clinical mental health counselors must create and maintain an on-going program for receiving feedback about their work from other mental health professionals.

In the process of acquiring the first 3,000 hours of client contact in postgraduate clinical experience, beginning clinical mental health counselors must obtain supervision at the rate of one hour of face-to-face supervision for every fifteen (15) hours of client contact, up to the required 200 hours of supervision.

After the first 3,000 hours of client contact, the ratio of supervision to client contact hours may be reduced to include a minimum of one (1) hour of face-to-face supervision for every 30 hours of face-to-face contact with clients. However, it is expected clinical mental health counselors will seek additional supervision as determined by the needs of individual clients, as difficulties beyond the normal range of expectation are perceived by supervisors, and as recommendations for additional supervision are made by supervisors.

Experienced clinical mental health counselors with the equivalent of five years of full-time supervised clinical work may elect supervision on an as needed basis. Need is to be determined by individual counselors; however, clinical mental health counselors must ensure a minimal but optimum level of consultation and supervision.

Qualified supervisors meet these standards, have a minimum of five years of clinical experience, are licensed by their state (where available), and can document training in supervision.

Clinical mental health counselors must maintain working relationships with other professionals who may complement their practice and provide assistance to clients. They must be knowledgeable of pharmacology and must know when to utilize the services of psychiatrists or other medical professionals. When appropriate, they must make referrals for medication and communicate the effects of psychoactive drugs to prescribing or consulting medical physicians.

K. Mental Health Continuum

Mental health counselors who deliver clinical services shall understand and utilize the continuum of mental health care.

COMMENT: Clinical mental health counselors must know, accept, and acknowledge the limits and uncertainties of current mental health treatment knowledge and techniques. Furthermore, they must be aware of the limits of their knowledge and techniques and must not practice outside the scope of their individual education, training, experience, national certification, licensure, certification or registration for any reason.

Clinical mental health counselors must acknowledge when their services are no longer benefiting a client or are beyond the scope of their education, training, experience, national certification, or statutory regulation, and must make this known to clients and other responsible parties. Thereafter, clinical mental health counselors must terminate treatment and make a referral to the appropriate resource. Should clients not wish to be referred, the counseling relationship must be terminated so as not to inhibit seeking assistance in the future.

L. Independent Practice

Mental health counselors who deliver clinical services have the right to establish an independent practice.

COMMENT: Clinical mental health counselors must be qualified for private or independent practice, whether full-time or on a limited basis while employed elsewhere. In both limited practice and full-time practice clinical mental health counselors are responsible for assuring that all clinical services, including diagnosis and treatment, provided by themselves, employees, consultants and others meet national standards for the clinical practice of mental health counseling.

Employed mental health counselors who deliver clinical services must not use their employment setting to establish or maintain a limited independent practice or to establish a full-time practice. For example, a clinical mental health counselor will not refer paying clients to themselves nor have the employing agency refer clients to their practice.

Prior to leaving an employment setting to enter independent practice, clinical mental health counselors must begin termination with clients in a timely manner. They must obtain written approval of a termination procedure that offers clients the following options: terminating treatment; remaining in treatment at the present setting and being transferred to another staff member; transferring to another professional outside the present setting, or continuing with the present clinical mental health counselor in the independent practice setting. Options must be discussed with clients in the presence of an agency staff member and all clients must be offered the same options.

After the choice has been made, mental health counselors who deliver clinical services must discuss the details of their independent practice in the first session at the independent practice location, not while on the job in the employment setting. Clinical mental health counselors must not use the employment setting to obtain clients or to encourage clients to leave the employment setting.

M. Qualification to Practice

Mental health counselors who deliver clinical services shall engage in the independent practice of clinical mental health counseling only when qualified to do so.

COMMENT: Most states regulate counselors. If mental health counselors who deliver clinical services practice in such states, they must be licensed in order to engage in independent practice. If a clinical license is available, they must be licensed at that level.

The American Mental Health Counselors Association's qualifications for clinical practice include:

- Completion of a minimum of 60 semester (90 quarter) hours of graduate study in counseling at a regionally accredited college or university. The sixty hours must include a master's degree in mental health counseling in a program accredited by the Council for Accreditation of Counseling and Related Educational Programs (CACREP), or an equivalent program;

- Completion of 3,000 hours of supervised postgraduate clinical experience over a minimum of two years with a minimum of 200 hours of face-to-face supervision;

- Approval of a work product sample;

- A passing score on an examination designated by the Clinical Mental Health Academy of the National Board of Certified Counselors;

- Adherence to all relevant codes of ethics;

- Adherence to the AMHCA standards for the clinical practice of mental health counseling; and

- Where available, state licensure; licensure at the clinical level of practice, if available.

N. Service Environment

Mental health counselors who deliver clinical services shall provide clients with a wholesome environment in which to receive services.

COMMENT: Clinical mental health counselors must ensure a reasonable degree of safety and comfort for their clients. They must take reasonable steps to assure the personal security of clients and themselves. Parking lots must be well lighted. The office space where services are rendered must be free of distractions and must be quiet and private. Waiting rooms and offices must be kept clean. Restroom facilities must be available and well-maintained. The area outside the office building must be clean and safe. The office must be easily accessible to the handicapped.

O. Advocacy

Mental health counselors who deliver clinical services shall assume the social responsibility of advocating for their clients.

COMMENT: Clinical mental health counselors must actively support public and private programs benefiting persons with mental and emotional problems and conducive to prevention and early intervention. They must be visible in local, state, regional and national mental health associations, and support legislation for prevention, early intervention, and diagnosis and treatment of mental and emotional disorders.

Clinical mental health counselors must be knowledgeable of available community-based services and resources. They must work toward gaining entry for clients in all needed community or school-based resources. Referrals will be made to meet the clients' needs. Clinical mental health counselors must serve as client advocates in order to obtain optimal benefits from needed resources.

Clinical mental health counselors must work in collaboration with other community-based providers with whom clients have contact. They must ensure coordination of services to help clients receive optimal benefits from all available resources.

Mental health counselors who deliver clinical services must maintain effective consultation with other health caregivers with whom clients have contact. However, clinical mental health counselors will not share information with these professionals without clients' informed, written consent.

P. Reimbursement for Services

Mental health counselors who deliver clinical services shall be considered competent to receive reimbursement from all available payment systems for services rendered.

COMMENT: Mental health counselors who deliver clinical services are qualified to be compensated for their services in all ways currently available to psychiatrists, clinical psychologists, clinical social workers, psychiatric nurses, and marriage and family therapists. Mechanisms of compensation include cash, credit cards and third-party payments through health maintenance organizations; preferred provider programs; employee assistance programs; business coalitions; contractual arrangements with local, state, and national mental health and rehabilitation programs; contractual arrangements with departments of human services and human resources; OCHAMPUS; Federal Employees Health Benefit Plans; Medicare; behavioral managed care systems; and others.

Clinical mental health counselors are as qualified to render diagnostic and treatment services as clinical psychologists and social workers, psychiatric nurses, and marriage and family therapists. In addition, clinical mental counselors are qualified to provide services provided by psychiatrists, except narcosynthesis, electroconvulsive therapy, and pharmacological management. Consumers have the right to select the services of clinical mental health counselors and receive the same financial consideration as when served by other mental health professionals.

Q. Evaluation of Effectiveness

Mental health counselors who deliver clinical services shall evaluate the effectiveness of their services.

COMMENT: Clinical mental health counselors must collect data on their delivery of services, to be used in modifying client treatment goals and strategies, and directing the individual counselor's plan for professional and personal growth and development. Evaluation begins with the initial interview of the client, and continues through case development and review, development of an effective treatment plan (including client input) and execution of the treatment plan.

Effective case management is essential to the ongoing evaluation of mental health counselors. It includes progress notes; continuous client feedback; periodic review and changes in goals, methods, and strategies; consultation, supervision, and peer review as needed; and personal evaluation.

Mental health counselors who deliver clinical services are responsible for gathering and using information concerning personal counseling effectiveness.

R. Counselor Issues and Impairment

Mental health counselors who deliver clinical services shall be aware of anything which might interfere with their effectiveness and shall refrain from any activity which might lead to inadequate performance or harm to anyone, including themselves and clients.

COMMENT: Clinical mental health counselors must be aware of personal problems, unresolved issues and conflicts. They must be cognizant of client-elicited emotions, countertransference and other issues that impact counseling relationships and must obtain appropriate assistance to deal with such in their personal lives. At the same time, clinical mental health counselors must not accept clients who are not compatible and who might induce or enhance unhealthy personal feelings.

If, after accepting a client, clinical mental health counselors find the counseling relationship is or may be impaired for any reason, they must terminate the counseling relation, transfer the client to another mental health professional, obtain appropriate supervision and include, as necessary, a co-counselor. Clients must be involved in the process and fully informed as to the purpose of any change in treatment.

Clinical mental health counselors who are impaired for any reason are encouraged to use necessary and appropriate rehabilitation and recovery mechanisms. They must be given the full support of the profession during the rehabilitation and recovery process.

Clinical mental health counselors who are impaired and who successfully complete an appropriate rehabilitation and recovery program will be expected to develop and maintain a comprehensive supervision plan equalling the ratio of one (1) hour of supervision for every fifteen (15) hours of direct client services for a minimum period of not less than three (3) years, and longer if deemed necessary by the counselor, supervisor, or any other authority.

❖ ❖ ❖ ❖ ❖ ❖ ❖ ❖ ❖ ❖ ❖ ❖ ❖ ❖

APPENDIX B

Guidelines For Ethical Behaviour

The Manitoba School Counsellors' Association

PREAMBLE

The Manitoba School Counsellors' Association is a Special Area Group of the Manitoba Teachers' Society.

The goals of the Association include:

- supporting and promoting school counselling and guidance programming.
- providing a representative voice regarding issues that are of importance to school counselling.
- promoting and providing professional development.

Role Of The School Counsellor

- A school counsellor must be principally concerned with the personal, social, educational and career needs of the students, keeping in mind the best interests of the student.
- A school counsellor provides counselling and guidance within an educational setting. Counselling and guidance provide opportunities for students to explore feelings, examine information and consider options for problem resolution and decision making.
- A school counsellor works in collaboration with school personnel, other professionals, and parents.

Basic Principles

This document is intended to provide guidelines for the ethical behaviour of school counsellors.

The guidelines complement the Manitoba Teachers' Society Code of Professional Practices by clarifying the nature of the ethical responsibilities of counsellors in a school setting.

The guidelines are based on the following principles:

- that each person has the right to be treated with respect, dignity and integrity.

- that each person is entitled to freedom of choice and, with that freedom, must accept responsibility for choices and decisions.
- that the achievement of full potential for each person depends upon the development of self-awareness, self-direction and skills in interpersonal relationships, problem solving and decision-making.
- that each person has the right to personal growth and development within the context of the personal liberties set out in the Canadian Charter of Rights and the United Nations Convention on the Rights of the Child.

ARTICLES

Article 1. Primary Responsibility

A school counsellor's first responsibility is to act in the best interest of the students.

Article 2. Informed Student

A school counsellor shall inform students of the purposes, goals, techniques, and specific policies under which they may receive counselling, at or before the time when the counselling relationship is entered.

Such information includes concerns about confidentiality, legal restraints on the counsellor, and the possible necessity for consulting with other professionals.

Article 3. Confidentiality

Information received through the counselling relationship is confidential. The school counsellor regards such information as confidential and does not voluntarily divulge such information without the student's prior consent.

This statement applies equally to interview notes, tapes of interviews, test data, and any other documents used to assist in the counselling process. Notes are to be kept as part of the counsellor's record but not part of the records kept in the office of the school.

Exceptions:

i) **Consent:** With the consent of the student, the counsellor may divulge information received through the counselling relationship.

ii) **Potential Harm:** If behaviour of the student threatens potential harm to him/herself or another person, the school counsellor shall take appropriate action to protect the student and/or the other person.

iii) **Child Protection:** A school counsellor, who has reason to believe that a child is or might be in need of protection, shall forthwith report the information to the appropriate authorities in accordance with legal obligations pursuant to child protection legislation.

iv) **Consultation & Collaboration:** A school counsellor many consult and collaborate with other professionals for purposes of more effectively helping the student. The counsellor shall share only such information that will serve the best interests of the student.

Article 4. Impartiality

The goal of counselling is to assist students in their decision making. The school counsellor shall be aware of his/her personal values, and shall strive to remain impartial in assisting students with decision-making and problem solving.

Article 5. Referrals

School counsellors recognize their boundaries of competence and provide only those services and use only those techniques for which they are qualified by training or experience.

School counsellors shall make appropriate referrals when their professional assistance cannot adequately meet the student's needs.

The school counsellor must be knowledgeable about referral resources.

Whenever possible and appropriate, the school counsellor makes referrals with the knowledge and consent of the student. At all times, the counsellor should be acting in the best interests of the student.

Article 6. Testing And Assessment

A school counsellor explains the nature, purposes and results of standardized tests in language that is understandable to the student. This obligation also must be observed in consulting with other professionals and parents about such test information.

A school counsellor adheres to established standards regarding the selection, administration and interpretation of standardized tests and assessment techniques.

Article 7. Programs & Services

A school counsellor shares with other educators the responsibility for establishing and maintaining counselling and guidance programs which are responsive to the needs of the students.

Article 8. Professional Standards

A school counsellor shall strive to attain the standards of *Formal Professional Preparation* that are recommended by the Manitoba School Counsellors' Association and the Manitoba Teachers' Society.

A school counsellor shall strive to maintain his/her professional competence by taking advantage of professional development opportunities.

School counsellors shall accept only those positions for which they are professionally qualified.

Article 9. Professional Relationships

A school counsellor does not knowingly enter or continue a counselling relationship with a student who is receiving counselling from another professional person, without consultation with that other professional, except where the best interests of the student clearly demand such an extraordinary intervention.

In his/her relationships with employers, colleagues, and professional organizations, a school counsellor shall abide by the Code of Professional Practice of the Manitoba Teachers' Society.

Article 10.

The school counsellor shall observe the spirit not just the letter of these guidelines.

APPENDIX C

Procedures for Processing Complaints of Ethical Violations

Canadian Guidance and Counselling Association

The "Guidelines for Ethical Behaviour" of the Canadian Guidance and Counselling Association (CGCA) are intended as a basis for the conduct of its members in providing guidance and counselling services. The basic principles underlying these "Guidelines for Ethical Behaviour" are the respect for the dignity and integrity of persons, responsible caring in counselling relationships and responsibility to society. Ethical principles and guidelines become meaningful only when they are interpreted in the light of these principles and within the context of the circumstances in which they are applied.

The purpose of this document is to facilitate the work of the Ethics Committee by specifying procedures for submitting and processing alleged violations of the CGCA "Guidelines for Ethical Behaviour." The intent of CGCA is to monitor the professional conduct of its members to ensure sound, ethical counselling practices.

The Ethics Committee
The role of the Ethics Committee of CGCA is to assist in the arbitration and conciliation of conflicts among members of CGCA. The Committee is also responsible for:

1. Educating the membership as to CGCA's Ethical Guidelines;
2. Periodically reviewing the Ethical Guidelines and the "Procedures for Processing Complaints of Ethical Violations";
3. Processing complaints of ethical violations; and
4. Receiving and processing questions.

The *Ethics Committee* consists of four (4) members (including the Chairperson) of the CGCA membership. Two (2) members are appointed annually for a two (2) year term by the President. Appointments must be confirmed by the CGCA Board of Directors.

The *Chairperson* of the four-member committee is appointed by the President subject to confirmation of the Board of Directors. The Chairperson has the responsibility of:

1. Receiving (via CGCA Headquarters) complaints about and from CGCA members,
2. Notifying the complainant and the accused of receipt of the case,
3. Notifying the members of the Ethics Committee of the case within two (2) weeks after it is received,
4. Presiding over the meetings of the Ethics Committee, and
5. Preparing and sending communications on the recommendations and decisions of the Committee.

Procedures for Submitting Complaints
The CGCA Ethics Committee will act only on those cases where the accused is a member of CGCA. The Committee will not act on anonymous complaints. All correspondence, records and activities of the CGCA Ethics Committee will remain confidential.

The procedures for submission of complaints to the Ethics Committee are as follows:

1. If feasible, the complainant should discuss with utmost confidentiality the nature of the complaint with a colleague to see if she/he views the situation as an ethical violation.
2. Whenever feasible, the complainant is to approach the accused directly to discuss and resolve the complaint.
3. In cases where a resolution is not forthcoming at the personal level, the complainant shall prepare a formal written statement of the complaint, stating the details of the alleged violation and shall submit it to the CGCA Ethics Committee.
4. Written statements must include a statement indicating the section or sections of the CGCA's "Guidelines For Ethical Behaviour" that are allegedly being violated as well as the date(s) of the alleged violation. The written statement shall also contain the accused member's full name and address.

5. All complaints shall be mailed to:

> The Ethics Chairperson
> Canadian Guidance &
> Counselling Association
> 600-220 Laurier Avenue
> OTTAWA, Ontario K1P 5Z9

The envelope must be marked "Confidential".

Procedures for Processing Complaints

The procedures for processing complaints are as follows:

1. Within two (2) weeks after a written complaint is received at CGCA Headquarters, the case is sent to the Chairperson of the CGCA Ethics Committee. CGCA staff verification of membership for the accused shall be included among the documents sent to the Ethics Chairperson.

2. Within two (2) weeks of receipt of the written statement of the alleged violation of ethical practices, the Chairperson of the Ethics Committee shall do the following:

   a) acknowledge receipt of the complaint,

   b) direct a letter to the complainant acknowledging receipt of the complaint, informing the complainant that the case will be investigated by the Committee, and outlining the procedures to be followed in the investigation,

   c) direct a letter to the accused member informing the member of accusations lodged against her/him, asking for a response and requesting that relevant information be submitted to the chairperson within thirty (30) days, and

   d) direct a letter to members of the CGCA Ethics Committee notifying them of the case and presenting them with an action plan for investigation.

3. The CGCA Ethics Committee will review the case and make recommendation for disposition and/or resolution of the case within two hundred (200) days following its receipt.

Disposition and/or Resolution Options

After reviewing the information submitted by the accused, the Ethics Committee shall have the power to:

1. dismiss the charges, find that no violation has occurred, and dismiss the complaint, or

2. find that the practice(s) in which the member engages is(are) the subject of the complaint and is(are) unethical, notify the accused of this determination, and request the member to voluntarily cease and desist the practice(s) without imposition of further sanctions, or

3. find the practice(s) in which the member engages, that is(are) the subject of the complaint, is(are) unethical, notify the accused of this determination, and impose sanctions. These sanctions include:

   a) issuing a reprimand with recommendations for corrective action, subject to review of the Ethics Committee, or

   b) withdrawing membership in CGCA for a specified period of time, or

   c) placing the member on probation for a specified period of time, subject to review by the committee, or

   d) expel the member from CGCA permanently.

4. At the conclusion of the deliberations of the Ethics Committee, the Chairperson shall notify the accused and the complainant of the Committee's decision in writing. All of the written evidence and a summary of the decision of the Committee shall be forwarded to CGCA Headquarters.

Appeal Procedures

Appeals will be heard only in such cases wherein the appellant presents evidence that the sanction imposed by the Ethics Committee has been arbitrary or capricious or that proper procedures have not been followed. The complainant and the accused shall be informed of the appeal procedure by the Chairperson of the Ethics Committee The following procedures shall govern appeals:

1. A three (3) member review committee is established, composed of the President, President-Elect and Past President of CGCA .

2. The appeal, with supporting documentation, must be made in writing within sixty(60) days to the President of CGCA and indicate the basis upon which it is made.

3. The review committee shall review all materials considered by the Ethics Committee.

4. Within sixty (60) days the review committee shall submit a written statement regarding the decision of the Ethics Committee from the following alternative:

   a) support the decision of the Ethics Committee,

   b) reverse the decision of the Ethics Committee.

5. The parties to the appeal shall be advised of the action in writing.

Procedures for Submitting and Interpreting Questions of Ethical Conduct

1. Whenever possible, the questioner is first advised to consult other colleagues seeking interpretation of questions.

2. If a national level resolution is deemed appropriate, the questioner shall prepare a written statement, detailing the conduct in question. Statements should include the section or sections of the "Guidelines for Ethical Behaviour" to be interpreted relative to the conduct in question. Questions are mailed to CGCA Headquarters to be forwarded to the Ethics Chairperson.

3. The Ethics Chairperson shall direct a letter to the questioner acknowledging receipt of the question, informing the member that the question will be interpreted by the Ethics Committee, and outlining the procedures to be involved in the interpretation.

4. The Ethics Committee will review and interpret the question and, if requested by the questioner, make recommendations for conduct.

Note: CGCA acknowledges with gratitude the gracious permission of the American Association for Counseling and Development to excerpt, modify or adopt parts of its 1988 "Policies and Procedures for Processing Complaints of Ethical Violation."